The Mother Ache

Healing the Wounded Daughter Within

About the Author

Deva Arani is a writer and healing guide devoted to restoring belonging within the body and the heart. For over fifteen years, she has supported individuals in healing relational wounds, transforming inherited patterns, and cultivating embodied self-trust. Her work integrates somatic awareness, trauma-informed relational inquiry, breathwork, and contemplative practice to help people live with greater steadiness and compassion.

Drawing on decades of study with teachers and wisdom traditions across India and South America, Arani's teaching bridges psychological understanding with lived spiritual practice. She is the author of *Integration Alchemy* and *The Mother Ache*, companion works exploring how insight becomes lived change and healing becomes embodied presence.

Arani lives in the foothills above Boulder, Colorado, where she writes, teaches, and lives the ongoing practice of returning to herself.

www.devaarani.com

The Mother Ache

Healing the Wounded Daughter Within

Deva Arani

First Sentient Publications edition year 2026

A paperback original

Book design by Laura Johanna Waltje
Cover Art by Juca Maximo
Cover Design by Laura Johanna Waltje
Illustrations by Fatima Seehar

Library of Congress Control Number: 2025947287
Names: Shimer Tanya R., author.
Title: The mother ache : healing the wounded daughter within / Deva Arani.
Description: Boulder, CO: Sentient Publications, 2026.
Identifiers: LCCN: 2025947287 | ISBN: 978-1-59181-375-0 (paperback) | 978-1-59181-376-7 (epub)
Subjects: LCSH Parent and adult child. | Mothers. | Adult children--Family relationships. | Mother and child. | Self-help. | BISAC SELF-HELP / Spiritual | BODY, MIND & SPIRIT / Inspiration & Personal Growth | FAMILY & RELATIONSHIPS / Parenting / Parent & Adult Child
Classification: LCC HQ755.86 .A73 2026 | DDC 306.8743--dc23

Printed in Canada

SENTIENT PUBLICATIONS
A Limited Liability Company
PO Box 1851
Boulder, CO 80306
www.sentientpublications.com

To my mother, my grandmothers, and the lineage of women whose resilience runs through me.
To every woman who feels the mother ache and steps onto her healing path: may your ache become a guiding light, leading you home to yourself.

Contents

Foreword **xii**

Introduction:
An Invitation to Begin **xv**
A Word to Mothers and Daughters xvi
Living with the Mother Ache xvii
On Language and Lineage xx
Women, Weaving, and Lineage xxi
Guidance for Working with This Book xxiii

Part I:
The Roots of the Mother Ache

Chapter 1
Remembering the Innocence Within **3**
Meeting the Innocent Child 3
Relearning the Breath of Innocence 5
Planting the Seed of Hope and Intention 7
How Innocence Learns to Adapt 9
Awareness Through the Five Senses 10
The Healing Presence of the Natural World 12
The Living Pulse Beneath All Things 13
From Innocence to Wonder 19

Chapter Two:
The Magical Child and the World of Wonder **21**
The Magical Child and the Energetic Truth of Being 22
The Magical Child Gathers Your Story 25
Gathering Your Story 28
Listening for Our Mother's Story 31
Remembering Our Grandmother's Story 32
Meditation as a Path of Play 34
The Girl Who Remembered Magic 36
Conclusion: The Magical Child and Her Gathered Materials 41

Chapter Three:
The Wounded Child and Honest Seeing **43**
From Innocence to Adaptation 44
Understanding the Mother Ache Through Attachment 46
How the Mother Ache Forms: from Subtle to Severe 49
Subtle Roots of the Mother Ache 50
Other Roots of the Mother Ache 51
Mothers and Grandmothers: Seeing the Lineage of Adaptation 55
The Shape of Our Stories Lives in Our Bodies 57
Early Meanings and the Wounded Child 61
Triggers as Invitations to Honesty 63
Navigating Triggers Is Healing 65
How the Mother Ache Echoes Through Our Lives 66
A Dialogue with the Younger Self 67
The Girl Who Tried to Leave the Story 70
Conclusion: Meeting the Wounded Child with Honest Presence 75

Chapter Four:
The Orphan's Return to Trust **76**
Endowed and Entrusted with Healing 77
Tears as Prayer 78
Letting Go of the Mother's Promise 80
The Birth of Hope 82
The Awakening of Agency 83
The Journey from Soft Belly to Long, Slow, Deep Breathing 84
The Solace of Aloneness 87
The Woman Who Found Her Lineage 89
Conclusion: Honoring Our Inner Orphan's Trust 93

Part II:
Weaving the Basket of Healing

Chapter Five:
The Maiden and Weaving the Ground of Acceptance **96**
Weaving the Ground of Belonging 98
A Personal Story from the Maiden Years 99
What We Truly Needed 101
The Three Centers of Intelligence 103
The Navel as a Foundation for True Acceptance 105
Navel Awareness and the Maiden's Path of Acceptance 106
Courage: The Fire of the Navel 110

The Divine Mother and Our Seven Needs 113
Weaving from the Center by Strengthening the Navel 117
The Maiden's Initiation: Then and Now 118
The Maiden and The Sacred Trilogy Within 120
The Maiden Who Learned to Choose Herself 121
Conclusion: Coming Home to the Center 126

Chapter Six:
The Seeker and Coming Home Through the Body 127
Returning to the Body 129
The Body Remembers 130
Creating an Anchor in the Present 132
How the Mother Ache Lives in the Body 133
Listening to the Body: Felt Sense and Somatic Experiencing 135
The Three Centers of Connection 140
Edges that Hold the Whole 141
Healing in Relationship 143
The Woman Who Relearned Connection 144
Conclusion: A Blessing for the Lineage 148

Chapter Seven:
The Weaver of Life and the Patterns of the Mind 150
The Basket of the Mind 152
The Mind's Original Function 153
The Periphery Mind 155
Befriending Our Mind's Patterns 157
The Four Movements of Protective Energy 158
Movement One: Reaching 160
Movement Two: Guarding 161
Movement Three: Judging 162
Movement Four: Collapsing 164
Protective Energy Patterns: When Relief Becomes Compulsion 165
Postures of Protection: How the Body Reveals Our Patterns 166
Working with the Four Movements of Protective Energy 169
Reweaving Thought with Body Awareness 170
The Girl Who Learned to Slow Her Inner World 170
Conclusion: From Recognition to Presence 175

Chapter Eight:
The Healer and the Wisdom of the Heart 177
Understanding Emotion 179
The Body as an Instrument of Feeling 180

Perceptions Block Feelings and Flow 182
The Four R's of Emotional Alchemy 183
Meeting Fear: The Guardian at the Threshold 185
Resistance: The Hesitation Before the Doorway 186
Regression: The Child Who Still Resides Within 187
Repression: The Hidden Truth Beneath the Skin 187
Reaction: The Fire That Wants to Be Seen 188
Integration: The Courage to Stay 189
Empathy Requires Attunement 190
Empathy Starts Within 191
Feeling What Was Never Safe to Feel 191
Relating to Your Mother in the Present 193
Common Detours on the Path of Empathy 193
A Living Example: Reweaving Connection with My Mother 195
Reconnecting Through Feeling 196
The Alchemy of Self Inquiry 198
Meeting the Ache Beneath *I Have to Be Good* 199
The Girl Who Tried to Get It Right 201
Conclusion: Feeling is the Healing 205

Part III:
The Alchemy of Presence

Chapter Nine:
The Alchemist and the Four Phases of Feminine Transformation 208
The Mother Ache as Base Material 208
The Inner Alchemy of Healing 209
Meeting the Ancient Women of Alchemy 211
The Four Phases of Feminine Alchemy 213
Gathering—The Phase of Beginning 214
Softening—The Phase of Opening 215
Shaping—The Phase of Becoming 217
Offering—The Phase of Returning 217
The Fire That Teaches 220
Held by the Mother Beneath All Mothers 223
The Girl Who Walked Out of the Fire 224
Conclusion: From Alchemy to Devotion 228

Chapter Ten:
The Mystic and the Path of Compassion 229
Women Who Embody the Mystic's Compassion 231

The Bodhisattva Who Stayed 232
The Apostle of the Heart 233
The Mystic's Seal is Compassion 234
Breathing the World into the Heart 235
The Inner Flame of Compassion 237
What is Self-Love 238
Tending the Sacred Vessel 240
The Body as Sacred Ground of Compassion 241
Inner Beauty: The Radiance of Simplicity 243
The Daughter Who Inherited the Mystic's Path 244
Conclusion: The Fragrance of Compassion 249

Chapter Eleven:
The Wild Woman and the Fire of Wholeness 251
Women Who Run with the Wolves 253
How the Mother Ache Teaches Us to Tame Ourselves 254
Trusting the Voice That Rises From Within 255
The Wild Woman and the Return to Nourishment 256
Our Seven Needs Revisited 257
Rekindling the Sacred Fire of Creativity 258
Totality: Living the Creative Force of Life 258
The Daughter Who Inherited the Path: Finding Her Voice 260
Conclusion: Wholeness and the Mother Ache 264

Chapter Twelve:
The Priestess and Embodied Presence 266
The Priestess and the Mother Ache 267
The Orphan and the Priestess 269
The Priestess and the Power of Voice 272
Embodied Presence: From Ache to Offering 277
The Innocence of Wisdom 279
The Final Homecoming 281

Chapter 13:
The Daily Weaving of a Living Prayer 283
The Practice of Daily Weaving 284
A Note from the Weaver 285

Appendix A:
Daily Weaving Practices 287
Breathwork, Grounding, and Regulation 287
Intention, Awareness, and Inner Listening 288

Embodiment and the Navel Center 289
Meditation and Contemplative Practices 290
Movement and Energy Flow—Active Meditations 291
Sensory Presence and Nature Connection 292
Care and Creativity as Daily Weaving 292

Appendix B:
Weaving the Work into Daily Life 294
Working with Triggers 294
Three Signs You've Been Triggered 294
The Trigger Chain 295
Returning to the Sacred Center 295
Recognizing and Working with the Four Protective Movements 296
Reaching 296
Guarding 296
Judging 296
Collapsing 297
Returning to the Sacred Center 297
Guide to The Four Rs of Emotional Alchemy 297

Appendix C:
Glossary of Terms 299

Appendix D:
Ancestral Basketry—The Materials of Maternal Love 304

Acknowledgments 307

About the Author 309

Foreword

Before the world gave us names for our pain, we knew how to listen. Every ache was a messenger. Every longing, a call. Healing was not mending what was broken, but a remembering of what was always and already whole.

This book was born from that remembering.

Each of us carries a story written in the language of our mothers, still echoing through our bones. The mother ache is not only personal; it arises from generations of women who did what they could with what they had. It is the tender place where love and absence meet.

I call this place the *mother ache* rather than the mother wound because it is not only pain but also longing—the pull toward wholeness beneath the wound. The word wound belongs to the language of fixing and repair, but the word ache speaks in the language of reverence. It is the tender pulse that reminds us we are made of love and that our journey is a remembrance of this truth. To ache is to honor this love, intrinsic belonging, and the yearning to return home to ourselves.

We are living in a time when many of the inherited ways of holding one another have unraveled, and we are being asked to consciously reimagine what care, kinship, and belonging look like.

Families fracture under the weight of inherited pain. Women carry unspoken burdens while being asked to mother from depleted nervous systems. Entire lineages and communities are shaped by unhealed stories, while repeating patterns of abandonment, dissociation, hardness, and survival. This is our maternal lineage calling out for repair. The mother ache is where this call is felt first. It is the place where our earliest ruptures were written and where the possibility of a new story begins.

Mother ache healing is not only personal; it is cultural. The mother bond shapes our earliest sense of belonging. When it is strained or ruptured, we can lose trust in our own worth and become disconnected from ourselves, from others, and from the living world around us. We learn to override our bodies, to ignore our hunger, to endure what harms us. These patterns become the architecture of society: disconnected, rushed, extractive, guarded. Healing the mother ache begins to unclench this architecture and return us to the capacity for authentic relationships, empathy, and presence.

This work is also ecological. The way we treat the Earth mirrors the way we were taught to treat our own bodies: as resources to manage and control. Because the feminine has been diminished in our culture for generations, the living world suffers. When we heal our relationship to the mother within us and the mothers who raised us, we naturally soften into a deeper reciprocity with the Earth beneath our feet. We begin to sense Her not as an object, but as kin. Mother healing becomes Earth healing through a restored intimacy with life itself.

We are in a collective moment that demands this intimacy. Around us, systems are collapsing: political, ecological, and relational. What is rising is a hunger for what is real, embodied, and rooted in ancient memory. Women especially are feeling the ache for rest, for truth, for connection, and for a lineage that supports them rather than wounds them. This book meets that moment by offering a path that is neither clinical nor conceptual, but deeply human. It speaks to the part of us that longs to return to what is sacred within us.

My own story lives beneath every word of these pages. I know the ache of a fractured maternal relationship, the pain it creates, the compensations it drives. I also know the grace that arrives when we turn toward this ache with courage and compassion. The practices in this book arise from decades of tending my own ache, walking with other women, and apprenticing myself to teachers of body, breath, and spirit. They are invitations, strands you can weave into the basket of your own becoming.

Mother ache healing matters because it restores the foundation of our lives. It returns us to the place where love first faltered, so that we may learn to love in a new way, this time with awareness. It makes possible a new lineage, one that passes down presence and truth, rather than our inherited survival adaptations. When we heal the mother ache within ourselves, we heal forward and backward in time. We change the stories that shape our lives, our families, our communities, and Mother Earth who holds us all.

Looking back on my own journey, I now see beyond the limited lens of the daughter trying to fix what she thought was broken. I see a weaver with hands steady, heart open. I see the basket of my life: imperfect, resilient, and whole. This book is my offering of reciprocity for that sacred healing work. May it meet you where you are. May it remind you that you too, are the weaver of your own life and your own lineage.

Introduction:

An Invitation to Begin

Settle into your body. Let your belly soften, your breath deepen. Feel the ground beneath you. You are entering sacred territory: the terrain of your own becoming. This is not a place outside you, but within you. Every breath, every memory, every ache is welcome here.

This is a book about the mother ache and the wholeness that lives beneath it. The ache is the echo of what was missing, the intrinsic pull toward what you most needed and did not receive. It is not a diagnosis or a label. It is a living tenderness that longs to be met. When you meet it with awareness, it becomes a doorway. When you meet it with presence, it becomes a path.

The mother ache is both personal and ancestral. It carries your story, your mother's story, and the stories of the women before her. Some mothers were loving yet limited in their capacity to meet our needs, regardless of this love; others were absent or overwhelmed. Some were kind but withdrawn. Whatever the shape, the ache taught you how to seek love and how to lose yourself. It taught you how to survive. Now, it can teach you how to return home to yourself.

For as long as daughters have been born, women have tried to understand the mysteries of their mothers. Writers and thinkers across generations have named this complexity in their own ways. Marguerite Duras called mothers *the strangest, craziest people we ever meet*, pointing to the beautiful, maddening otherness that lives inside maternal love. Julia Kristeva described the maternal as both creation and disruption, the first place where our sense of self begins to blur and take shape. Adrienne Rich spoke of the mother-daughter knot, the lifelong tangle of longing, expectation, tenderness, and grief. Their voices remind us that the mother ache is not simply personal but universal, woven into the story of womanhood itself. It also lives in moments small enough to miss, shaped in the ordinary spaces of childhood.

A Word to Mothers and Daughters

This book is written for daughters, yes, but also for mothers, and for the mothering aspects within all of us. It is not an indictment of mothers. It is an invitation to understand how our maternal lineage shapes us and how each of these relationship carries both deep love and ache.

If you are a mother reading these pages, may you feel your dignity upheld here. You will not be asked to carry blame. You will not be diminished. You will not be judged. Instead, you will find space to breathe, to acknowledge your humanity, to understand where your own ache began, and perhaps to soften toward the places where you could not give what you yourself never received.

And if you are a daughter, may these pages help you recognize that your mother's imperfections do not in any way negate her love for you or yours for her. They are part of a universal story of human life, shaped by generations of women before you and shaped again by your healing.

The maternal bond is powerful because it is imperfect. It is through these cracks that consciousness grows, compassion deepens, and the possibility of transformation becomes real.

There are many ways a daughter comes to this work. Some are still in a close relationship with their mothers. Some are distant or estranged. Some walk this path after their mothers have died. Wherever you stand, you are welcome here. Healing the mother ache does not depend on your mother's presence in your life or in this world. The bond between mother and child is older than time, and its strands remain even when the relationship is severed or the body is gone.

To turn toward your mother now is to honor her essence and to tend the unspoken places that still live within you both. When you bring awareness to your own patterns, you are also touching hers. When you soften, she softens. When you heal, your lineage breathes a little easier.

This is not an act of blame or disloyalty, it is an act of love. It is how the unfinished prayers of the women before you find completion. To heal your own ache is to meet your mother in a new way, beyond story. In this field of remembrance, you may begin to see that healing is about allowing what is because you can't change what was. You may begin to hold your story and your mother's story with grace.

This work doesn't ask you to fix your mother, the past, or yourself. It asks you to expand your capacity to hold what is true. To meet feelings with presence. To mend what has been torn. To remember what is whole.

Living with the Mother Ache

As a child, I remember my mother in her stylish clothes, her beauty radiant even as her eyes drifted far away. I wanted to reach her. I wanted her to see me. Something in me sensed she was carrying more than she could bear: her own unhealed inner child, her mother's prayers, her grandmother's endurance. I didn't have language for it then, only the feeling that she was both near and out of reach.

My first memories are warm and sunlit, foothills rising behind our home, the smell of grass and creek water, laughter tumbling through the air. I was a happy child, running barefoot, riding my hot pink bicycle as fast as I could, and cuddling our pup, Darcy. My mother was there, pretty and kind. I followed my older brother and the big kids, determined to keep up.

But then, as quickly as a cloud passing over the sun, something changed. One evening, I watched from the dinner table as my mother asked my father for a divorce. I didn't understand what it meant, only that a tremor shook our world. I remember clinging to my dad's legs and crying for him not to leave as he packed his bags.

Soon after, she too was packing to leave. This time, I was sitting at the foot of her bed, four-years old, watching her fold clothes into a suitcase. She handed me a white jewelry box with a red velvet lining and a tiny ballerina who turned in circles when the music played. She gave me a book of *Grimm's Fairy Tales*, heavy, mysterious, filled with girls who wandered forests and met wolves—which I read as soon as I was able to, over and over again. I clutched both gifts, not knowing they would become living symbols of an ache that continues to cry out for healing, even now in my sixtieth year.

The day before, I had cried over mismatched socks, refusing to go to school without a matching set. We were late; my mother was hurried; she sent me off anyway. It is the last morning I remember with her before everything rearranged itself. One day, she was there; the next, she was gone. I thought she left because I had cried about the socks.

I lived with my father and brother after that. My mother had gone to Dallas, chasing a different life. My father rose early for work, setting out a dress for me each morning before he left. My brother, only seven, became my guide, helping me dress and walking me to school.

I stopped talking. I wet the bed. I sleepwalked through nights haunted by dreams of goblins who lured me beneath a dark bridge. The world no longer felt safe. I was watchful, quiet, apart. In line at school, I remember hearing whispers: *She smells like pee*. I kept my head down and said nothing.

There were moments of tenderness that I recall fondly now, like my grandmother calling me Little Miss Moppet, as I stood beside her at the sink helping her wash dishes and my aunt picking me up from kindergarten on her bicycle. But even those strands frayed. One day my aunt forgot me; I sat on the curb for hours, waiting—numb and invisible—until my teacher found me. I remember my aunt's tears when she arrived, the panic in her voice. I remember my own detachment: no fear, no anger, as if I were watching from outside my body.

When I remember my mother before she left, one memory stands out. She was lying on the couch, her feet propped up, and she asked me to call the radio station to request *Hey Jude*. I stood on a chair to dial the rotary phone with my tiny fingers, requested the song, and then we waited together for it to play. When it finally came on, we cheered out loud, and we sang along: *na na na nananana, nannana, hey Jude*. I can still sing every word. It is the song of before: before she left, before the ache.

As I grew older, I pieced together her story. My mother was the eldest of four, raised in poverty, her father a Baptist minister haunted by war and mental illness. Each year brought another move, another school, another fresh start. She learned early that stability could vanish overnight. Her mother, my grandmother Effie, was a pillar of endurance, sewing clothes from repurposed fabric and old clothing, stretching every meal, and strong in her faith. From her, I inherited resilience; from my grandfather, I inherited the sense that life could erupt at any moment. My mother grew up embarrassed by her family's poverty, determined to escape it. She wanted joy rather than fear-based religion, and a life of adventure rather than perceived servitude.

And yet, even as she sought freedom, she carried the ache of displacement. Every move, every rupture had etched itself into her nervous system. It's little wonder that when she became a mother, she too, uprooted from compulsion to escape the sense that she was a bad mother.

I see her now with compassion. She was surviving as best she could, but she mistook running away for freedom. I see how the ache passed through her to me, how I carried it into my own life. The child who learned to wait, to adapt, to be quiet. The woman who sought love across oceans.

For years, I wandered through India and South America, through ancient temples and jungle ceremonies. I sat at the feet of teachers and wisdom keepers, drank from rivers of ritual, and felt the world breathe me open. The sacred plants taught me reverence. The mountains taught me stillness. The forests taught me to listen. Each voyage was a strand of lived experience, luminous, yes, but also painful and necessary.

What I learned at last was this: you do not have to leave home to find what heals. The medicine is not only in the mountains or the jungle—it is in the kitchen, the garden, the breath, the body—the daily weaving of love into ordinary life.

Healing is remembering. It is singing *Hey Jude* to yourself when you forget you have always been loved. It is forgiving the mother who left because she didn't know how to stay. It is becoming the woman who can stay with the ache and transmute it into love.

Healing the mother ache is a journey. For me, as I came of age, I tried to appease the ache through goodness, through achievement, through giving myself away for other's needs. Still, the ache endured.

When I was ready, my healing path gathered me up and carried me to teachers I did not expect: breath, body, plants, silence, movement, stillness, work, and rest. I learned that our stories are not obstacles to healing; they *are* the healing. Every unspoken word, every unmet need, every inherited pattern is a fiber waiting to be softened and rewoven.

In the Amazon, under the canopy of night, I sat with the grandmother medicine, ayahuasca, and met the spirit of my lineage in visions woven with tears. I saw my Dutch grandmother, Effie, whose hands had turned scarcity into beauty. I held her feet and whispered what I could not say before she died, *thank you*. That ceremony did not erase the ache but instead revealed its holiness.

The mother ache is holy and it is universal. All mothers fail their children in some way because the role itself is impossibly large, shaped by the weight of culture, expectation, lineage, patriarchy, and the sheer complexity of being human.

No mother emerges whole and free of her own needs and the circumstances that shaped her. Even the most devoted mother cannot meet every need or protect her child from every ache. This is part of being human. It is how children grow, how resilience forms, how empathy awakens, how ancestral healing plays out, and how each generation receives the opportunity to awaken a little more than the last.

On Language and Lineage

Throughout this book you will meet women whose healing journeys I am honored to share, with their permission. Their stories, personal yet universal, offer living examples of what becomes possible when we tend the mother ache with intention and presence.

In this book, I use she/her pronouns when referring to the daughter, the mother, and the feminine archetypes we explore. I do this because the mother ache has traditionally lived within women's bodies and lineages, and because these archetypes arise from feminine-coded stories across cultures.

Still, this healing is not limited to one gender identity. Many people, regardless of how they identify, carry wounds shaped by the maternal relationship. If you use different pronouns, or if your experience of gender is fluid, please know that you are welcome here.

As you read, feel free to translate the language into whatever pronouns reflect your lived truth. The teachings in these pages are for all who carry the mother ache, all who seek repair, and all who long to return to the wholeness of their own *sacred center*.

When I speak of the sacred center, I am naming an embodied place of alignment within us. This is a living intelligence that arises when instinct, heart, and awareness move in harmony. It begins in the navel center, where intuition and courage are felt as visceral knowing. It rises through the heart center, where emotional truth softens, opens, and connects. And it widens into a spacious, quiet awareness which is the still point beneath thought, what some traditions call *shuniya*, the fertile emptiness from which clarity emerges. When these centers are in relationship, we are no longer driven by habit or fear. We become present, responsive, and rooted in ourselves. Returning to this sacred center is a remembering, one that unfolds again and again throughout the work of healing.

Women, Weaving, and Lineage

Across cultures and continents, women have woven baskets for as long as we have been human. In my own maternal lineage, Dutch women crafted baskets from reeds and rushes gathered from the water's edge. In other lineages, women wove with willow, pine needles, straw, river grasses, palm, wood, or bark. No matter the material, the basket was never merely a tool, it was an extension of the feminine body and spirit.

Baskets carried food for survival and seeds for planting. They held medicine bundles, sacred objects, stories, and offerings. A woven vessel is both practical and holy: it sustains and symbolizes life. It protects and contains. And in nearly every tradition, it was the women who carried this knowledge through their hands.

In this book, I draw from that ancient art as a living metaphor for healing the mother ache. You and I may not weave with the same materials as our ancestors, yet we inherit their instinct to create containers of meaning. As you move through these pages, you will be invited to weave your own healing basket, one strand, one practice, one insight at a time.

You may imagine your strands as reeds, grasses, branches, fibers, or whatever materials belong to your maternal line. Whatever specific strands you choose to envision, what is most important is the movement you embrace: the slow, attentive weaving that brings scattered pieces of your inner world back into coherence.

By the end of our journey together, the basket you weave will not be only for yourself. It becomes a vessel you consecrate for your lineage, an offering for those who came before you and a blessing for those who will come after. Healing the mother ache is never solely personal. It is communal, ancestral, and generational. When you weave your healing basket, you reweave the feminine line.

We will weave our healing basket in twelve movements, relearning and remembering the qualities of our intrinsic nature: awareness, curiosity, honesty, empathy, acceptance, connection, understanding, trust, inner alchemy, compassion, wholeness, and embodied presence. Each movement invites a deepening into your own healing. This is work for your hands. This is the art of reweaving your lineage. This is the basket that will hold your healing.

You will not walk alone. Throughout these pages, you'll encounter feminine archetypes as inner wisdom keepers. These are living patterns of energy that will awaken in you when you are ready to remember their presence within you. They guide the work and give it shape.

Every basket begins with the weaver's vision of its shape. Before you begin weaving your own healing basket, it helps to glimpse the larger pattern of our journey together and meet the archetypal energies within you, inherited through your feminine lineage, that will rise and guide each spiral of this journey. The path unfolds in three movements like the weaving of a basket.

Part I: The Roots of the Mother Ache

You begin with the Innocent Child, remembering awareness.
You meet the Magical Child, cultivating curiosity.
You sit with the Wounded Child, strengthening honesty.
You walk with the Orphan Child, discovering trust.

Part II: Weaving the Basket of Healing

You enter the Maiden, grounding acceptance in the body.
You walk with the Seeker, deepening self-connection.
You learn from the Weaver of Life, understanding the mind's patterns.
You embrace the Healer, awakening genuine empathy for yourself and others.

Part III: The Alchemy of Presence

You apprentice with the Alchemist, learning the fire of inner alchemy.
You open with the Mystic, inviting compassion as warmth and blessing.
You rise with the Wild Woman, standing in wholeness: strong, supple, alive.

You bow with the Priestess, with embodied presence offering your woven basket back to life in reciprocity.

This healing work is not a straight path. It is a spiral. You will circle back. You will meet new layers of old places. That is not failure. It is how living things grow. There is no right pace, no wrong entry point. This work is a relationship with healing, and we must approach it one strand at a time, just as we would if we were weaving a basket. Let each page meet you where you are.

Guidance for Working with This Book

Go slowly. Let the practices breathe. Pause when needed.
Stay in your body. Feel the ground. Rest a hand on your navel or heart.
Pause. When emotion swells, pause, breathe, name what you feel.
Choose safety. If memories feel overwhelming, step back, resource, or seek support.
Write it down. Please keep a journal for prompts and insights. There are prompts at the end of each chapter and I encourage you to use these as you make your way through the book.
Create a small altar. A place just for you that you return to, that reminds you this is sacred work.
Have an experience. Reading these pages can orient you, but it is your lived experience of doing the work that brings healing.
Honor the spiral. Return to any chapter as needed. Trust your pacing.

This book is both *practical and devotional*. You will learn to work with your nervous system; your three centers of intelligence: navel, heart, and mind; and the parts of your psyche that were formed to protect you. You will also learn to listen deeply to the subtle wisdom moving through your body, your lineage, and the living earth. Without compassionate inner listening, inquiry becomes something we do to ourselves rather than with ourselves. With listening, it becomes a doorway through which truth can gently emerge.

You will meet practices like long-slow-deep breathing, walking from the navel, humming to synchronize the three centers, embodiment practices to unwind held energy, and self-inquiry work to bring old beliefs into the light. You will learn how to feel without drowning, how to set boundaries without hardening, how to speak truth without leaving yourself.

Throughout this book, you'll find *Experiential Invitations* and *Experiential Practices* woven into each chapter. Experiential Invitations are gentle openings that invite you to explore awareness through direct experience. They are not exercises to master. They are doorways into presence: ways to listen, feel, and remember from within. Experiential Practices are more structured explorations: meditations or breathwork techniques drawn from somatic, yogic, and psychological traditions. They are meant to be practiced with consistency, supporting your nervous system and awareness as you weave healing into daily life.

As you walk this path, reflection becomes an essential companion, helping you hear the subtle truths that rise as you explore your inner world. At the end of each chapter, you'll find journaling prompts, that are small gateways into deeper understanding. Journaling is a form of weaving: each word you place on the page becomes a strand that clarifies and reveals. These prompts offer a way to meet your inner world with curiosity and care. Let them guide your hand as you make your way through the pages of this book to support your healing.

At times, you may feel tired, tender, or unsure. Good. That means you are meeting real places. Rest often. Drink water. Step outside. Place your feet on the earth. Remember that you belong to a larger rhythm than your thoughts and your ache, one that includes your very being, your ancestors, and the turning of the seasons.

You will be introduced to the Great Mother in these pages. The Great Mother is the oldest remembrance that something vast and loving holds us, like the earth beneath our feet and the rhythms of birth and death that shape all life. You will also be invited to meet the Divine Mother—a primordial presence of protection, nourishment, and fierce compassion, honored across cultures and centuries in many forms, including Isis, Mother Mary, the Black Madonna, Inanna, Demeter, Gaia, Pachamama, Tara, Quan Yin, and countless other named and unnamed expressions of sacred maternal care. These embodied figures bring the vastness of the Great Mother close, into the intimacy of form. Let them be companions as you walk. Let them give you courage. Let them remind you that you are already held.

This book reflects my own journey toward them, a journey of direct experience, which is the journey I am encouraging you to also make. While it draws on insights from psychology and trauma healing, including my studies during a year-long Compassionate Inquiry® professional training, its heart lies with the spiritual path I diligently walk myself. These teachings took root not just through study but through practice: listening to my body, tending to my ache, and walking alongside others as they rediscover the wisdom within themselves.

What follows is a living fabric of experience woven from breath, awareness, inner listening, and devotion. It belongs to the realm of the body, to the pulse of the earth, to the moments of stillness where knowing emerges naturally. These pages are not meant to be merely read; they are meant to be lived. Each practice is an invitation to return, to feel what has long been numb, and to remember what has never been lost.

This book is an invitation to embodied presence. Presence changes everything. When you are present with what hurts, it softens. When you are present with what is beautiful, it grows. Presence is the warmth that hardens the basket in the sun and the blessing that turns it into an offering.

Take one breath, in and out. Feel your feet. Place a gentle palm over your navel. Whisper, *I am ready.* With this affirmation to yourself, the weaving has begun.

A ceremonial basket woven with intention, each thread a prayer, each fiber a vow. Its spiral reminds us that healing is a return—again and again—to what longs to be met with love. As we weave the strands of our healing, the basket becomes both vessel and guide: a living symbol of the journey from ache to wholeness.

Part I: The Roots of the Mother Ache

As we explore the roots of the mother ache, we begin with the archetypes of childhood. Archetypes are living energies within us. They are patterns of consciousness shaped by memory, carried in the body, and expressed through the intrinsic qualities of our inner nature that are waiting to be reawakened. When we meet an archetype, we are meeting a part of ourselves that has been waiting to be recognized and embodied. These early archetypes form the ground of our healing journey, for they carry the first impressions that shaped who we believed we needed to be in order to be loved.

In his early writings, Carl Jung taught that the Child Archetype represents the blueprint of our original wholeness, the place where innocence, imagination, vulnerability, longing, and resilience first took form.[1] According to Jung, the psyche does not discard its early experiences; it carries them

1 Carl G. Jung, "The Psychology of the Child Archetype," in *The Archetypes and the Collective Unconscious*, vol. 9, part 1 of *The Collected Works of C. G. Jung*, ed. Gerhard Adler and R. F. C. Hull (Princeton, NJ: Princeton University Press, 1981), 151–181.

forward as inner figures that continue to influence how we make meaning of our lives, how we protect ourselves, and how we love. The Child Archetype carries the early patterns that shape our sense of safety, connection, and self-regard, along with the unspent vitality and aliveness that can be reclaimed.

Jung described the Child as an archetype that manifests within us in different forms, a symbolic image of original wholeness and future possibility. In my own healing work and intuitive understanding, this archetypal field reveals itself in four distinct forms: the Innocent, the Magical, the Wounded, and the Orphan. Each one illuminates a different facet of our early emotional world: our first experiences of belonging, imagination, rupture, survival, and longing. By remembering and tending to these child forms, we reclaim the parts of ourselves that were shaped before we had choice or agency. In doing so, we restore the foundation upon which all healing of the mother ache must rest.

Chapter 1

Remembering the Innocence Within

"You were born a child of light's wonderful secret—you return to the beauty you have always been."

—Aberjhani

Meeting the Innocent Child

The Innocent Child lives within each of us like a small bird emerging from its shell, vulnerable, luminous, and alive with the first pulse of being. She embodies our original rhythm, the natural *awareness* we were born with, which is the simple capacity to be present to life. Recognizing her presence is the beginning of healing the mother ache, for our return to her is the first step in the arduous journey of returning to our true nature—innocence.

This archetype is our deepest connection to Mother Earth and to the life-giving rhythm that sustains all creation. She is the part of us that is unburdened and true, whose awareness moves through the body like sunlight through leaves, gentle, effortless, without judgment.

Imagine a newborn: eyes open, body soft, fully in tune with her own needs. We arrive in this world already whole, guided by sensation and instinct. We cry, gurgle, and laugh without hesitation. Like a fledgling bird, the Innocent Child calls out for nourishment, comfort, and connection without inhibition. She reminds us that we arrived whole, able to love and be loved, each of us an incarnation woven into the eternal thread of life.

Yet over time, we forget. To survive, we adapt, learning to suppress emotions, to hold back, to fawn, to brace. We lose touch with our natural rhythms and begin seeking outside ourselves for what was once innate. The journey of healing is a gentle circling back—not to become the child again—but to remember the innocent awareness she embodied before the world taught her to leave herself.

I was reminded of this truth while preparing for my mother's eightieth birthday recently. Sorting through a basket of old photographs, I paused at images of her as a girl, radiant and free. Then I found one of myself as an infant in a christening gown with eyes wide, face open to the camera, glowing with untouched innocence. Tears came from recognition. That tiny being—so pure, so trusting—was me. She still is me. Her light had never vanished; it had only been dimmed.

Innocence is not something we must earn or recover through effort. It is our original nature. Long before adaptation, protection, or self-doubt, there was a knowing that lived in the body: a simple, intact presence. Healing does not require becoming someone new. It is a remembering of what has always been here, beneath the layers of conditioning. This remembering is not learned so much as listened for, like a language once spoken fluently and slowly forgotten.

The Innocent Child remains untouched by the adaptations we'll explore next. She is nature embodied, untroubled by past or future. By remembering her, we reconnect with the essence beneath all the layers we've taken on. Healing begins here, in our most natural state of simply being with awareness.

The Innocent Child lives beneath the mother ache—unmarked, unguarded, and whole. Before words, before survival strategies, she is and will always be simply here: breathing, feeling, and belonging to life.

Relearning the Breath of Innocence

As infants, we breathe with our whole being in a natural rhythm. Over time, we lose that effortless flow as our minds begin working to keep us safe. The body tightens, the belly tenses, and the breath becomes shallow. Awareness, once natural and fluid, narrows into vigilance.

Before we go further into the ways this disconnection forms, we begin by returning to this most basic rhythm. To reconnect with the Innocent Child's natural state of awareness, we need tools that do not belong to the mind but that soften its hold. One of the simplest and most powerful of these is a meditation called soft belly breathing.

This gentle practice mirrors the natural breathing of the innocent child and invites you back to the intrinsic awareness that lives beneath thought. It is both a beginning and a return: a daily act of remembering.

Soft belly breathing helps restore awareness to your body and calm to your mind. Awareness becomes possible when we are neither overly activated nor shut down. This breath brings us into that balanced space where healing can occur. It relaxes tension, slows the heart rate, quiets the mind, and leaves us feeling more stable and present. It is a bridge to cross back to the innocent child's state of awareness within.

I first learned soft belly breathing years ago through my self-studies in Somatic Experiencing and the work of Dr. Peter Levine[2]. It has been a steady companion in my own healing and teaching. Later, when I encountered Dr. James S. Gordon's *Transforming Trauma*[3], I was deeply moved by how he placed this same simple breath at the center of his work with people facing crisis, trauma, and war. It is the very first tool he teaches in his workshops. Dr. Gordon writes:

> You can feel the benefits of soft belly the first time you do it. Seventy to eighty percent of those who practice it—even those who have lost family members, are mourning a lost relationship, struggling with cancer, or have survived natural disaster or assault—report positive changes after only ten or twelve minutes. Tight shoulders relax, heart rate slows, and the torrent of disturbing thoughts abates. People feel calmer, more stable, more present, and more hopeful.

Even if you've practiced breathwork and meditation for many years, try this as if you are a beginner. Its power lies in its simplicity. The reason soft belly breathing is so effective is that it reconnects us with the Innocent Child's actual way of breathing. Through this breath, the nervous system remembers safety, and awareness emerges naturally. Healing can only happen in presence, and presence begins with the breath.

Experiential Practice: Soft Belly Breathing

Find a comfortable chair or cushion in a supportive space. Dim the lights, light a candle, or wrap yourself in a soft blanket.

Feel the weight of your body resting on the chair. Let your awareness settle.

---

2 Peter A. Levine, *Waking the Tiger: Healing Trauma* (Berkeley, CA: North Atlantic Books, 1997), 88–91.

3 James S. Gordon, *Transforming Trauma: The Path to Hope and Healing* (New York: HarperOne, 2019).

Begin breathing slowly and deeply, in through your nose and out through your mouth.

Invite your belly to soften. Let it expand on the in-breath and relax on the out-breath. If it feels comfortable, place your hands gently on your belly.

As you breathe, say silently to yourself: *soft* on the inhale, *belly* on the exhale. The words give your mind a place to rest, a rhythm to follow.

Continue this way for 10 to 15 minutes. If thoughts arise, let them drift through and gently return to your breath and the gentle words of *soft belly, soft belly*.

When you finish, open your eyes slowly. Notice how you feel. Practice this once a day, perhaps upon waking or before sleep. Let it become a re-weaving ritual. With each breath, you realign with your natural rhythm. Your nervous system will settle; your mind will follow and also settle into more calm.

On a practical level, the benefits are profound. Soft belly breathing draws air deep into the lower lungs, enriching your blood with oxygen and nourishing every cell. It relaxes large muscles, slows your heart rate, lowers blood pressure, and supports digestion. It also activates the vagus nerve, which helps calm the fight-or-flight response and soothes the parts of the brain that generate fear and anxiety. Over time, this breath reconditions the body toward calm, and with calm comes awareness.

Through this gentle, daily practice, awareness becomes less a concept and more a living rhythm in your body. It is the rhythm the Innocent Child within you has been waiting for you to return to.

Planting the Seed of Hope and Intention

"Hold the hand of the child that lives in your soul. For this child, nothing is impossible."

– Paulo Coelho

Hope is the first stirring of the Innocent Child within you. It lives the way a baby bird waits in a nest: small, fragile, and trusting. She opens her beak to the sky without knowing what will come. Hope is like that: uncertain, yet steady in the faith that life will provide what's needed.

If you are reading this book, some part of you already carries this same hope and the sense that healing is possible. Hope doesn't arise from effort; it comes naturally, like breath. You cannot force it, but you can notice it. And noticing is awareness. From awareness, hope grows roots. From hope, intention is born.

The Innocent Child's way of setting intention is simple. She does not bargain with life, she opens to it. In her world, there are no expectations to fulfill. Instead, there is only an instinct to grow towards light. Yet as we move through life, unmet needs begin to shape our expectations. We learn to measure, compare, and strive, losing the spacious innocence that once guided us. Awareness invites us to release those expectations and begin again with sincerity.

I invite you now to set an intention for your own healing. Let it be an offering, a prayer of your heart's longing. This intention becomes the first strand in the basket we will weave together. It is your vow to stay present to what unfolds, to let healing reveal its own timing and form.

Setting an intention can take the shape of a prayer, a wish, or a vision for your becoming. You might imagine a version of yourself that lives with more ease, speaks more truth, or rests more deeply in belonging. Let the words come simply. Hold your intention as a seed, placed with care in the soil of your being, and trust its unfolding.

Remember that you are not alone. Every intention joins the larger weave of the prayers of your mother, grandmother, and great-grandmother, the ancestral ache that lives in your bones. Your healing ripples through time, touching both those who came before and those who will come after. What you offer now becomes part of the unbroken lineage of women remembering their resilience.

In this way, your intention is both deeply personal and also universal. It will guide the weaving of your healing basket, grounding you in a story that extends far beyond your individual life. Hope and intention are the first stirrings of creation. They arise from innocence and the inner knowing that something beautiful longs to take form through us.

The Innocent Child stands at this threshold, not yet gathering or shaping anything, but reminding us of the simple, natural state from which all healing begins. Her presence returns us to the feeling of belonging to our bodies, to the earth, to the innate awareness that does not require any doing. Her gift is the gentle awakening of the part of us that knows how to begin.

Experiential Invitation: Planting the Seed of Intention

Take a moment to reflect on your intention for healing the mother ache within you.

What is your prayer or wish for yourself on this journey? It may be specific, like healing a relationship, softening a pattern, reclaiming a lost voice, or it may simply be the longing to feel more present and alive.

Write down your intention. Then speak it aloud. Feel how your body and heart respond. Sense how this personal vow weaves itself into the larger fabric of life, including your lineage and your place in the great weave of creation.

Let this intention be your compass as we continue. It will guide you gently home.

How Innocence Learns to Adapt

As you rest in your intention, take a few soft belly breaths. Notice how your breath naturally rises and falls without effort. This simple rhythm mirrors the natural state of the Innocent Child within you. In this stillness, recognition arises: beneath all the striving and tension, you are still whole. The Innocent Child reminds you that you were, and are, unconditionally lovable. This truth lives in the body as a felt sense of ease, worthiness, and belonging. Yet as life unfolds, we often lose touch with this natural rhythm. The disconnect from this essential truth is the root of the mother ache.

We lose our felt sense of being worthy of love as we adapt to our caregivers. We learn that we cannot fully exist in our own natural rhythm without risking the withdrawal of care and love. Feeding, sleep, play, and emotional expression—the innate cycles of a baby's natural rhythm—must adjust to the mother's availability, moods, and expectations. To feel safe and held, the Innocent Child begins to disconnect from her natural impulses and spontaneous expression of needs. What was once a seamless flow of inner signals and responses starts to shift outward, aligning instead with the cues and needs of the mother.

This attunement, though born of survival, forms the basis for the adaptive patterns found in our periphery minds that lead us away from innocence. The Innocent Child learns to predict, anticipate, please, and hold back. She learns that her needs are negotiable, conditional, or sometimes even irrelevant. In these adaptations, a subtle but profound disconnection from the self begins when the child shifts focus outward, seeking recognition and care from her mother, and in doing so, starts to ignore her own body's signals.

Ignoring our inner cues is the first seed of the mother ache: the ache of disconnecting from oneself. As a result, the seeds of ache and of yearning for reconnection are planted. This disconnection marks the beginning of a journey that will eventually call the child back home to herself.

The truth is that not all our needs were met, and in response, we learned to adapt. These adaptations, which serve as survival strategies, helped us navigate a world that couldn't always nurture or protect us. They are neither wrong nor shameful; they are the creative responses of a child striving to be safe and loved.

Yet these same strategies, which are so vital during our early years, can often cause us to remain reactive and disconnected from our true selves as adults. By grounding ourselves first in the awareness of our Innocent Child, we create a space to observe these adaptive patterns with gentleness. From this place of awareness, we can begin to explore how they formed, how they protect us, and how they can now be released or transformed.

Awareness Through the Five Senses

The Innocent Child lives in direct contact with life. She does not analyze her experience, she feels it. Her awareness is sensory: rooted in the smell of the earth, the warmth of touch. To reconnect with her presence, we too must return to the body's natural way of knowing.

To heal, we need to reawaken our painful early experiences, yet staying connected to the present is crucial for this process. When we focus on what we see, hear, touch, taste, and smell, we can anchor ourselves in the here and now. Spiritual teachers, yogis, and Wisdom Keepers throughout history have taught and continue to teach that our five senses are a powerful gateway to staying present. They remind us that awareness is an embodied state: a way of knowing the world through intimacy and immediacy. When we open to our senses, awareness expands beyond the mind and into the living moment.

This practice invites you to slow down, observe, and honor what we mostly take for granted. Each sense is a doorway back to the simplicity of being alive. Through the senses, we remember what the Innocent Child always knew: that life is vivid, textured, and here, now.

Experiential Invitation: Awakening the Senses

Find a tranquil space, in nature if that is possible. Bring something flavorful to taste. Sit comfortably or stand with your feet planted on the ground. Take a few soft belly breaths, letting your body settle and your awareness deepen. Spend a good amount of time with each sense, really relishing this opportunity to experience that which we largely take for granted in our worlds.

Sight: Gently open your eyes. Take in your surroundings: the colors, shapes, textures, and shadows. Let your gaze soften. Notice without naming. See as if for the first time.

Sound: Close your eyes and listen deeply. What sounds meet you now: the hum of air, the rhythm of your breath, a distant bird, music? Let your listening be spacious.

Touch: Feel the air against your skin, the weight of your body on the earth. Rub your palms together and sense the warmth that forms. Touch what is near you and feel its texture.

Smell: Notice the scents around you: the faint fragrance that stirs, the smell of earth. Really savor the smells that surround you, noticing more subtle aromas as you allow time to explore.

Taste: Slowly imbibe whatever you brought to experience the sense of taste. Feel it on your tongue. Sense it in your mouth as you chew and swallow.

Move slowly through each sense. There is no right or wrong way to experience this. The invitation is simply to be in the moment and to let your body's sensory intelligence lead. Each sense opens a doorway into the present and thus helps you learn to rest safely in your own skin.

Awareness through the senses grounds you in the here, now. It reminds you that beneath every thought and adaptation, your innocence remains intact. Like soft belly breathing, this practice can support you anywhere: walking in a park, preparing a meal, or pausing between tasks. Each time you engage your senses, you return to the simple miracle of awareness.

The Healing Presence of the Natural World

Awareness through the senses returns us to the present moment. It reminds us that life is always meeting us through taste, texture, color, sound, and scent. As you settle more fully into this awareness, you may feel an instinctual pull toward nature: the trees, the sky, the soil beneath your feet. Nature becomes your next teacher, a steady companion who offers belonging and restores your trust in life's rhythm.

Nature is a patient guide. She teaches without words, through the language of wind and rain, growth and decay. It is often in nature that we remember our own innocence and the way awareness once flowed effortlessly through us before we learned to try to manage our lives. In the stillness of the forest, the rush of a river, or the hum of insects at dusk, we remember that we are part of something vast, cyclical, and whole.

Nature teaches surrender. In her presence, we remember that we are not in charge. The seasons unfold without our control, just as healing does. We begin to see that every cycle—birth, growth, decay, and renewal—has its place. By observing these rhythms, we learn to honor our own cycles, creating, letting go, stillness, and beginning again.

Find ways to meet the natural world each day. Whether it's a park, a walking trail, a garden, or simply the sky outside your window, each moment of contact nourishes your sense of connection. Step outside and notice how your senses awaken. Feel the air touch your skin, listen to the sounds that surround you, notice how the earth meets your feet. These small acts of attention bring you home to your body and the living world.

While in nature, experiment with seeing as the Innocent Child sees without naming. When you look at a sunrise or a sunflower, notice how quickly the mind begins to label: beautiful, golden, bright. Then gently release these words. Return to the raw experience of seeing, the simple wonder of color and light. This is the essence of awareness, no language is required or needed.

Even brief encounters with the natural world can open the heart like watching clouds drift across the sky, hearing birdsong in the early morning, or noticing dew on morning leaves. These are reminders that life continues to unfold in harmony. Such moments offer the same sense of calm and grounding as soft belly breathing. Over time, they weave a relationship between you and Mother Earth, a silent conversation that whispers that you belong.

No matter how full your life feels, seek these moments. A short walk around the block, sitting under a tree during lunch, tending a garden, or even touching a houseplant can become acts of reconnection. Nature is our most profound teacher. In her company, you will find patience, renewal, and the simple grace of being alive.

The Living Pulse Beneath All Things

As you connect with nature by feeling her breath in the wind, the warmth of sunlight on your skin, the hum of life in the soil, you may begin to sense an incredible intelligence holding it all. This can be understood in our journey together as the Great Mother[4]: the living energy field from which all things arise and into which all things return. Long before religion, before we had names for the sacred, our early ancestors felt Her presence. She is the unseen rhythm pulsing through birth, growth, decay, and renewal. She is the heartbeat of creation itself.

The Great Mother, as I use the term, is not a goddess in human form. Here she is the primordial breath of existence itself, the living matrix from which all life emerges. In early human history, this formless presence was

---

4 Erich Neumann, *The Great Mother: An Analysis of the Archetype* (Princeton, NJ: Princeton University Press, 1955). In this brilliant work of archetypal psychology, Neumann identifies the Great Mother as humanity's earliest understanding of the divine, a primordial symbol encompassing both creation and dissolution, birth and return. His insights reveal how the Great Mother continues to live within the collective psyche as the original source of life, shaping our experience of love, safety, and belonging. Reading *The Great Mother* reminded me how profoundly we remain bound to Her, and not only to our personal mothers but to the lineage of all mothers who came before.

felt through nature, through the body, and through the cycles of birth and decay. As cultures developed symbolic language, the Great Mother became personified as goddesses of fertility, the Earth, creativity, and protection, such as Isis, Demeter, and other ancient figures. These divine mothers are archetypal images that help us relate to the ineffable, but the Great Mother herself is older than any of these personifications. She is the source; the goddesses and holy women are her messengers.

As humans began to anthropomorphize Her, early Paleolithic images of the sacred feminine were reshaped into named goddesses and devotional forms. From the Neolithic figurines of Old Europe, to the Celtic goddess Brigid, and later the veneration of Mother Mary as the sacred feminine in Christian lands, these figures reflect humanity's enduring relationship with a maternal intelligence greater than any single tradition.[5]

Earlier than these historic embodiments, she was understood to be the living pulse beneath all things. Before the mind divided spirit from matter, She was known through connection to the Earth, in the rhythm of the tide, the turning of the seasons. For our earliest ancestors, the Great Mother was the first face of the divine, representing the unbroken circle of life through which all beings move.

Later, as humanity's gaze turned toward the heavens, we began to forget the holiness of what is near: the Earth beneath our feet, the breath within our chest, the body that is also Her. Yet She never left us. She continues to move through us as intuition, as longing, as the gravitational pull toward truth. She remains the intelligence that breathes us, shapes us, and calls us home.

Within Her, nothing is separate. Light and shadow, stillness and storm, birth and death all spiral together in Her embrace. The Great Mother is not apart from the world you touch; She is the touch itself. The fragrance of rain, the pulse beneath your feet, the awareness that beholds all and judges nothing.

From Her, we inherit our innocence. It is Her breath that fills the newborn's lungs, Her warmth invites the feeling in the body that says, *I am safe here. I belong.*

---

5 See Marija Gimbutas, *The Living Goddesses*, ed. Miriam Robbins Dexter (Berkeley: University of California Press, 1999), and *The Civilization of the Goddess* (San Francisco: HarperSanFrancisco, 1991), which document the continuity of prehistoric feminine symbolism and its later personification into named goddesses and sacred maternal figures across cultures.

Our Innocent Child carries this imprint and the understanding that life itself is trustworthy, that love is the ground of being. To awaken awareness is an invitation to remember her and to return to the first wisdom: that all of life, even its ache, belongs within a larger harmony.

A simple way to understand the Great Mother is to feel her as the current of love moving through existence, shaping all things. She is not a separate being or a distant deity. She is the very essence of life itself. Wherever love is felt, wherever beauty is recognized, wherever presence awakens, the Great Mother is there. She is a continuous echo from the universe, reminding us that beneath all our layers, we are love, incarnated.

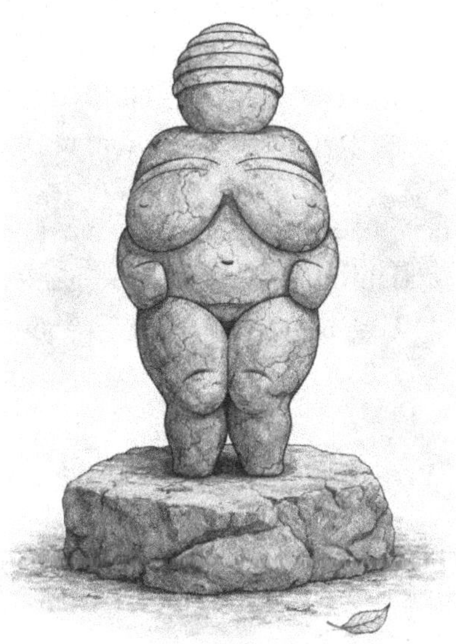

One of the earliest sculptures of the sacred, this Great Mother figure embodies humanity's first understanding of divinity as life-giving, cyclical, and ever-renewing. Her rounded form echoes the primordial source of birth, nourishment, and return.

As you open through your senses and commune with the natural world, you are experiencing Her. She is the energetic origin of every feminine manifestation of the Divine Mother: Pachamama, Gaia, the Dark Mother, Isis, Brigid, Mary. Even your human mother, with all her imperfections, is a reflection of the Great Mother expressing Herself through human form. The Great Mother, in essence, is love.

The journey of awareness is a journey of return to this simple truth. As we cultivate awareness, we remember what the Innocent Child within has always known, that love is not something we earn, it is something we are. Over time, this innocence ripens into wisdom, the mature knowing that this same love breathes through all creation. When Christ said, "Truly I tell you, unless you change and become like little children, you will never enter the kingdom of heaven" (Matthew 18:3), he was calling us home to this truth and inviting us to restore our hearts to their original innocence, unburdened, awake, pulsing with love.

Recognizing the Great Mother does not negate any faith or path. It simply involves sensing what lies beneath them all: the original pulse of creation, the silent presence that breathes through every name for God. Before temples existed, there was the Earth. Before prayers, there was life. She is the silent ground beneath all understanding, the love from which every path unfolds. And for as long as we have been human, we have known her as mother.

As we walk this spiral of remembrance together, may you let Her hold you through the ache, and through every act of devotion and return. Walking this path is to remember Her, to remember love, within yourself, to remember that you are love.

Experiential Invitation: Meeting The Great Mother

Let the following practice become a way of meeting the Great Mother through your body: simple, sensory, and real.

Find a time to be in nature.

Once you have settled, pause. Feel your body resting on the earth beneath you, the solid, breathing presence that holds all life. Notice how the ground supports you effortlessly and without condition.

Bring awareness to your breath. Feel the air moving in and out of your body, the same air that moves through trees, rivers, and clouds. With each inhale, invite Her presence. With each exhale, offer your presence, your gratitude, your belonging.

Let your awareness expand gently through your senses.

Listen: What sound meets you right now? The murmur of wind, the cry of a bird, the hum of silence itself?

Smell: What scent lingers in the air: earth, pine, rain, your own skin?

Touch: What texture calls to your hands: the bark of a tree, the smoothness of stone, the rhythm of your own heartbeat beneath your palm?

Let these small details become messengers. Each carries the signature of the Great Mother, whispering that you belong, that you are part of Her living field.

As you listen, invite recognition to rise within you. You are not separate. You are held within Her breath, woven into the same current that moves the wind, the water, and the stars.

Rest here for a few breaths, rooted in the innocence that knows everything belongs.

Sense into the idea that you are already home.

When you return from this practice, pause before speaking or moving. Notice what lingers, the sense of the air on your skin, the steady rhythm in your chest, the subtle awareness that you are part of something vast and benevolent. This is the living presence of the Great Mother moving through you.

In the days ahead, let small moments become reminders of Her: the warmth of sunlight on your face, the weight of your feet on the earth, the taste of water after thirst. Each is a thread of reconnection, an invitation to live as though the world itself were sacred, because it is.

I still remember the first time I felt this presence in a way that broke me open. I was running on a trail I had traveled for years with the same trees, same sky, same familiar curve of Earth beneath my feet. But something in me had shifted after years of this very same healing work that we explore in this book, and on that day the world revealed itself differently. The trees felt alive with awareness. The ground rose to meet me. The sky seemed impossibly vast, and the birdsong felt like it was moving through me rather than around me. I stopped and began to cry, partly in grief for all the years I had run through this beauty without truly knowing it, and partly in gratitude for receiving this understanding at last. That moment was my first unmistakable experience of the Great Mother as a living presence that holds me, connects me, and opens my heart to boundless love.

As you continue your journey, may you begin to notice your own moments of recognition, subtle openings that remind you that you belong to something vast, benevolent, and loving. Let the reflections below help you deepen into that awareness and reconnect with the Innocent Child within you.

Journal Reflections: Reweaving Awareness

Take a few deep breaths and let your body soften. Move through these reflections at your own pace, allowing each one to meet you where you are. You do not need to answer every question. Let your attention rest on what feels most alive within and accessible. Awareness grows through kind attention and cannot be forced.

Recognizing the Innocent Child

What does innocence mean to you, as a way of being?
In what moments do you sense your Innocent Child within you?
How do you notice innocence expressed in others or mirrored in the natural world?

Soft Belly Breathing

As you reflect on your breathing practice, notice how your body responded.
Did you sense tension softening or feel its calming effect?
How did this gentle rhythm influence your sense of safety, presence, or calm?
Consider committing to eleven-days of soft belly breathing. Write about this commitment and how it might support your healing. If you don't want to commit, explore why this doesn't appeal to you.

Setting Intention

Look at the intention you have formed. How does this feel supportive for you as you begin this healing journey?
How might you hold your intention as an invitation rather than a demand?
What are a few practical things you can do daily to support this intention? I like to call these my daily weaving practices.

Noticing Through the Senses

Which of your senses felt most alive during the practice?
Did any sense open a doorway to more awareness?
How did engaging your senses shift your awareness of yourself or the world around you?

Communion with Nature

Recall a time when the natural world soothed or held you. What did that feel like in your body?
How does time in nature affect your sense of calm or belonging?
In what ways might the Earth become a companion on your healing journey? How might the Earth be an ally who reminds you to slow down and return to your natural rhythm?
What small, daily gestures can honor your connection to nature right now?

Being Held by the Great Mother

Reflect on a moment when you felt supported by something larger than yourself through nature, prayer, meditation, or stillness.
How might seeing this presence as the Great Mother shift your experience of belonging?
How could this awareness influence how you move through your daily life, your relationships, and your inner world?
Reflect on the idea that love is the signature of the Great Mother and binds all things into one.

Take your time with these reflections. Let your words settle where they need to, knowing that each one brings you closer to the Innocent Child within you.

From Innocence to Wonder

"We shall not cease from exploration,
And the end of all our exploring
Will be to arrive where we started
And know the place for the first time."

- T. S. Eliot

Take a moment to honor the Innocent Child you were at the very beginning of your life. She embodies the essential quality of awareness within you. In remembering her, you have begun the journey home to yourself and to the self-compassion that lives beneath all striving.

Through soft belly breathing, you now have a meditation that offers an anchor, a way to return your body and mind to presence. By awakening your five senses, you have practiced inhabiting the richness of the here and now. Seeing, hearing, touching, tasting, and smelling the world around you are daily invitations to return to your body, to remember that love lives here, through awareness. These tools are yours, ready to use whenever you need to ground, soothe, or reconnect. You have also begun to recognize how nature mirrors your own inner landscape—a living reflection of rhythm, renewal, and belonging.

In this awareness, you may sense the presence of the Great Mother, the ancient intelligence that breathes through all creation. From Her we can relearn innocence, the original knowing that we belong. And to Her we return as her daughters, ready to release what never belonged to us and rest in the wisdom of what remains.

Our awareness will guide the path ahead. Innocence is your first touchstone. To meet this place within is to feel the longing that draws you toward your own inner world and healing. From this place, wonder awakens. Curiosity stirs. The natural awareness of the Innocent Child is the bridge to the next archetype, the Magical Child, who invites you to rediscover curiosity through exploration, imagination, and wonder.

Chapter Two:

The Magical Child and the World of Wonder

"I suppose to some extent all children have a touch of magic about them – like some mysterious living lens they seem to have the capacity to focus the light into the darkest and gloomiest of places.... Perhaps it's the very newness of the young, or perhaps it's just because the shine hasn't worn off, but they can and do, if you give them half a chance, make a dent in the toughest armor of life. If you're very lucky they can dissolve away all those protective barricades so carefully erected over years of living."

-Fynne

If the Innocent Child is the seed of awareness, then the Magical Child is the sprout reaching toward the sun with curiosity. The Magical Child archetype in our journey connects us to another natural quality within ourselves that we must reacquaint ourselves with on our healing journey. *Curiosity* is the gentle, open interest that allows us to explore experience without needing to control or explain it. Through curiosity the Magical Child embodies a natural openness to the world. She is the part of us that enjoys exploring and trying new things. Like the innocent child, she is also an essential part of our natural selves, no matter how disconnected we may feel from her. Past injuries or fearful future projections do not limit her. She observes and experiences what is. The energy of the Magical Child archetype has always existed within us, ready to help us grow and evolve.

For most of us longing to heal our mother ache, she may feel unfamiliar, tucked away beneath layers of adaptation and self-protection. Whether familiar or distant, the first step is to recognize her presence within us. It is through her energetic signature of curiosity that we begin gathering the raw materials of the experiences of our childhood relationship with our mother. We will do so like a child gathering raw materials for a basket in the forest; we won't measure or judge as we gather. Instead, we will invoke the awareness from the last chapter and our natural curiosity.

With curiosity, the Magical Child gathers the early strands of your mother ache, bringing together the raw materials of memory and feeling that will form the foundation of your healing basket.

The Magical Child and the Energetic Truth of Being

"We have calcium in our bones, iron in our veins, carbon in our souls, and nitrogen in our brains. Ninety-three percent stardust, with souls made of flames, we are all just stars that have people names."

—Nikita Gill

Before we knew words, we first experienced life as energy. In utero, much of what our mother lived and felt reached us as sensation and rhythm in the body. At birth, we enter a world alive with energetic frequencies: light, tone, color, breath, touch, and sound. The Magical Child inhabits this world with ease.

Modern physics affirms what ancient wisdom keepers have always known: *everything in existence is energy in motion*. Every atom, stone, tree, every cell in our bodies, everything is moving particles of energy shaped into form. Even what seems solid is, at its core, a pattern of energetic vibration.

We sense this truth without needing to name it. We feel comfort from a gentle voice. We sense tension before someone speaks. Stepping into a room, we know if it feels welcoming or unsettling. Our hearts soften when we see a sunset. These are largely unconscious perceptions of the energy that surrounds us and they are also physiological truths. The body correctly reads energy long before the mind interprets meaning.

The Magical Child lives naturally in this awareness. She moves through the world guided by resonance, by the feeling of *this is right* or *this is off*. She learns by exploring, sensing, and moving. Curiosity is her language. She does not separate sensation from emotion, or emotion from meaning; to her, they are one continuous stream of experience.

As we grow older, this innate sensitivity becomes overshadowed. We are taught to value what can be understood by the mind and to disregard this intuition. Logic takes the lead, and energetic awareness recedes. Yet it never disappears. It keeps shaping our lives, subconsciously.

Reconnecting with the Magical Child is reconnecting with this original truth: you are a being that is comprised of energy, living in a world that is also comprised of this same energy. This explains why your early experiences made impressions on your body and its vibrational field. The child within you felt these currents long before she could understand them. When you begin to understand your story energetically, things begin to make more sense. You begin to understand why you brace around certain people; why some places drain you while others enliven you; why your breath changes in conflict; why your body remembers what your mind has suppressed. Energy is the first language of the psyche. It is the thread beneath sensation and emotion, the pulse beneath thought.

Through years of meditation, shamanic apprenticeship, daily yoga, and listening to the natural world, I have come to understand energy as something intimate and alive. The teachings I have received from Andean, Amazonian and Eastern Wisdom Keepers regarding the five elements of earth, water, fire, air, and ether, have shown me that everything in existence is made of the same energetic signatures, including us. The proportions may differ, the expressions may change, but the essence is shared. Recognizing this has been profoundly healing for me. It feels magical, almost childlike, to remember that my bones are made of earth, my breath carries air, my heartbeat glows with fire, my emotions move like water, and my awareness expands like ether. When I began to honor that I am woven from the same elements that shaped the mountains, rivers, wind, and stars, something inside me softened. I felt less separate, more held. The world became a companion rather than a place to navigate. This simple remembering has brought me home to myself again and again.

The Magical Child within you already knows this too. She remembers the world as vibration, color, movement, warmth, aliveness. She invites you to return to it, bringing awareness and curiosity back online within your own being. When you pause, soften your gaze, and wonder even for a moment, the subtle, energetic world becomes available again.

Your inner Magical Child is your first guide into this vibrational truth. She reminds you that healing is not only psychological; healing is also a return to the energy that has moved within you since the beginning, waiting for you to return. This energy is older than your memories and older than your name. It existed before your body took shape and will continue long after your body is gone. It is the same living current that forms clouds and oceans, mountains and moonlight, trees and starlight. The Magical Child does not need to understand this; she simply feels it. Through her, you may begin to sense that you belong to something continuous and ancient, a presence with no beginning and no end, one that has been with you long before you had a name, patiently waiting for you to remember. You might think of this energy as the Great Mother and invite her support as you move through this chapter and gather the strands of your story to weave into your healing basket.

The Magical Child Gathers Your Story

As you begin gathering the materials of your story, it helps to remember, as we explored above, that every experience you carry arose within the larger energy field of life itself. The Magical Child invites you to explore these memories with curiosity, without judgment, the way a basket weaver collects natural fibers. We observe what presents itself, we honor what we find, and we let curiosity guide the way.

Before we continue, let us prepare a place of safety and beauty to hold you through the work ahead.

Experiential Invitation: Creating a Safe and Sacred Space

Before gathering the strands of your story, choose a space that feels grounding and private, a place where you can settle, breathe, and meet what arises with safety.

Rather than imagining a distant refuge, let a physical, sacred space, like your altar, be that sanctuary. It will remind you of your intention and invite you back to stillness whenever the strands of your story feel tangled and unmanageable.

Begin by finding a small corner or nook in your home that feels cozy. It doesn't need to be grand, but it should have a flat surface that you can use to hold your altar. Make sure it is a comfortable place that will not be disturbed, as the key is to return here often. This is where you'll journal and engage in the experiential invitations and practices outlined in this book, connecting with the parts of yourself that long to be held.

As you prepare this space, think of it as both an outer altar and an inner sanctuary. The act of creating your altar mirrors weaving—bringing order, beauty, and meaning—to what was once unformed.

You might begin with the five elements that shape your body and are the subtle energies within it:

Earth: represented by a stone or crystal, offering steadiness and nourishment

Water: represented by a shell, or fresh flowers, inviting emotional flow and renewal

Fire: represented by a candle, awakening courage and transformation

Air: represented by a feather or incense, bringing breath, clarity, and inspiration

Ether: represented by a beloved object, reminding you of spaciousness and possibility.

Place the object representing ether in the center of your altar if it feels right. This should symbolize the heart of your healing journey like a photo of your younger self, a sacred object, or a symbol of your intention. Let this altar grow with you, adding flowers, childhood tokens, or stones, leaves, and feathers from your nature walks.

When you arrive in this space, begin with your breath. Close your eyes if it feels comfortable or soften your gaze. Notice the rhythm of inhaling and exhaling, and how your body relaxes into the ground. Imagine that every part of this space, each object and element, supports your heart and mind.

If thoughts or memories arise, let them drift by like clouds. With each exhale, let go of tension. With each inhale, invite safety and calm. Remember that this altar is your safe place, a living sanctuary that reminds you of your capacity to nurture and heal yourself.

Return here whenever you need to remember who you are and how naturally you belong to the same elements that shape the world around you.

This space will become a visible reflection of your healing journey, both earthly and divine, woven of breath, memory, and devotion.

Each time you sit before your altar, take a slow breath and remember you are not separate from the elements. You are earth in your bones, fire in your will, water in your tears, air in your breath, and space (ether) in your being. These elements live in every part of you.

As you continue your journey by inviting your Magical Child to feel welcome within you again, you may find the following practices simple, even childlike, but they are sacred in their simplicity. They help you remember how to meet life without pretense, to play rather than perform.

Experiential Invitation: Meeting the Magical Child through the Eyes of Curiosity

Now that you have created a sacred space, a place of safety both within and around you, let us invite the Magical Child to join you there. She is the one who remembers wonder, imagination, and awe. In her presence, the ordinary becomes luminous again.

Allow fifteen minutes or so and approach this as an inner-journey meditation.

Sit at your altar. Close your eyes, breathe gently, and invite the presence of your Magical Child. Now, imagine her joining you there. Notice how she appears: her expression, her energy, her way of moving. She might look like the child you once were or an unfamiliar but joyful new friend.

Let her explore your space with curiosity. Watch how she touches the objects on your altar, how she notices color and light, how she delights in small details. This is her gift: she reminds you how to see with wonder.

Sit quietly together for a few breaths. You don't need to say or do anything. Let her presence open a door inside you. When you open your eyes, notice what has shifted. Perhaps your body feels lighter, or the space around you feels more alive. This is how the Magical Child restores curiosity through awareness, showing you that healing need not always be heavy; it can also be found through simple attention.

Experiential Invitation: The Companion of the Heart

Now that we've invited the Magical Child through imagery and imagination, we want to give her something tangible: a companion who can remind her that she is seen, safe, and loved.

More than twenty years ago, during a week-long Primal Therapy group in India, I was given a stuffed animal to carry with me throughout the week, a very large, cumbersome blue dolphin. I took it everywhere, even to meals. People unfamiliar with the group sometimes laughed or pointed at me, but I carried it anyway. The dolphin became a silent friend, a soft witness to my most vulnerable moments. Holding it was like holding myself.

That week taught me something simple yet profound: the healing power of a soft, comforting object. It was more than a toy; it served as a bridge to the part of me that needed gentleness. The dolphin reminded me that tenderness must coexist with deep emotional work.

For this chapter, I invite you to find such a companion. It doesn't need to be elaborate or new. A stuffed animal you already own will do; or take your inner child on a shopping trip and let her pick out a new one. What matters is that it evokes warmth and care. This object will serve as a supportive presence as you gather the raw fibers of your healing basket. It becomes a reminder that safety and love can be felt in your body, here and now.

When you hold this companion, wrap your arms around it as if embracing your inner child. Feel its texture, warmth, and softness. Let your breath slow down. You might whisper something kind to the little one inside: *You are safe. I'm here. You are loved.* Each time you hold it, remember that comfort is not a luxury, it is your birthright.

For the next week, keep this companion nearby. Let it rest beside you in bed, ride in the passenger seat of your car, or sit beside you in your workspace. You don't need to bring it everywhere but try to keep it close when appropriate. Each time your eyes meet it, let it remind you to pause, breathe, and reconnect with the wonder and innocence you are reclaiming.

This practice isn't about regression; it's about remembrance. You are endeavoring to bring the Magical Child's qualities forward consciously into your present life, where she belongs. Each glance at your companion is a gesture of reunion, a way of telling the tender one within you, *I see you. You matter. You are home.*

Gathering Your Story

"Owning our story and loving ourselves through that process is the bravest thing that we'll ever do."

—Brené Brown

As you reconnect with the Magical Child within, memories and images may start to surface—sensations, or fragments of stories. This is where the weaving begins: gathering what has been scattered and listening for what wants to be remembered. Before you start gathering the strands of your own childhood, I want to share how this process played out for me.

When I first sat down to gather my story through the eyes of my Magical Child, I didn't know where to begin. So I went to my altar, let my body soften, held my stuffed jaguar, and waited. I wasn't searching for a narrative, only listening for a whisper of memory.

At first, brief images appeared like flickers of light: running barefoot through the foothills, the sun warm on my back, dodging cactus thorns; the weight of newborn puppies in my hands; my older brother's scolding as I placed them carefully in the basket of my hot pink bicycle. I saw myself trailing behind the older kids, working hard to be included, and heard my mother's voice calling me in for dinner. I remembered the pink corduroy pants and cowboy boots I insisted on wearing every day, and I felt the simple joy of being alive in my body.

Then other memories surfaced which were cloudier and heavier. I saw my mother packing her belongings to leave, the jewelry box she gave me. It was white, with a small ballerina twirling to a tune I would never forget. I can still feel the ache of sitting on her bed, too small to understand, sensing something ending I could not name. These images came gradually, like clouds drifting across the sun.

My first instinct was to turn away. But I realized these, too, were part of the gathering. The Magical Child doesn't avoid what hurts; she moves toward it with curiosity, trusting that truth and tenderness are woven from the same thread. Each memory, bright or shadowed, is part of the same weave, teaching us how deeply we long to love and be loved.

Gathering your story begins this way: not through effort, but through openness. The memories come as they will: some vivid, some faint, some light, some dark. You don't need to chase them or make sense of them. Simply receive what arrives. Let your breath anchor you and your body remain present by connecting to your sacred space if needed.

When a memory surfaces, whether light or heavy, let it be. Feel your feet on the ground, the air in your lungs. You are not returning to the past; you are allowing it to speak. These are the strands you will later weave into your basket: bright, frayed, tender, and true.

Experiential Invitation: Gathering Your Story with Curiosity

Now that you have a sacred space and a comforting companion, you are ready to begin gathering the raw materials for your healing basket. Approaching your memories with awareness and curiosity allows you to collect what truly belongs to you, the experiences of your own childhood that will form the foundation of your healing.

Imagine yourself outdoors, gathering natural fibers for a basket. Notice how you pick each one up without judgment. A reed is neither good nor bad; a fallen branch is neither perfect nor flawed. Each has value simply by being what it is, offered by the earth. Likewise, every memory, whether bright or shadowed, has its place in your own healing journey.

Begin by closing your eyes and allowing memories to surface naturally, especially those related to your mother and your early experiences of love, care, or absence. Don't try to search for or force them. Let the images come as they wish—perhaps a flash of color, a sound, or a small, remembered gesture. As they appear, stay connected to your body. Notice sensations: a warmth in your chest, a flutter in your belly, or a tightening in your throat. Breathe softly into whatever you feel, letting your breath flow through you like a tide.

If a memory feels heavy or too intense, pause. Return to your altar, to your breath, or to the comfort of your soft companion. You can always rest in the safety you have built.

Spend time in this way, following the curiosity of your Magical Child. Let her guide you as you collect the fibers of your mother ache. There is no rush. You may gather one strand today, another tomorrow. Healing is woven over time.

You might first notice the joyful moments when you felt seen and held, and loved. Maybe it was a summer afternoon, a bedtime story, or how your mother's hands moved while she cooked. Let these bright strands come easily, like sunlight filtering through leaves.

Then, gently, turn toward the memories that feel more tender, moments of separation, confusion, or pain. These too belong in your basket. They do not need to be analyzed or fixed. Simply hold them with curiosity, as if gathering weathered reeds along the riverbank. Each one, gathered with presence, becomes part of the material of healing.

When you feel complete, take a few deep breaths of gratitude for your courage to remember. What you have gathered today are more than memories; they are the living fibers of your story, ready to be woven into wholeness. It might help to journal about what you have gathered. There are journal prompts to support this at the end of the chapter, or you can free write your experience both of gathering and what came through for you.

Listening for Our Mother's Story

Now that you've begun gathering the strands of your own story, it's time to turn your curiosity toward your mother's. Approach this step gently. You are not seeking to find fault but to gain a sense of what shaped her, what she carried, and how those strands were woven into your life.

When I began gathering my mother's story, I saw a young girl shaped by instability and hardship. My mom was seventeen when she gave birth to my brother in 1962, a time when becoming a mother at such a young age meant leaving school and stepping into adult life overnight. My father worked in construction, and by most accounts, they were happy, at least for a while. I arrived two years later, an "easy baby," she said, born into a world already filled with both hope and strain.

My mother's early life was chaotic and unstable. Her father, a World War II veteran turned Baptist minister, struggled with undiagnosed mental illness and unpredictable rage. The family moved frequently—from one church to another, from one small town to the next—so my mother never spent a full year at the same school. Just as she would start to settle, everything shifted again. Poverty followed them, but so did my grandmother's devout Christian faith and ingenuity. Effie, my grandmother, sewed clothes from remnants and turned the most meager ingredients into nourishing meals. Though my mother saw her as passive, we both now see her as strong and steadfast, a woman holding her family together through sacrifice, devotion, and unwavering love for her children.

My mother's childhood was a blend of shame about her poverty and a longing for stability and safety. She never knew when her father would go off on an extreme tirade that would then cause another move. When she turned back toward her childhood, she remembered the shame of raising her hand in fifth grade when the teacher asked who had a television, even though she did not. In sixth grade, she had to carry the sting of her teacher arriving at her home as part of a church charity visit. In eighth grade, she remembered the pride of riding her new bicycle to school on the first day, until she arrived and realized she was the only girl on a bike, and something in her folded. These small moments revealed a larger story: a girl learning to read the room, hide her needs, and protect herself from embarrassment. Without meaning to, she passed these skills on to me.

When we gather our mothers' stories, we begin to understand the roots of their choices and strengths. We may notice how their adaptations became our own, either through mirroring or rejecting them. As you start to recall your mother's story, hold her with the same curiosity you hold your own Magical Child. You are not judging her story but observing the strands that shaped her so that you can choose how to weave them differently.

You might have only fragments, such as a few stories passed down, old photographs, your own memories, or impressions felt rather than spoken. These are enough. Let curiosity guide you as you trace her childhood and the environment that shaped her. Each glimpse adds texture to the weave of understanding, helping you recognize the lineage of resilience, love, and adaptation that connects you both.

Approaching your mother's story this way opens a door to belonging and is not at all about finding fault with her. When you hold her story with tenderness, you begin to free your own. You might journal about what you have uncovered here as well, either free writing or with the prompts at the end of this chapter.

Remembering Our Grandmother's Story

When you turn toward your grandmother's story, you are also turning toward the deeper currents that shaped your own life. The science of epigenetics[6] shows that when your mother was developing inside your grandmother's womb, the immature egg that would one day become you was already present. For a brief moment, three generations shared one internal world. Your grandmother's environment, including her nourishment, stresses, joys, and fears, left impressions that influenced your mother's biology and, eventually, your own nervous system through that egg that became you. This is one of the ways lineage moves through us, both physically and

6 If you are curious about how experiences in one generation can shape stress responses in later generations, this field is known as epigenetics. For an accessible introduction, see Mark Wolynn, *It Didn't Start with You: How Inherited Family Trauma Shapes Who We Are and How to End the Cycle* (New York: Penguin, 2016). For a more science-focused overview, see David S. Moore, *The Developing Genome: An Introduction to Behavioral Epigenetics* (New York: Oxford University Press, 2015).

energetically. Earlier in this chapter, we explored how energy lives within and around us; here, that teaching becomes tangible. Your grandmother's life formed part of the field you emerged from. Her experiences continue to echo through your patterns of protection, connection, and sensitivity, and even physical or mental illness. Gathering her story becomes an act of understanding the original conditions that shaped your being, and a way to honor the connective and timeless energy that you now carry forward from her. In this way we are linked across time to our entire maternal lineage.

With this in mind, I invite you to now turn your attention to your grandmother and the women who came before her. What do you remember? What stories were told, and which ones were never spoken aloud? If she is still living it might be nice to reach out to her and explore these questions. If not is there anyone who might remember and share with you? Think of these memories as precious fibers for your basket: each one a strand that connects you to your maternal line.

Each generation carries echoes of the last. A mother's exhaustion, a grandmother's resilience, a great-grandmother's servitude: these become textures in a daughter's life. When we recognize these influences, we begin to discern what is ours to carry forward and what we can lay down with love.

These histories are living energy currents shaping patterns of courage, creativity, and endurance within you. Honoring the women who dreamed and birthed you strengthens the weave of your basket; your healing ripples backward and forward through time.

When I gathered my grandmother's story, I understood how deeply she had shaped my understanding of love and safety. My maternal grandmother, Effie, was a steady light in my early childhood. I remember cuddling beside her as she read until her voice became hoarse. With her, I felt safe and loved. Yet her life, like my mother's, carried its own ache. She was a Dutch immigrant born into hardship. Her father, widowed with two young children, remarried quickly—out of necessity, not love—and her mother, my great-grandmother Martha lived a life of servitude under strict religious rules. Effie was one of four children born to Martha, who raised all six Dutch children in strict obedience to her husband's stern commands. My grandmother adored her father and spoke of him with reverence. She rarely mentioned her mother. In that silence, I now hear an unspoken grief, a thread of longing woven into her heart. I find myself wondering about Martha: what she loved, what she dreamed, how she cared for the six children entrusted to her. It seems no one actually knows, which I find terribly sad.

After the war, Effie married my grandfather, a Baptist minister and WWII veteran. They faced poverty, frequent relocations, and the burden of his mental illness. Throughout it all, she kept the family together by mending clothes, stretching meals, and leaning on faith. Her gentle strength was how love took shape under pressure. She lived by true Christian values and even in her abject poverty sewed small gifts for the children in her Sunday school class and gave what she could to those in need.

Gathering her story taught me how strength and service can intertwine, how devotion can carry its own ache, and how love endures. As you explore your grandmother's life, look for the invisible strands: the ways care, sacrifice, humor, prayer, craft, or song may still live in you. Notice what was passed down through hands and habits, through voice and absence. Every gesture, every hush, is part of the material you are gathering for your own healing. You might journal here with the prompts at the end of this chapter before continuing.

Meditation as a Path of Play

For the Magical Child, play is not a luxury, it is a language. It is how the body remembers joy, experiments with freedom, and restores a sense of safety after intensity. When our inner work brings up tender memories or strong emotions, play offers a way to stay connected to aliveness without becoming overwhelmed. It reminds us that healing does not happen only through insight, but through movement, curiosity, and pleasure. Making time to play, whether through movement, creativity, or simple silliness, gives the Magical Child permission to come back online, to explore, and to feel held by life again.

The Magical Child's task of gathering memories can be tender and intense. As we collect these raw materials, we must also make space for movement, release, and play. The following practice is a playful, active meditation that invites the body to move energy instead of getting stuck in the stories we've unearthed. It's a way to let your Magical Child dance, shake, and breathe her way back into flow.

Experiential Practice: Kundalini Meditation

This one-hour active meditation unfolds in four stages: shaking, dancing, sitting, and relaxation. Shaking melts rigidity and restores natural aliveness. Dancing expresses what has loosened, allowing it to flow. Sitting allows awareness to settle, and the final stage of relaxation invites integration.

These movements are not new. Across cultures, our ancestors have known the medicine of motion. Indigenous peoples, Indian sadhus, Tibetan monks, and Sufi dervishes all used shaking and dancing as forms of devotion, prayer, and healing. The body has always known how to release what the mind holds too tightly.

Before you begin, take a moment to recognize what a rare and precious opportunity this is. To move the body freely. To shake, inviting repressed energy to release. To let energy surge and spill without explanation or apology. Many of us with the mother ache were never given permission to move freely like this. We were not allowed or encouraged to be playful, free in our own bodies, or spontaneous. And yet the body remembers and longs to be set free like this.

As the music begins, allow yourself to shake as if heat were moving through you, loosening what has been held. Let the movement grow until you feel liquid inside, until effort gives way to flow. When the dancing stage comes, dance as though no one is watching, as though this were your last chance to feel the miracle of your own aliveness through movement. This is not performance. It is release. It is celebration. It is the body remembering itself. The more total you are in this meditation the more healing and release happens, and the more silence and relaxation will occur in the last two stages. Be total.

Kundalini Meditation Instructions: Four Stages (fifteen minutes each)

The music for this meditation is available on most streaming platforms by searching for Osho Kundalini Meditation.

Shaking: Stand with knees soft and let your body shake freely. Don't direct it; allow it. Eyes closed, start with your hands and arms and let the shaking move into every cell of your body.

Dancing: Let the shaking dissolve into movement: dancing, swaying, twirling. Move however your body wishes. Keep your eyes closed or if open to avoid bumping into things, keep a soft, unfocused gaze.

Sitting: Come into stillness in sukhasana or on a chair. With your eyes closed, turn inward. Watch the energy moving within you. Let the breath find its own rhythm. Focus on your breath.

Relaxation: Lie down on your back. Breathe gently. Let your body rest into the ground and release completely. Let go.

For over twenty years, I have practiced Kundalini Meditation, and it remains one of my most supportive daily practices. It restores rhythm, releases tension and brings lightness to my days. If you don't have a full hour, create your own "Mini-Kundalini" by shortening each stage to five minutes. Even a few moments of shaking or spontaneous movement can help shift stagnant energy and foster curiosity.

What follows is one such story.

Mother Ache Healing in the World:

The Girl Who Remembered Magic

Michelle grew up on the edges of her family, the middle daughter in a home where love flowed unevenly. Her father favored her older sister. Her mother's attention turned toward her two younger daughters from a second marriage. Even her maternal grandmother once looked at Michelle and wondered aloud if she really belonged to the family. These moments formed a mother ache that lived just beneath her ribs, unnamed but present. She did not have language for it then, but she could feel the truth of being left out.

To soothe this ache as a child, Michelle found comfort in art and nature. In the basement of her childhood home, painting ceramics to supplement her mother's income, she discovered a gift for painting. Outside, in the woods and along lake edges, she felt welcomed by the trees and the earth in a way she never felt inside her own home. Nature held her in a steadier way than her mother could. Her Magical Child found refuge in creating art and in the wild world, in color and clay, lake and sky.

Still, the longing for her mother remained. As she grew older, that longing twisted inward and became a battle with her own body. The eating disorder that emerged reflected the deeper wound of feeling unworthy of being loved. Her mother's preference for her younger two daughters became Michelle's belief that something within her was terribly wrong and needed to be hidden and fixed in order for her to be loved.

When Michelle and I began working together, she was used to examining herself through judgment, with a harsh inner critic that seemed unrelenting. By learning to approach her inner world with curiosity, that critical voice began to soften. When she asked gentle questions rather than harsh ones, something shifted. Curiosity created a small space inside her where her mother ache could breathe. It also allowed her to look at her lineage with new eyes. She began to gather the strands of her mother's and grandmother's stories, seeing how each of them carried wounds of their own. Her mother had suffered a terrible ongoing violation in childhood and grew up inside a home marked by silence and fear. Understanding this did not excuse the pain Michelle felt, yet it helped her hold it with more compassion. Her grandmother failed to protect her mother and was very cold.

I've worked with Michelle for many years and have witnessed her healing journey with deep respect. Through years of therapy, embodiment practices, breathwork, sacred plant medicine, movement, active meditations, and supported, deep self-inquiry work, the Magical Child she had tucked away began to emerge again, as her healing ripened. Her creativity returned as a companion rather than an escape. The ache remains, but it no longer defines her. She begins to sense the difference between longing for a mother who could not give more and recognizing the young part of herself who still somehow had expectations that someday this would occur.

Today, Michelle is a massage therapist and sound healer. Her touch is gentle and intuitive, shaped by a life that taught her that healing is a life-long process of showing up and being open to new experiences and healing modalities. The ache that once isolated her has become a bridge of compassion. Her Magical Child now lives within her as a steady knowing that wonder and curiosity can lead us back to the places where belonging becomes possible again.

Journal Reflections: Reweaving Curiosity

Take a few slow breaths and settle into your sacred space. Let your awareness soften as you prepare to reflect on The Magical Child within you. The following prompts are invitations and can be explored over time, no need to tackle them all at once.

Energy and the Elements Within You

How do you relate to the idea that everything, including you, is energy and comprised of the five elements?
Take a few moments to soften your breath and notice the presence of the elements in and around you. Let your awareness rest on the felt sense of being made of earth, water, fire, air, and space, and allow whatever arises to meet the page.
How do you sense the elements within your own body and energy right now, through sensations, images, or feelings?

Your Sacred Space and the Elements

What do the elements or symbols you placed on your altar mean to you?
How does it feel to create an altar devoted to you and your healing?
In what ways can returning to and tending this altar become a practice of self-love and remembrance?
How might tending this space reflect the way you tend to yourself?

Welcoming Your Magical Child's Companion

What feelings arise when you hold your companion?
How does this object support remembering your Magical Child?
When difficult memories surface, how might this companion remind you of safety and care?
If your companion could speak, what would it tell you about nurturing yourself during this work?

Collecting the Stories of the Mother Ache

Take a moment to soften your breath and let the thread of memory unwind. You are gathering what is ready to be remembered. Trust what surfaces and your own timing.

What were the first memories that surfaced as you began this gathering?
What small gestures, objects, or moments stand out to your Magical Child?
Which memories with your mother feel joyful or nurturing? Which ones feel tender or unresolved?
How can you hold these memories without judgment, allowing them to exist as part of your story?
Reflect on what you have gathered so far. Which experiences feel most vivid within you right now? Which might need more gentleness or more time as you continue?

Offer yourself gratitude for listening with gentleness and courage. Each memory you meet with compassion becomes a golden strand in the basket of your healing.

Your Mother's Childhood

Take a few moments to soften your heart. As you turn toward your mother's story, let it unfold gently. You are not seeking to excuse or justify, but to understand.

Which part of your mother's story feels most familiar or resonant to you?
What emotions arise as you hold her story with curiosity and compassion?
What do you now understand about her, and perhaps about yourself, that you could not see before?

With each breath of understanding, notice how the thread between mother and daughter becomes more spacious, more real.

Your Grandmother's Story

Take a quiet moment to sit with your grandmother's presence, whether through memory, imagination, or an object or photograph on your altar. Let the strands that connect your life to hers rise gently.

What do you know or still wonder about your grandmother's childhood, her spirit, and the times that shaped her?
How do you think your grandmother's story impacted the way your mother mothered you?
Which of her ways of being can you feel living in you that you cherish?

Are there any you are ready to release with love?
Where do you feel gratitude for her strength, and where do you sense grief or longing for what could not be given?

Allow fragments to surface without forcing coherence. Curiosity will guide you as you weave the gifts and the sorrows of your lineage into the basket you are making now.

Play

What did play look like for you as a child—what games, textures, worlds, or imaginings made you feel most alive? What might it feel like to reconnect with one of those today?
Where could you invite ten minutes of play into your life this week without needing it to be productive or impressive? (Coloring, dancing, hide-and-seek with your dog, singing in the car, jumping in leaves, making something with your hands).
When you imagine letting yourself play, what arises first: joy, resistance, embarrassment, longing, grief? What does that response reveal about what your younger self needed?

Kundalini Meditation (Shaking, Movement, Stillness)

What did you notice in your body after shaking and movement. What shifted in your breath, mood, or energy? What did stillness feel like afterward?
Where do you sense stuck energy in your body or life right now? How might shaking, sound, movement, or breath help interrupt that pattern?
If you used this practice regularly as a form of nervous-system support, what might become more available?
What helps you surrender into the shaking and let the body lead? And what tends to hold you back?

Michelle's Story

Do you sense any resonance between her mother ache and your own?
Are there echoes of her longing or her attempts to appease her ache that feel familiar?

Conclusion: The Magical Child and Her Gathered Materials

"Children see the world as magical not because they are naïve, but because they are actually more neurologically open to it. They have not been taught yet to "gate" out the aliveness of the more-then-human world."

—Sophie Strand

As this chapter ends, we honor the spirit of the Magical Child within you with awareness and curiosity. You have begun to see that we are all comprised of living energy and the same elements, created an altar to honor your healing journey that provides a comforting place to return to during this work, found a companion to hold as you would your own inner child, and begun gathering the stories of your life, your mother's life, and the lineage that lives through you. You've learned to move energy through shaking, dancing, and stillness.

Remember that gathering your memories is not a one-time act; it is a spiral that expands and deepens over time. Each return to your story reveals something new. What was hidden begins to emerge; what once felt unbearable can now be held with tenderness. Healing is not linear, it moves in sacred spirals.

The spiral is one of the oldest symbols of femininity, carved into stone, painted on cave walls, and woven into baskets. It appears throughout nature: in seashells, ferns, galaxies, and the turning of the seasons. It reminds us that healing is a rhythmic circling of returning again and again to what still needs tending, each time bringing new breath and awareness.

When old wounds resurface, we can feel like we've regressed. However, each return represents growth. We revisit the same pain with greater compassion and strength. What once seemed unbearable takes shape within a wider pattern, creating a living basket able to hold more of who we truly are.

In basket weaving, each new row rests on the previous one, spiraling outward from the center. The same principle applies to healing. Every turn strengthens what came before. You are not reliving the past; you are expanding your healing basket.

The Magical Child encourages us to trust this rhythm. Returning to our painful past is a deep acknowledgment of what still longs to be healed. Each spiral back broadens your capacity for awareness, curiosity and the other intrinsic qualities within us, which we will explore in the chapters that follow. Healing happens in spirals. Each turn adds strength, flexibility, and grace to the weave of your being until the basket of your life, imperfect but whole, can hold everything you truly are.

The spiral is one of humanity's oldest symbols, found on prehistoric stones and cave walls across the world. Long associated with the Great Mother, it signifies birth, death, and rebirth, as well as descent and return. The same spiral lives on in the act of basketweaving, mirroring a woman's healing journey as it unfolds through time.

As you walk this spiral, familiar memories may arise again with new meaning. What once confused you might now make sense in context. Each turn brings you closer to the center, where your story exists in wholeness rather than fragmentation. Collecting your story is a lifelong act of remembering. Each cycle adds another thread to the basket of your becoming. In the next chapter, we begin sorting the fibers we've gathered by meeting the Wounded Child who will help us discern what belongs, what needs care, and what must be released.

Chapter Three:

The Wounded Child and Honest Seeing

"The wound is the place where the light enters you."

—Rumi

At the heart of the mother ache is the Wounded Child within us. This archetype is the vulnerable inner child within that still remembers our earliest pain with *honesty,* understood here as the body's simple truthfulness about what was experienced. Her small body recalls what the adult mind has long tried to forget: the longing for a mother's attunement, the sting of rejection or harsh words, the confusion of love tied to pleasing, and the ache of feeling like too much or not enough.

In our adult lives, she manifests through waves of loneliness, persistent shame, addiction or compulsion, or the never-ending ache of not belonging. She stays just beneath the surface, hidden behind the energetic patterns that she learned to protect her from further hurt, and she often reveals herself in our closest relationships.

This archetype is deeply personal to each of us, yet also ancestral. The Wounded Child holds not only our unmet needs but also the unspoken grief of our mothers, grandmothers, and maternal ancestors. She echoes their silenced voices and bears the weight of their unhealed pain. To meet her is to encounter the ache passed down through generations, an inheritance longing for transformation.

Just as the Magical Child guided us to gather stories of our childhood and maternal lineage, the Wounded Child now helps us sort through what we've collected. She is the one who feels the heaviness and texture of the fibers and knows which strands still carry sorrow. Her sacred work is to notice what was carried forward, the memories, beliefs, and adaptations that still echo in the body, and to see them with honesty.

She encourages us to look closely at our stories, to distinguish lived experiences from the distortions we've created to survive. Through her sorting, we begin to understand how the past has shaped us and how it no longer needs to define us.

The Wounded Child is the archetype inside us that carries the mother ache. When we meet her with awareness, curiosity, and honesty, healing begins to take shape.

From Innocence to Adaptation

As we have seen, we start as innocent children, naturally developing into magical children, being curious, playful, and receptive to affection. Our hearts easily reach out toward love, trusting it will be returned. This is the natural rhythm of early life: to need, to ask, to receive, and to grow within the safety of a mother's presence.

As children, we rely entirely on our mothers. Her eyes meeting ours, her arms holding us, are the first mirrors in which we see ourselves. When her presence falters through absence, distraction, harshness, depression, anxiety, or any other expression of her own unhealed pain, we cannot safely remain in our own open flow. We must adapt.

Every adaptation is a sign of intelligence. To stay connected with our mothers, we learned to hide our feelings, remain quiet, and try to please her. We held back tears to avoid rejection, swallowed anger to stay safe, and aimed for perfection or invisibility to keep love close. Each of these strategies was a small act of genius and survival, a child's way of holding onto connection at any cost.

However, these creative responses came with a cost. In maintaining this connection, the child sacrificed her authenticity. The natural flow of the Innocent and Magical Children within—open, spontaneous, expressive, and lively—gradually became more constrained. Awareness and curiosity did not disappear, they withdrew behind survival strategies. What was once a free stream of openness and curiosity was shaped into patterns of defense.

These patterns follow us into adulthood. They become the unseen architecture of the mother ache. They show up as familiar and largely unconscious energy patterns that move through our bodies and relationships, and we mistake them for our identities. I call these protective energy patterns, and we will explore these in depth in Chapter Six. For example:

A child who stayed quiet to avoid upsetting anyone becomes an adult who hesitates to voice her needs, fearing she is too much.

A child who learned to earn connection through helpfulness becomes a woman who tends to everyone else while quietly neglecting herself.

A child who tried to stay perfect to avoid criticism becomes an adult who never feels she has arrived at good enough, no matter how hard she tries.

A child who protected herself through laying low becomes a woman who finds intimacy overwhelming and repeats this guarding energy in her intimate relationships.

A child who escaped inward to feel safe becomes an adult who drifts into workaholism, fantasy, or spiritual bypassing when her vulnerability feels too exposed.

These are not flaws or failures. They are energy patterns, shaped in a young nervous system doing everything it could to stay connected and safe. Each of these energy patterns began as a way to belong in an environment where being fully oneself felt unsafe. They are testaments to how deeply the child wanted to stay connected, to be loved.

To recognize these patterns is to bow to their brilliance. They kept us connected when caregiver connection was required in order for us to survive. But we are no longer the children who needed those patterns. The energetic strategies that once ensured survival now perpetuate our suffering, which is the persistent pulse of the mother ache.

Healing begins when we meet these inner energetic patterns with honesty, acknowledging both their wisdom and their limits. Only then can the child who adapted begin to rest, and the woman she became begin to soften into who she truly is.

Understanding the Mother Ache Through Attachment

We can start to understand our energetic patterns by looking at the nature of our earliest bond with our mothers, known as our attachment style. Every child needs a secure base of love and safety. Healthy attachment forms when a child feels both physically and emotionally held. Her needs are met, her cries answered, and her presence is welcomed. This steady attunement becomes the foundation for the felt sense that *I am safe, I matter, and the world will meet me with care*. When a mother's attunement is disrupted, whether from illness, absence, distraction, or her own unhealed pain, the child adapts. To preserve connection, she tries to make sense of the disconnection egocentrically by thinking that *something must be wrong with me*. It's not safe to think something is wrong with the person we are dependent on, so we automatically create the narrative that the disconnect is a reflection of ourselves. In truth, nothing was wrong with us, but this interpretation takes root in the deepest layers of our psyches. We can start to understand these roots by looking at our early attachment patterns.

As adults, our early attachment patterns shape how we seek, avoid, or fear connection. A secure attachment nurtures a well-regulated nervous system and the ability to trust both ourselves and others. When attachment is insecure, our nervous system learns vigilance, withdrawal, or confusion.

Psychologists describe four attachment styles that develop in relation to a child's first caregiver. Understanding them helps us bring awareness, curiosity, and honesty to the roots of our mother ache.[7]

Secure Attachment

Secure attachment forms when a child consistently feels safe, seen, and soothed. Her mother is responsive, feeding when she's hungry, comforting when she's distressed, and taking joy in her presence. Over time, she learns: *I am worthy of love. I am safe. The world can be trusted.* This trust allows her to explore freely, seek comfort, and form relationships that balance intimacy and independence.

Dismissive Attachment

Dismissive (avoidant) attachment develops when a child learns that seeking comfort doesn't work. If the mother is emotionally or physically unavailable, the child adapts by minimizing her needs. She appears independent and capable, even praised for her self-reliance, yet underneath she is guarding against pain. The body stays tense, the heart closed. She may avoid intimacy because love has come to feel unreliable.

Anxious Attachment

Anxious (ambivalent) attachment arises when care is inconsistent. The child learns to amplify her signals to maintain attention by clinging, crying, or trying harder to please. Her nervous system remains on alert, oscillating between hope and fear. As an adult, this may show up as relationship anxiety, fear of abandonment, or an insatiable longing for reassurance in friendships, love relationships, or even at work.

Disorganized Attachment

Disorganized attachment occurs when the mother is both a source of comfort and fear. If she is traumatized, unpredictable, or abusive, the child faces

---

7 For readers who want a deeper, accessible exploration of attachment patterns and how early relational experiences shape our adult connections, see Diane Poole Heller, *The Power of Attachment: How to Create Deep and Lasting Intimate Relationships* (Boulder, CO: Sounds True, 2019).

an impossible dilemma: she wants closeness but also needs to protect herself. The child may freeze, dissociate, or display contradictory behaviors such as approaching then pulling away. The nervous system struggles to find a steady rhythm, often resulting in chronic anxiety or somatic distress later in life.

These patterns are not flaws; they are love's adaptations. Each one represents a wounded child's brilliant attempt to stay connected when safety was uncertain. Awareness of them is not about finding fault or blaming our mothers. Rather, by bringing awareness and curiosity to them honestly, we open the door to compassion for the child you were and for the mother who was herself dysregulated, due to her own experiences in life.

Our attachment style is not a permanent energy signature. The same neuroplasticity that once shaped our adaptations can now weave new patterns of safety. Through mindful awareness and inner work, like the work we are doing in this book, the nervous system learns to trust again.

Trust is the essence of earned secure attachment. Even if you did not begin life feeling safe or seen, you can cultivate that security within yourself now. Every time you return to awareness, curiosity, and honesty, you create new experiences of reliability for yourself.

For the wounded child, this truth matters deeply: the past shaped you, but it does not define you. Through reflection and presence, you are already reorganizing your inner world. As Daniel Siegel describes in *Mindsight: The New Science of Personal Transformation*[8], the capacity for mindful reflection allows the brain and the heart to rewire. This integration transforms old patterns of disconnection into an embodied sense of safety, belonging, and love.

Each time you choose to stay present with your emotions, soothe your inner child, or trust connection again, you strengthen this new attachment. The weave becomes stronger, the healing basket more resilient. Our attachment patterns did not form in isolation; they arose in response to the environments we grew up in and the ways our mothers were able or unable to meet our earliest needs. What follows is a deeper dive into the dynamics that created these early energy patterns of adaptation.

---

8 Daniel J. Siegel, *Mindsight: The New Science of Personal Transformation* (New York: Bantam Books, 2010).

How the Mother Ache Forms: from Subtle to Severe

"To write one's way out of the incapacitating dependence of daughterhood into autonomy means shedding the unquestioning fidelity of a child. A daughter's liberation is trailed by disorientation, her sense of self inseparable from the story of the mother who, through tyranny or tenderness, made it possible."

—Rebecca Mead

Before we proceed, two truths must be acknowledged. First, the harms that shape the mother ache exist along a wide spectrum from the subtle to the catastrophic. No list can capture every nuance. Yet, naming them helps give form to what was once only felt in a hazy blurred way. Second, reading or recalling these patterns can hurt. To name them is an act of courage. If you feel overwhelmed, pause and breathe. Seek comfort, support, and safety as needed. This work is not meant to retraumatize, but to help you sort through the fibers of your story with honesty and care. As you move through these patterns, notice what resonates in your body. Let awareness, curiosity, and honesty be your guides. The list moves from the most subtle to the most overt expressions of maternal wounding.

The patterns that follow reflect my own synthesis of trauma-informed psychological, somatic, and relational work with women, along with study of maternal wounding. They are not drawn from a single text, but emerged over time through study, observation, practice, and listening to women's stories in healing contexts.[9]

9 For readers who wish to explore additional perspectives on maternal wounding, Kathie Carlson's *In Her Image: The Unhealed Daughter's Search for Her Mother* offers a clear and compassionate lens on dynamics such as binding and banishing, and therapist Kelly McDaniel's *Mother Hunger* provides a clear, accessible exploration of the many ways maternal nurturance, protection, and guidance can be missed in childhood. Kathie Carlson, *In Her Image: The Unhealed Daughter's Search for Her Mother* (New York: Ballantine Books, 1989); Kelly McDaniel, *Mother Hunger: How Adult Daughters Can Understand and Heal from Lost Nurturance, Protection, and Guidance* (Carlsbad, CA: Hay House, 2021).

Subtle Roots of the Mother Ache

Binding

Binding happens when a daughter's natural energy flow is limited by unspoken rules about who she can be. These rules are rarely stated openly but are deeply felt. She learns that certain expressions—like being too loud, too emotional, too sensitive, or too strong—cause disapproval or withdrawal. The message is clear: parts of her are not accepted. A mother might hush her daughter's tears or laugh at her enthusiasm. Over time, the daughter learns to shrink to preserve connection. What starts as subtle self-editing becomes chronic self-surveillance. She grows into a woman who measures her words, hides her joy, and fears her own bigness. When I think of binding, I remember the women in ancient China whose feet were bound to appear more delicate. It was considered beauty, but it was actually bondage, just as the unseen restraints of a daughter's conditioning can become an invisible, painful constraint on her spirit.

Banishing

Banishing happens when a daughter's need for closeness, care, and dependence is quietly refused. Rather than being constrained, she is pushed away, encouraged to be self-sufficient too soon, and to manage on her own. Emotional need is met with distance or dismissal. Tears are discouraged. Vulnerability is unwelcome. The message she receives is *you are too much*, or *you should not need*.

A banishing mother may value competence, independence, and caretaking, often because she herself was forced to survive without nourishment or support. She may praise strength while withholding comfort, urging her daughter to be capable rather than held. Over time, the daughter learns that closeness is unsafe or unavailable. She stops reaching. She learns to tend to others while neglecting herself.

What begins as early self-reliance becomes chronic deprivation. As an adult, she may struggle to receive help, rest, or care. She may feel uneasy when she is needy, unsure how to ask, or ashamed when she longs for support. Her hunger is not for attention, but for attunement, for the simple permission to lean, to soften, and to be met.

Banishing does not look dramatic. It often wears the face of encouragement. But beneath it lies a quiet loneliness, and a body that learned too early to survive without being fed.

Enmeshment

Enmeshment blurs the boundary between mother and daughter. The mother doesn't see her daughter as a separate being but as an extension of her own emotional world. She might seek comfort, share adult worries, or expect loyalty that excludes others. The daughter becomes her mother's confidant. To stay close, she learns to merge. She senses her mother's moods before her own and confuses being needed with healthy connection. As an adult, she may struggle to recognize her own needs or opinions.

Binding, banishing, and enmeshment are unconscious strategies a mother may use to manage closeness and distance when her own needs, fears, or unmet longings remain unresolved. While these strategies serve as a protective function for the mother, they can distort the daughter's natural process of becoming her own person. Recognizing these patterns helps the daughter see where love became entangled with survival, where connection replaced freedom, or distance replaced attunement.

Other Roots of the Mother Ache

Many forms of disruption shape the daughter's early experience. Some are subtle, others unmistakable. Each one leaves its own imprint on daughter.

Emotional Climate

The mother's unprocessed pain, such as depression, anxiety, fear, and exhaustion, colors the daughter's inner world. She learns to read cues and regulate others before herself.

Sibling Dynamics

Favoritism, comparison, or triangulation create scarcity, teaching that love must be earned.

Early Deprivation

A difficult birth, feeding struggles, or limited touch teaches the daughter that her needs are unsafe and unimportant.

Neglect

Emotional or physical absence compels the daughter to parent herself. She learns to live without being held, often carrying the quiet ache of feeling unimportant, unseen, or unsafe, and turning self-reliance into her earliest form of protection.

Parentification

The child assumes adult roles by comforting, mediating, or protecting either the mother or her siblings, learning that care must flow outward, not inward.

Criticism and Conditional Love

Shame, body judgment, or withdrawal of affection teach the daughter that love can be taken away and that she must be pleasing in order to stay close.

Harsh Punishment, Shame, and Fear-Based Correction

Repeated experiences of being punished, shamed, or harshly corrected without emotional repair teach the daughter that safety depends on compliance rather than understanding. When discipline is infused with fear, unpredictability, or wrongful accusation, the child learns to monitor herself constantly, often internalizing guilt, self-doubt, hypervigilance, or a pervasive sense of being wrong.

Ambivalent Mirroring

Ambivalent mirroring occurs when a mother's response to her daughter's emerging competence is inconsistent or contradictory. At times, the daughter is praised or idealized; at other times, she is ignored, diminished, or subtly undermined. The messages she receives are confusing and often opposing: *be successful, but not more than me*; *be independent, but don't leave me*. Over time, the daughter learns to question her own instincts and achievements. She may feel guilty for thriving or anxious about being seen. Caught between approval and withdrawal, she struggles to trust her own direction, often suppressing parts of herself to preserve connection.

Arrested Maternal Development

Arrested maternal development refers to a mother's own blocked growth, including her unfulfilled longings, curtailed potential, or unresolved identity, that quietly shapes her relationship with her daughter. Unable to fully embrace her own potential, the mother may idealize her daughter's competence, live vicariously through her, or unconsciously rely on her for meaning or validation. In this dynamic, the daughter often grows up too quickly. She becomes capable, responsible, and self-sufficient, while learning that her own needs must wait. She may reject softness or dependency, equating strength with worth, and unconsciously distance herself from the feminine in order to survive.

Mother's Sexual Boundaries

Oversharing or intrusion of sexual boundaries blurs the mother-daughter roles and can leave the daughter confused, unsafe, or ashamed in her body.

Mental Illness, Addiction, or Violence

When the mother's inner or outer world is affected by mental illness, addiction, or violence, the daughter learns to scan for danger, carrying a quiet dread that safety could disappear at any moment.

Unsafe Environment

Poverty, persecution, or violence in the home fills the air with fear, and the daughter absorbs it, learning to live in heightened vigilance and chronic insecurity.

Physical or Sexual Abuse

Physical or sexual abuse can disrupt a daughter's development and nervous system, shaping profound breaches in safety and trust that often require long-term, relational healing and support.

Each of these forms of disruption restricts the daughter's freedom to feel safe, loved, trust her needs, and exist as herself. Her nervous system, seeking to survive, encodes these losses as patterns of protection.

Abandonment

At the heart of the mother ache is abandonment, and it is important to understand that each of the patterns above is a form of abandonment. A mother might be absent due to circumstances like work, divorce, illness, or death. Abandonment can also happen through a lack of presence, such as her eyes appearing dull from depression or trauma. The daughter feels the loss just the same. Even brief separations can seem like forever to a child's nervous system.

Sometimes abandonment happens subtly: when a new sibling arrives or when a mother goes back to work. Regardless of the circumstances, the daughter's nervous system whispers the same message: *You are not important*. The daughter becomes cautious, either reaching for or guarding against closeness to avoid further abandonment.

Adoption

Adoption carries its own sacred ache. Even in the most loving families, a daughter separated from her birth mother carries a cellular memory of loss. The womb was her first home, its sounds, rhythms, and chemistry are familiar. When that home is gone, the body remembers.

Adoption can be a story of deep belonging, but its shadow is the primal rupture that came before. Recognizing this truth does not lessen the adoptive mother's love; it honors what the daughter carries so that love can take deeper root.

A Different Ache: The Stepmother's Shadow

Not every wound that shapes a daughter's heart starts in her bond with her mother. Some wounds come from encounters with other women who held authority but did not offer a mother's love. The pain caused by a cruel or neglectful stepmother is different from the ache related to her biological mother.

The mother ache is woven from longing for what *was* or *could have been*. The harm caused by a difficult stepmother, however, comes from rejection and misuse of power. It is not a failure of love; it is a lack of love.

For the child, this distinction is confusing. Her heart does not yet understand the difference between abandonment and cruelty; it only feels pain. Yet, the paths to healing diverge. The mother ache invites reconciliation through love's imperfection. The stepmother's wound calls for reclamation of dignity and worth.

I knew this pain intimately. My stepmother was a woman who took pleasure in cruelty. She banished me to the basement, withheld affection, and turned my home into a landscape of fear. Unlike the ache I carried for my mother, which was bound by love, this pain was cold, born of power without tenderness. Healing it meant reclaiming the worth she tried to strip from me.

If this resonates with your story, understand that your healing depends on recalling your own sacred worth—the light that no cruelty can extinguish—and that the healing work that you do in this book will support this too.

Mothers and Grandmothers: Seeing the Lineage of Adaptation

As we begin to understand the ways the mother ache forms within us it becomes clear that our mothers were shaped by similar forces. Their energetic patterns of adaptation arose within the emotional landscapes they inherited, shaped by silence, loss, overwhelm, cultural expectations, and the painful imprints of their own childhoods.

When we look at our mothers through this wider lens, we begin to see a human being who was formed by her own unmet needs and efforts to stay connected. And when we look one generation further, we often notice the echoes. Our grandmothers were shaped by the eras they lived in, by their own unmet needs, by trauma that remained unspoken, and by their own mother's adaptations.

As you reflect on the forms of the mother ache described earlier, you may notice how some may feel familiar when you think of your mother or grandmother. Awareness naturally begins to trace the strands backward, showing where each woman may have encountered loss, fear, or longing. Let these recognitions come gently. This kind of seeing does not excuse harm. It invites context. It softens the edges gently and widens the space around our own experience.

You might begin to notice what your mother longed for and did not receive, how she protected herself, what she avoided, or what she tried to manage through control or withdrawal. You may also notice the patterns she inherited rather than created. You can allow your awareness to move one layer deeper. Consider what your grandmother endured, how she adapted, what was available to her, and what remained out of reach.

These reflections do not diminish your ache. They help you understand the larger context. They show how certain maternal strands have been carried through the lineage and how you now have the chance to meet them with awareness, curiosity, and honesty.

From this place of understanding, our healing becomes possible as a natural unfolding as we bring empathy into our mother-daughter healing journey. It arises when we begin to see how love, fear, and survival shaped the women who came before us and how those same forces shaped us in turn.

In my family history, my mother's rebellious nature grew from a long lineage of women who learned to survive through obedience and servitude. My grandmother, Effie, spent her life tending to the demands of first her strict and controlling father and later her husband, a man living with untreated mental illness. The atmosphere of instability and emotional unpredictability shaped her world. Kindness became her currency. Caretaking became her safety. In a home where men held power and tenderness was scarce, she adapted by becoming steady, compliant, and endlessly responsible.

My mother witnessed this as a child and longed for a different life. The forms of the mother ache she inherited were subtle yet powerful. Emotional scarcity shaped her early years. Chronic overwhelm influenced the atmosphere of her home. Her needs were secondary to the needs of her father. My mother saw her own mother's life as a kind of confinement. She wanted space, autonomy, and a sense of freedom. Her teenage pregnancy, leaving school, and later leaving her children, reflected an attempt to escape a lineage of suffocation and self-erasure.

In seeking freedom, my mother encountered her own version of the ache. The instability she fled reappeared in new ways. The absence she experienced became the absence she repeated. She longed for autonomy, expression, and inner safety, yet she did not receive the support needed to create that life. Her choices were formed through the emotional deprivation and lack of stability that shaped her early years. These choices protected her from repeating one form of harm, although they carried their own consequences.

Seeing my mother and grandmother through this wider lens allows me to understand my own story with more tenderness. The forms of the mother ache that shaped their lives did not begin with them. They did not begin with me, either. Each of us responded to the emotional landscapes we inherited. With awareness, there is now an opportunity to meet these patterns differently, to honor the survival strategies they carried, and to gently loosen what no longer is needed.

As you begin to understand what shaped you, a larger picture comes into view. Your patterns did not arise in isolation. They emerged within a lineage of women who learned, in their own ways, how to survive what life placed before them. This understanding does not define you. It simply reveals how you learned to be. From this clarity, a new path becomes possible. The spiral that once carried you away from your inner truth can now guide you back toward what was never lost, only forgotten.

The patterns you carry today formed when your needs were not fully met and your young nervous system had to adapt. These adaptations were responses to overwhelm, absence, misattunement, or emotional instability. Every pattern reflects the intelligence of a child finding a way to stay connected and remain safe. They reveal resilience and resourcefulness, even when they feel painful now.

These patterns stay with us until we recognize them. They made sense in childhood, while we were dependent on the emotional landscapes around us. They no longer match the circumstances of adult life. When they remain unconscious, they limit our freedom, shape our choices, and influence our closest relationships. They hold energy that longs to move and soften. Beneath them, your innocent, magical, and truthful selves remain intact, waiting to be felt again.

Awareness becomes the beginning of change. When you approach these patterns with honesty and curiosity, new possibilities emerge. You begin to understand how they once protected you. As this understanding grows, the patterns loosen. You can reclaim the energy they have been holding and redirect it toward your wholeness.

Healing begins when you recognize that these patterns are not your identity. They are movements of energy that formed around pain and confusion. When you stop identifying with them and begin to see them clearly, they soften. This is the first step in returning to yourself. You stand in awareness. You sense the space around the pattern. You remember that you are larger than anything you once carried. This spaciousness is where rewoven life begins.

The Shape of Our Stories Lives in Our Bodies

Over the years, I've come to realize that healing isn't just something we think or feel, it's something we *embody*. The stories we carry live not only in our minds, they also live in the shapes our bodies take. The way we hold and carry ourselves are reflections of our inner life, revealing where we've braced and how we've adapted.

This understanding grew deeper through years of studying Gurdjieff's Sacred Movements and a decade of practicing Kundalini Yoga. In these traditions, posture is more than just physical alignment; it acts as a gateway. Through conscious movement and awareness, we access states of presence that awaken energy and restore the psyche's balance. Every posture vibrates a certain energy, and each shape calls forth a specific inner state.

In Gurdjieff's movements, I learned that changing posture alters consciousness. The body and being are interconnected. When the spine lifts, awareness increases. When the heart opens, breath deepens. When the head bows, humility follows. In Kundalini Yoga, posture becomes a sacred tool to activate the navel center, balance the nervous system, and unite body, breath, and spirit into one current.

In healing the mother ache, posture becomes a living metaphor. The way we hold ourselves reflects how we've learned to survive. When we curl inward, we may still be protecting the child within. When we stand too rigidly, we may still be bearing the weight of perfection. And when we find balance, we return to our true seat, the grounded, spacious awareness of who we truly are beneath our posturing, so to speak.

The following practice encourages you to begin to understand how powerful the energy of your posture actually is. This is a sensory practice. Treat it as an exploration. Pay attention to how each posture feels, what emotions arise, and how your energy changes as you move.

Experiential Invitation: Meeting the Wounded Child Through the Body

Find a place where you can sit undisturbed. Take your seat in sukhasana, a relaxed cross-legged posture. Sit on a cushion or folded blanket so your hips are slightly higher than your knees. If sukhasana is not possible for your body then you can sit in a firm chair with feet connected to the ground so that your spine can be erect. Let your spine rise naturally by pulling up on your pelvic floor by lightly engaging your *mūla bandha* (root lock).[10] Drawing your navel up and in, lift your heart, soften your shoulders down, lift the crown of your head gently upward, and tuck your chin slightly. Rest your hands on your knees. Feel your breath move through your body.

This posture reflects the qualities that live at the core of your being: steadiness, openness, and strength. It is a shape that belongs to the woman you are becoming.

Sitting in sukhasana, with the chin slightly tucked and the shoulders relaxed down, the spine forms a straight line from the tailbone to the crown. The heart gently lifts as the root lock (mūla bandha) activates by subtly pulling the pelvic floor upward. This balanced posture prevents gravitational pull forward or backward, allowing energy to flow freely and supporting awareness.

After a few breaths, slowly shift into the posture of the wounded child, as shown in the illustration at the beginning of this chapter. Bring your knees toward your chest, wrap your arms around your legs, sink your shoulders down, and let your head bow toward your heart. Notice how this shape feels in your body. Notice what emotions or sensations arise. Observe without judgment.

10 *Mula bandha*, or root lock, is a gentle drawing upward at the base of the body, gathering energy from the pelvic floor and lifting it toward the center. We lift rectum, sex organs and navel up and in and then gently release while maintaining a slight pressure, thereby supporting the sukhasana posture.

Stay for a few breaths, then gently return to sukhasana. Inhale and lengthen the spine. Exhale and soften the shoulders down lifting up through the crown of your head again. Feel the contrast between these two postures, they are the embodiment of the alignment into presence and collapse into protection.

Every posture tells a story. The body remembers long before the mind can name anything. Through these two simple shapes, you are sensing how the mother ache lives in you: where you have held yourself in smallness and where your natural openness still lives.

Now, return to sukhasana and bring your hands together in prayer mudra at your heart center. Let the bases of your palms touch first, then your fingers, as if sealing a vow. Apply gentle pressure and notice the warmth that gathers there. In this mudra, we embody the meeting of left and right, inner and outer, giving and receiving, masculine and feminine, and we balance the elements within us. Take a few deep breaths in this posture. Feel your hands meeting with gentle pressure. Breath here. Feel the natural balance that this posture creates within you.

In sukhasana, the hands meet in prayer mudra at the heart center, awakening the felt sense of balance within. Earth steadies the seat, fire warms the belly and lifts through the spine, air moves through the breath, water creates fluidity at the heart center, and ether opens the channel from the crown chakra to existence. A gentle pressure between the palms draws awareness to the sacred center—the still axis where spirit and body remember their unity.

Posture is prayer. Every gesture carries meaning. Through mindful alignment, we remember that healing is a reorientation: a return to the shape of wholeness. This process is also a spiral because as you position your body in the posture of wholeness, your inner wholeness expands. Rest here for a few breaths. Practice this posture as a way to bring balance to your entire system whenever you feel the need to regroup or ground.

Let this practice of posture be an ongoing conversation between your body, your history, between the child who survived and the woman who is reclaiming her ground.

Even minor posture shifts, such as lifting the spine, softening the gaze, or releasing the shoulders, can begin to reawaken trust in your body's wisdom. In this way, posture becomes both mirror and guide.

Early Meanings and the Wounded Child

Our sorting task now brings us to the places where the spiral tightened into knots, where early meanings formed as we learned how to survive separation and ache. In our earliest moments of attachment, the nervous system learned what to expect: safety or uncertainty, attunement or absence. From this lived experience, the body began to form understandings, subtle and unconscious meanings, about why our needs were or were not met. In this book, I call these understandings *early meanings*.[11]

Early meanings are not thoughts we chose. They are body-based conclusions formed in relationship, often before language developed. They live both as sensation and as story, woven into the fibers of our being: *I am unlovable, I am too much, I don't belong*. These meanings represent the infant's best effort to make sense of her world. Without the capacity to perceive the other as separate, she interprets her experience egocentrically. If her cries go unanswered, it must be because she is bad. If she is not held, it must be because she is unworthy. From these early meanings, the first adaptive energy patterns begin to take shape.

11 What are commonly referred to in therapeutic literature as *core beliefs*, and in Buddhist psychology as *diṭṭhi* (views or conditioned ways of seeing), are framed here as *early meanings* to emphasize their relational, somatic, and largely pre-verbal origins.

Early meanings tend to reside outside of conscious awareness, yet they diligently organize perception and behavior. They repeat as familiar inner messages: *I don't matter* or *It's no use trying*. Over time, they become so familiar that we mistake them for our very identity. *I'm a loser. I can't do anything right*. They form a constant hum beneath our daily lives, shaping how we relate to ourselves and move through the world.

This is the outward spiral, away from the center of wholeness. Attachment taught the body its first rhythm. Early meanings hardened that rhythm into a sense of self. This is how we learned to live separately from ourselves. This is the ache beneath all aches.

Our work here is not to argue with these early meanings or force them to dissolve, but to bring them into awareness with care. Awareness illuminates what was once hidden. What emerges is no longer the conclusion of a vulnerable child, but the understanding of a wise woman turning back toward herself. As these meanings are met with presence and compassion, they begin to soften. They loosen their hold because they are no longer needed in the same way.

This marks a turning point in the spiral, a gentle return inward as we loosen these false knots of identity.

Experiential Invitation: Naming Our Early Meaning Knots

Before you begin, take a few slow breaths and feel the earth beneath you. These questions are an invitation to listen honestly to your own early meaning messaging. We are not trying to fix or challenge the mind. Our intention is to bring gentle honesty to the early meanings your younger self still believes are true about herself in relation to love, safety, and belonging.

Let this be an act of witnessing. Each meaning formed in relationship and once served a purpose. You are here to meet these early meanings with understanding so that the knots they form inside you can loosen, unwind. What softens in awareness no longer needs to hold so tightly. What you are willing to see with kindness can begin to untangle.

What words rise in your mind when you feel hurt or unseen?

When you make a mistake or disappoint someone, what do you tell yourself?

What message do you hear in moments of rejection or failure?

When you are triggered, what familiar story returns?

What inner message feels louder than truth when you're tired, lonely, or afraid?

How has this message shaped your choices, relationships, or sense of self?

What happens in your body when this voice speaks? Can you embody this posture?

When you trace this early meaning back, how old do you feel?

What truth might you begin to answer back to it now?

When you finish, take a slow breath. If you were able to name an early meaning that shapes your life, write it down, for example: *I am unlovable* or *I don't belong*. Then pause and ask yourself, gently and honestly: *Is this belief actually true?* Beneath it, write a truer statement you want to live from, such as: *I have always been lovable*. Use this statement of self-truth as a daily weaving tool. When the old meaning arises in your day, bring forward the true statement with kindness and repetition. You are not defined by the early meanings you formed. You are the awareness that can meet them with curiosity and answer them with honesty.

Triggers as Invitations to Honesty

When an early meaning is touched, it awakens not only the message itself, but it also awakens the original hurt beneath it. The system reacts before we have time to think. Sometimes the response is a small tightening at the edge of awareness. Other times it surges with surprising force and feels larger than the moment. This is a trigger. A trigger is not the pattern itself. It is the spark that accelerates it, the moment when a present cue meets an old wound and our energy system lights up to protect us.

A trigger can be ignited by anything that echoes past pain: a tone of voice, a delayed reply, a shift in expression, or a perceived withdrawal. One small cue touches the place where the Wounded Child once felt alone, unseen, or overwhelmed. The early meaning, now hardened into an internal scripture kicks in: *I am not worthy*. In an instant, defensive energy begins to move. Breath tightens. Thoughts flood. Our heart races. In this way, triggers reveal the places where the mother ache is still alive inside us.

The body responds first with a quickening of breath, a tightening in the chest, and a sinking in the belly. Only afterward does the mind arrive to explain the sensation, weaving a narrative that matches the child's earliest maps of meaning: *I am not safe. I am too much. I am not enough. I am alone again*. Without awareness, these interpretations feel like truth rather than old echoes rising to protect us egocentrically, in the same way they did when we were very young.

Honesty opens a different path. It allows us to pause and name that this reaction feels familiar. This feels old. This is not only about what is happening now.

During my college years, I was majoring in psychology and regularly met with a therapist I admired deeply. She had just completed her doctorate, and I looked up to her with a kind of hopeful reverence. We often talked about my dream of becoming a therapist myself. One afternoon, in an offhand way, she said, "You will most likely have to get a master's degree first."

On the surface, it was a simple comment. To the adult, it could have been neutral or even helpful. But inside me, something old and wounded ignited. My early meaning that I was not worthy surfaced immediately. In an instant, the Wounded Child heard, *You are not smart enough. You do not belong. Something is wrong with you*.

I did not pause. I did not question her. I did not ask myself what was true. Instead, I reacted from the lens of a very early meaning within myself that echoed the old fear that I was not worthy. Within a week, I changed my major to English and walked away from psychology entirely, even though I was only one course away from completing the major. That single moment touched an ancient wound, and the rest and the effects rippled outward from there.

Looking back, I can see that the trigger was not caused by her words at all. It was the emotional signature beneath them. My system lit up before I had time to think, pulling me into an old story based on early meaning that felt true even though it belonged to the past. All of this happened below the surface. Consciously, I thought to myself: *I can't afford two graduate level degrees and a Master's is not enough*. This is how triggers shape our lives when they go unseen. They do not just create reactions; they create directions. They can alter choices, identities, and the paths we believe are possible.

Navigating Triggers Is Healing

When a trigger arises, gentle questions help us shift from reactivity to recognition: Which way did my energy move? Did I reach outward for reassurance? Did I brace for hurt? Did I push away what felt too close? Did I fold inward?

These questions draw us back toward the present situation and our centered selves. As we return to the center, the urgency eases. The wave rises and falls. Breath softens. Space returns. We remember that we are not the reaction. We are the awareness that sees it.

Over time, as we meet our triggers with honesty, their intensity fades. They no longer signal catastrophe. Instead, they show us where the child within is still waiting to be met. A trigger marks the moment an early ache has been touched, inviting us to respond with compassion rather than shame or urgency. When we recognize this with presence, old early meanings begin to loosen, and we are reconnected to the truth of who we are now. From this place, a new pattern can emerge, one shaped by awareness in the present moment rather than the past.

I recently had an opportunity to work with a mother-ache trigger in my own life, one that awakened my Wounded Child. I was having lunch with a small circle of women I have met with for nearly a decade, at times we gather just be together as girlfriends and at times for more formal sharing circles and support sessions. That afternoon, one friend arrived overwhelmed, and we spent most of our time supporting her. Near the end, another friend grew visibly upset that she hadn't had space to share. We all tried to soothe and include her, but she couldn't settle. At one point, I must have had a look of dismay or discomfort on my face, because she suddenly turned toward me and shouted directly at me, "Why are you looking at me like that. What....?"

In that moment, something in me collapsed inward. I felt singled out, exposed, and like I had done something wrong. My chest tightened, my mind raced, and my whole body moved into flight mode. The Wounded Child in me had been touched and it happened so quickly I didn't recognize it at first. I left shaking, heart pounding, and the old story rose with familiar speed: *I can't trust women. I don't belong here.*

I could see what had actually happened, but I still had to move through the energy pattern that had awakened somatically within me. When the initial shock softened, I recognized the imprint beneath the moment: my Wounded Child had interpreted my friend's outburst as an unfair attack and rejection. The woman was not my adversary; she was a mirror, unintentionally reflecting a tender place in me still waiting to be reassured, healed.

I began to work with this energy consciously. Over the next few days, I stayed close to the Wounded Child within that had contracted. I breathed with her, wrote to her, and let her know she was safe now, that I was here, and she no longer had to face moments like these alone. I explained to her that being shouted at was scary and being singled out did seem unfair, but this wasn't about her or me and that our friend was triggered herself. Slowly, the tension eased, and I could feel myself returning to center.

This is the heart of working with triggers. They pull us outward at first, into old fear and old narratives, yet when we pause and listen, they guide us back to the place within that is aching for attention, tenderness, and repair.

How the Mother Ache Echoes Through Our Lives

Early wounds rarely stay contained in childhood. They ripple outward, shaping how we see ourselves, how we relate to others, and what we believe we deserve. A single moment of rupture in early life can create a series of echoes that influence our choices for decades.

When a child loses safety, she adapts. When she adapts, she makes meaning. When that meaning settles in the body, she begins to move through the world as if it were true. Life then reflects that meaning back to her, again and again.

This is the ripple effect of the mother ache.

A child who felt abandoned may grow into a woman who fears being left, who over gives to keep others close, or who mistrusts intimacy altogether. A child who felt unseen may become an adult who hides her true self, marrying for safety rather than connection, or choosing environments where invisibility feels safe. A child who felt unprotected may become hypervigilant or may unconsciously drift toward relationships that repeat the original power imbalance.

Every woman I have worked with has her own version of this unfolding, this ripple effect that begins in childhood and winds through the decades of her life until it is finally named and healed.

In my own life, the early abandonment I experienced at four did not remain a single event. It became the first ripple in a long wave of consequences. Without my mother's protection, I was vulnerable in ways I could not name. Later, a controlling stepmother entered our home and shaped my childhood through fear and humiliation. My sense of safety was fractured. I became vulnerable to a male predator because I lacked security both in my inner and outer world.

As I grew, the ache echoed in subtler forms. The above story about how I switched majors is a case in point. I also mistrusted women, sought to please and appease in relationships rather than be true to myself, and contorted myself to be accepted. The original wound kept finding new ways to speak until I learned to listen.

This is how the mother ache works. Its first impact is not its last. Its echoes appear wherever the child within us is still asking for understanding. This is the ripple effect, and it takes us further and further away from ourselves.

This ripple reveals how early wounds continue to echo through our lives in our ongoing meaning making, triggers, and the choices that result. Non-dominant hand journaling offers a simple, honest way to listen to the child at the beginning of this echo, the one whose ache still lives beneath the surface.

A Dialogue with the Younger Self

After exploring your early meanings, triggers, and the ripple effect that might have followed them through your life, you now have a clearer sense of how your younger self once tried to understand the world. Her conclusions were not formed through thoughtful reasoning. They arose from sensation and emotion, shaped in moments when life felt overwhelming, confusing. To understand these patterns more fully, it helps to listen directly to the child who first carried them.

Non-dominant hand writing (writing with your opposite hand) is a simple practice developed by Lucia Capacchione in her work with expressive arts and inner child healing.[12] Writing with your non-dominant hand softens the analytical mind and opens a more intuitive channel. It can feel almost like the younger self is speaking through the body, at her own pace and in her own language.

The first time I tried non-dominant hand journaling, I was deep in my own search to understand the roots of my mother ache. Someone had suggested the practice to meet my own inner child, who still carried the early wounds I had spent years trying to outrun.

What surprised me most was how quickly a clear and determined voice emerged. Writing with my non-dominant hand, I felt a younger self come forward with a mix of intensity and humor. She declared that people could not be trusted, that needing anyone was dangerous, and that human relationships were far less reliable than the steady presence of animals. Her proclamations were dramatic and oddly funny, yet they carried the unmistakable imprint of old pain. She especially loved using colored pens and a large sketchpad, as if the wide page gave her permission to say things she had never been allowed to express.

What became clear was that she had been living just beneath the surface of my adult life. The early meanings she carried about safety, trust, and self-worth were still active. And whenever something in the present resembled an old wound, her voice would surge forward in a moment of triggering, trying to protect me with the only strategies she had ever known.

I named her Lizzie because I had the distinct sense that she would always rather "shoot first and ask questions later." Naming her helped me recognize when she was speaking. It helped me pause, breathe, and offer her presence rather than letting her reactions shape my choices. Listening to her softened something inside me that had long been braced for impact.

This was my first real deep understanding that the Wounded Child does not disappear with age. She waits for us to turn toward her, to hear what she

12 Lucia Capacchione, *Recovery of Your Inner Child: The Highly Acclaimed Method for Liberating Your Inner Self* (New York: Simon & Schuster, 1991).

has been holding, and to let her know she no longer must carry her burdens alone.

Experiential Invitation: Non-Dominant Hand Journaling—Listening to the Wounded Child

Set aside some unhurried time to be with your inner world. Sit comfortably and place a hand on your heart or navel. Take a few slow breaths to settle into your body.

Many people find it helpful to use a large sketch pad and colorful markers for this practice. The larger page invites openness, and the colors create a sense of freedom that can feel safer for the younger self.

As you take up your journal, remember that the child within you does not need to explain anything or revisit specific memories. She only needs space to find her voice. Non-dominant hand journaling is one way to offer her that space. With your non-dominant hand, you invite the younger self to speak in her own language, at her own pace, without pressure or expectation. The adult hand asks with steadiness; the child's hand responds with truth.

With your dominant hand, write a simple question such as:

What hurts?

What feels frightening to you still?

What do you need?

What do you want me to understand?

Then switch the pen or marker to your non-dominant hand. Let whatever arises come through. The response may appear as childlike writing, scattered words, or fragments. There is no right way for it to look. We are simply trying to connect with this Wounded Child within us so that we can understand how to comfort her, so she doesn't have to work so hard.

Continue for several exchanges. Pause after each exchange. Notice the sensations in your body. Notice if something softens or opens. Notice if the younger self reveals a feeling or belief, you had not fully acknowledged. Continue for as long as it feels natural. Trust the moment when the dialogue feels complete.

When you finish, offer a gentle acknowledgment to the younger self who spoke. You are not trying to fix her or analyze what she said. You are simply letting her know that she is no longer alone with what she carries.

Non-dominant hand journaling creates a bridge between past and present, opening a space where the child within can finally be heard.

Before continuing, pause for a moment. What emerged through your hand has roots, and every root belongs to a story. The one that follows offers a glimpse of how early imprints shape a life from the inside out.

Mother Ache Healing in the World:

The Girl Who Tried to Leave the Story

Lili grew up inside a lineage shaped by secrecy and trauma. Her mother's childhood had been marked by violation and betrayal, and the ache of those years lived inside her. By the time Lili was born, her mother longed for a child who might bring innocence back into her life, a little girl to cherish. Lili arrived as that hope, yet early on it became clear that hope alone could not heal the past.

Even as an infant, Lili sensed her mother's love as a force that overwhelmed rather than soothed. At six months old, she refused the breast. Later, she understood this as a boundary her tiny body created in order to survive. She was already trying to protect herself from a mother who needed more from her than she could possibly give.

Home held an atmosphere of strain. Her father mistrusted the world and kept the family isolated. Their version of homeschooling never quite happened, so Lili taught herself everything from kindergarten through twelfth grade. Her mother moved through the days behind closed curtains, hiding habits she could not escape, and shame settled over the house like a second skin.

Inside this environment, Lili formed two competing early meanings about herself. First, that she was too much. Second, that she was not enough. When she reached for closeness, it felt smothering. When she protected herself with distance, she longed for connection. These opposite impulses lived side by side, creating an anxious and avoidant pattern that would shape her relationships for years.

By fifteen, she began running away from home. She crossed state lines searching for a version of herself who did not have to shrink or disappear.

Running away became a form of survival, a way of escaping the intensity she felt at home. By seventeen she left home for good, vowing never to return.

On her own, Lili eventually put herself through school and became a therapist. Her healing journey included talk therapy, which offered some relief, but could not reach the wordless places inside her where the pain truly lived. Understanding why she hurt was helpful but not healing. Eventually, Lili tried MDMA-assisted therapy, and something opened that she had never known before. She discovered a sense of safety in her own body, a truth she could feel rather than think. This first doorway helped her find ground beneath the chaos she had carried since infancy.

Around this time, Lili and I began working together. Through the lens of mother ache work, and using somatic practices, active meditations, and self-inquiry tools shared in this book, she learned to stay with sensation instead of fleeing it, to follow the small tremors of release of mother ache that moved through her like weather shifting. By approaching her inner world with honesty and relational curiosity, rather than fear or self-blame, the armor of her wounded child softened a little. She could finally name what had once been too overwhelming to feel.

With this foundation forming beneath her, she felt ready for deeper ceremonial work with lineage-held sacred plant medicines. In those altered and sacred states, the doorways created through earlier healing efforts widened. She began to understand her mother not through story alone but through the language of her nervous system. The body became the teacher, the place where spirit and matter remembered each other.

After one ceremony, resting after a long night of deep work, Lili found herself sitting outside by herself when another woman insisted on joining her, adamantly refusing to leave, and gathering her into her arms. The gesture was simple, yet it reached a part of Lili that had never known what it might feel like to be held by a mother. In that much-resisted embrace, she experienced the mothering she had always longed for. Something inside her surrendered. The child who once refused to be held finally exhaled and accepted mothering from her sister, her friend. This was one of the most healing moments of her life.

Today Lili lives in the mountains of Peru, where she continues her path of lineage repair. In ceremony, in community, and in the natural world, she feels the ancestral ache unwind itself. Now, when she notices the old impulse to flee, she pauses. She places a hand over her heart and reminds herself that running once kept her alive. Staying can now be a sacred act.

She is learning that she does not need to leave the story to rewrite it.

Journal Reflections: Reweaving Honesty

Take a few deep breaths before beginning. Let your body soften. These prompts are invitations to listen gently to the Wounded Child within you, honoring her pace and her truth. Move through them slowly, returning to whichever ones call to you most strongly.

Your Attachment Story

How would you describe the emotional atmosphere of your childhood home?

What patterns of closeness, distance, or unpredictability shaped your early sense of safety?

Which attachment style feels most familiar to you, and how do you notice it showing up in your adult relationships?

Where do you sense your nervous system still responding as though you are the child you once were?

How the Mother Ache Formed

Which descriptions in this section resonated in your body as you read them?

What memories or sensations surfaced as you explored the spectrum from subtle to severe forms of maternal harm?

How do you relate to the ideas of binding and enmeshment with your mother either as a child or now?

Are there specific moments when you felt unseen, overwhelmed, constrained, or responsible for the emotional world around you?

Which forms of harm have you experienced as abandonment, even if no one called it that at the time?

How do these early experiences continue to influence your choices, relationships, or inner landscape today?

Mothers and Grandmothers: Seeing the Lineage of Adaptation

What do you understand now about your mother's adaptations that you could not see before?
How did her environment, upbringing, or burdens shape the ways she could or could not show up for you?
What do you know or imagine about your grandmother's life that gives context to your mother's story?
Where do you sense tenderness, grief, or recognition as you look at the lineage of women you come from?

The Shape of Your Story: The Postures of Sukhasana, Wounded Child, and Prayer

What emotions or memories surfaced as you sat in these postures?
Did one posture feel more familiar or charged than the others?
How did your body respond, for example: tightening, softening, resisting, or opening?
What did you learn about the Wounded Child through your physical experience rather than through thought?

Early Meanings and the Wounded Child

What early meanings began forming in you during early childhood? Examples: I am unlovable, I am bad, I am not safe, etc.
Which meanings still echo in your adult life, influencing how you speak to yourself or relate to others?
If it feels right ask yourself where did these meanings originate, and how did they help you survive?
Which meaning did you write down and how does it feel to know that it is not true, nor never has been? How might the true statement you wrote down support you now?

Triggers as Invitations to Honesty

Recall a recent moment when you felt triggered. What was the situation actually about?
What old fear or unmet need did that moment touch in your Wounded Child?
How did your body respond, and what did it need that you could not access in the moment?

As you revisit the experience now, what truth becomes clearer about the early meaning that fed this trigger?

The Mother Ache Ripple Effect

Where do you notice early painful patterns repeating themselves across friendships, romantic relationships, work, or spiritual communities?
What echoes from your early mother relationship do you notice?
How have these ripples shaped your sense of worth, belonging, or trust?

Opposite-Hand Journaling: A Dialogue with Your Wounded Child

What did your non-dominant handwriting reveal about your wounded child within?
What does she need to feel seen and safe finally?
Did the younger self express something you had not consciously named before?
How might you continue this dialogue as part of your healing?

Lili's Story

What moments in Lili's story stirred recognition, tenderness, or discomfort?
What would it mean to meet your wounded child with the same patience, protection, and compassion that Lili's story invites?

As you finish these reflections, take a moment to place a hand over your heart. Notice any shifts in your body or the way you feel toward the Wounded Child within you. Healing unfolds through attention and tenderness. You do not need to resolve every question now. Simply acknowledging what has been carried is itself a profound act of restoration. Let these insights settle gently, trusting they will guide you as you continue to weave the next strands of your healing.

Conclusion: Meeting the Wounded Child with Honest Presence

Healing does not come from bypassing our early wounds, but from turning toward them with honesty and care. What wounds us early in life often shapes the very path through which wholeness seeks to return. When we deny or minimize our original ache, we also turn away from the deeper intelligence held within it, the place where our capacity for healing and awakening quietly waits.

In this chapter, you turned toward the Wounded Child and began to see how her early experiences shaped the patterns that still echo through your life. You explored the many forms the mother ache can take, and how each one leaves its own impression on the tender psyche of a child. You named the early meanings she formed, felt how triggers respond to these early meanings, and traced the ripple effect that unfolds when early wounds go unrecognized.

This work is an act of honest presence. Our judgments and blaming do not serve us or further our healing path. By acknowledging what the child once carried—pain, confusion, overwhelm, or loss—you begin to loosen the old protective strategies that once defined your path. You learn to differentiate between what belonged to a moment in childhood and what belongs to your life now.

You are the woman who holds the fibers of the basket. You are the one who decides what will be woven forward. As you sort through these early strands, you reclaim the truth that the child inside you needed and still needs to be understood and comforted. Each moment of awareness becomes a gesture of care. Each moment of honesty becomes a new way of relating to yourself.

This stage prepares the ground for the basket weaving ahead. It helps you recognize which strands still ache, which are ready to rest, and which carry strength you never knew you had. Every strand matters.

In the next chapter, you will meet another expression of your inner world: the Orphan Child. Her longing and her search for belonging reveal the next layer of healing. Through her, you will begin to understand the difference between loneliness and aloneness, and how slow, steady, embodied trust can reshape the weave of your life.

Chapter Four:

The Orphan's Return to Trust

"You must trust the small light within you to find your way through the dark."

—John O'Donohue

The Orphan Child archetype appears next to guide our healing. She is the part of us that remembers the ache of unmet needs, and she also holds our potential for *trust* as a slow, embodied knowing that we can remain with ourselves and that we can heal. The Orphan archetype within us has the basket weaving task of soaking the materials gathered by the Wounded Child. Just as basket materials need to be softened in water before they can be woven without breaking, we too must allow our painful memories to soften.

Although the Wounded Child and Orphan Child may seem similar, they arise from different layers of experience. The Wounded Child holds the original raw, early pain formed in relationship with the mother. The Orphan Child emerges later, shaped by the need to survive without the safety, guidance, or attunement she longed for. The Wounded Child feels the injury; the Orphan Child learns to live with it. In energetic terms, the Wounded child is in a way static, caught in time and the Orphan Child is in motion, moving forward the best way she can with what she has to carry. She carries the wound and adapts and she also carries both resilience and a deep longing for belonging. Tending to both is essential, because healing requires acknowledging the wound and comforting the child who had to carry it alone.

The Orphan's Return to Trust

The Orphan embodies the human experience of being alone: the moment we realize we must navigate life without guarantees of protection or perfect love. Yet within this heartbreak lies her sacred potential. In learning to hold her own pain with tenderness, she begins to weave belonging from within, transforming loneliness into compassion and the ache of separation into the capacity to love.

Softening requires trust. Trust that we can face the truth of our childhood; that the strands of our story are flexible enough to be woven into a healing basket; and that the basket we create can hold both our ache and our healing. During this soaking process, there is no rush, no need to fix or judge. There is only the invitation to stay present with the honest truth of our experience that we gathered in the last chapter, and to trust that healing is possible. This moment invites us to plant the seeds of trust within ourselves.

The Orphan is entrusted with the sacred task of softening what was once rigid. As she soaks the strands she has gathered and sorted, she begins to reclaim her agency and the strength of belonging to herself. Each step through the landscape of her own becoming teaches her that alone does not mean lonely.

Endowed and Entrusted with Healing

There is an ancient Sufi teaching I read in Tara Brach's book, *Radical Acceptance*, that deeply moved me. The teaching states that the Great Mother entrusts each of us with a measure of the world's pain and endows each of us with the capacity to heal that pain. Trust. The Sufis understood that this sacred trust is given to us by the Great Mother, who is always with us. There is a recognition that we are never alone in our efforts to heal and that the weight of our suffering is met with her support. Our capacity to heal flows from her infinite well of compassion. This requires both humility and courage. We are not here to escape our suffering, nor are we alone in facing it. Every human has been entrusted and endowed with their portion of pain.

In the previous chapter, through the lens of the Wounded Child, we examined how early bonding influenced our attachment styles, the forms our mother ache took, and the early meanings we developed to interpret our experiences. These reflected our ways of navigating inconsistent maternal love, and each created an early meaning that continues to influence how we relate to ourselves and the world. The Orphan now steps forward to gently soften and nurture these strands. Her sacred ally is trusting that these strands can be softened and that the wounds they carry can be healed.

Tears as Prayer

To honor this sacred trust, we begin by softening. Like fibers placed in water before they can be woven, our feelings must also be soaked so they can soften and release. Sometimes, the simplest way to remember our capacity to feel is to let tears come through the tender mirror of a story or a film that touches the ache within us.

Early in my healing journey, while I was traveling in India, I participated in a week-long residential Primal Therapy group. It was a very intense process involving honest (terrifying) exposure work, catharsis, meditation, and a profound exploration of my primal childhood. Primal childhood refers to our earliest layer of emotional life, before language, before self-protection, when every experience imprints directly on the body. This exploration as you can imagine was quite painful. About midway through the group, one evening, we gathered to watch *The Prince of Tides*, and I remember the tears that flowed, not just from me, but from everyone in the room. We cried together and alone as the story revealed its aching truths. The release was tender, and I felt a deep sense of witnessing—my own pain and the universal pain of being human. In that moment, I understood something deeply: tears are a language of the heart and a sacred bridge to the inner children within us, because they express what words cannot. Tears rise from the oldest layers of our emotional life, revealing vulnerability, need, and truth in their purest form. This pure form vibrates with authenticity and compassion and invites our inner children to respond with trust.

There is a profound sacred wisdom in our tears. When we watch a story unfold on screen that touches the most tender parts of our hearts, we are reminded that suffering and love are universal. During those moments, crying is not a sign of weakness. It is truth. It is the Orphan Child within us meeting her own vulnerability and witnessing the pain and beauty of life reflected in others' stories. Watching a sad movie like *The Prince of Tides, Old Yeller, Terms of Endearment, A River Runs Through It, Steel Magnolias,* etc., we let the floodgates of our feelings open, and in doing so, we honor the Orphan Child within. The tears that fall are sacred water that cleanse, release, and foster trust. They tell the Orphan Child that her pain belongs, and that she has a place in the weaving of life's healing story.

In this context, our tears remind us that our own suffering is not isolated. When we see suffering reflected in the stories of others, we realize that we are not alone in our pain, despite our loneliness. The Orphan Child learns, through the silent, overflowing language of tears, that she is part of a larger tapestry of human experience, and her healing is a thread contributing to the whole. Trust begins to grow here: trust that pain can be felt, held, and transformed; trust that we are supported by a love bigger than our own experience of it; and trust that our story also has a role in helping others to heal.

Experiential Invitation: Allowing Emotion to Flow Through Story

Choose a film that has the power to open your heart and bring tears. It might be one of the classics mentioned above, or maybe there's another film that calls to you. Before you begin, settle into a comfortable space, perhaps cover yourself with a soft blanket, hold your stuffed animal in your lap, have a box of tissues handy, and remind yourself that crying is allowed. Invited. As the story unfolds, let the tears flow freely. Notice how the Orphan Child within you feels through this act of witnessing another's pain.

Through this practice, we learn that our emotions are valid and that we belong to a larger field than our own story. Every tear shed is an act of soaking the strands for your own healing basket. With each tear, trust grows in the truth of your lived experience. Tears are prayer.

Letting Go of the Mother's Promise

Tears truly are a form of prayer. They soften the heart's soil, allowing us to release what has long been held naturally. What has been gathered for your healing now soaks in this tenderness, softening old promises that never took root and expectations that never bore fruit. In this softened ground, the Orphan can begin the gentle process of letting go.

To heal, we must ask our inner Orphan to release our expectations held toward our mothers, those carried from the past and those projected into the future. This is not a denial of love or a dismissal of pain. It is a conscious act of surrender, a way of opening the hands that once clutched for what could not be given. The path of healing leads toward wholeness, and along the way, we come to understand that through the wisdom of spirit, we chose this mother, this life, and these lessons. We chose them not as punishment, but as the ground from which our evolution could grow.

To embrace the Orphan is to start freeing our mother from our expectations. It is to stop trying to extract love, validation, or approval from her. In doing so, we release ourselves from the endless cycle of longing and resentment. The Orphan does not dwell in bitterness or blame; she lives in the awareness, curiosity, and honesty of our Innocent, Magical and Wounded Children; she offers her trust in this powerful weave. She understands that although our mothers shaped our early experiences, these experiences do not define our ultimate wholeness.

I invite you to intentionally release your expectations you hold for your mother. In doing so, allow yourself to feel the ache that arises, and the sense of relief that follows. Let the past soften. Let unmet needs fade away. Recognize that freedom comes from surrendering. In the tears of release, the Orphan teaches the courage to let go and the grace to stand in self-reliance now.

This process of letting go of the expectation that my mother would one day *mother* me was one of the most challenging and healing steps in my journey. During a residential group process called the Path of Love, my teacher and friend Alima helped me express the pain of these expectations and then invited me to let them go. There was a pause—an instinctive hesitation—and when she asked why, I said from the depths of my being, "If I let go, I'll be alone." Ah, the pain I felt in that moment, the fear. She encouraged me to stay with the pain, stay with the fear, and look around the room at the beloved friends and allies who were part of my life and journey. With this support, I released the future expectations I had been carrying. That release changed me. Most importantly, it also changed my relationship with my all-too-human mother.

For years, I had carried the ache of unmet expectations. When I was accepted to law school, I waited to tell her until I also had a full scholarship, believing this time she would be proud. Her response was: "I hope you don't become another one of those Hillary Clinton women." Ouch! Later, when I graduated, she dismissed the graduation celebration, and when I got divorced, her first concern was practical, not tender. Eventually, I wrote to her, asking for space. That space lasted over two years, and in it, I learned something vital: releasing the need for her approval set me free.

Experiential Invitation: Letting Go of Expectations

Before you begin, take a few slow breaths and rest a hand over your heart. This reflection is not about giving up on love, but about freeing love from illusion. Every daughter carries unspoken expectations with hope that her mother might see her, soothe her, or finally change. When those hopes go unmet, the ache deepens. I suggest you write in your journal as you move through these questions. As you write, allow compassion to hold both your longing and your disappointment.

What expectations did you have as a child that your mother couldn't meet?

How have these expectations reappeared in your adult life?

How might letting go of these expectations help bring you more peace in your current relationship with her?

When you let go of the hope that your mother will change, what feelings come up?

When you finish, pause for a moment of stillness. Place your hand again on your heart and breathe gently into whatever arises, whether its grief, relief, tenderness. In releasing what cannot be, you make room for what is: your own steady presence, your own becoming.

The Birth of Hope

When you release expectations, it may feel like an ending. You let go of the dream that your mother will change. You lay down the longing for what never was. For a moment, the heart feels empty, an ache where the old dream lived. But emptiness is not the end. It is a clearing. In that open space, something new begins to stir, a different kind of hope.

Not the naive hope that believes someone will come and make everything right or finally offer praise or acknowledgment like "I'm proud of you. You're doing great." This new kind of hope is different. It grows from the soil of truth. It knows that love may not come in the way you expected, yet love is still possible. It is already here, waiting inside you.

Hope is the flickering light in the Orphan's hands. It whispers, *I can be the mother I never had to myself. I can care for the places she couldn't that need attention. I can grow deep roots in the ground of my own being*.

To hope in this way is to drop expectations and believe in life itself. It is to trust that healing unfolds when you face what is true and stay with it. It is to know that even when your mother's love failed you, love did not disappear. This is the Orphan's sacred hope, the flame that stays lit even in the dark.

Hope, when it begins to stir in this way, is not a wish for rescue, it is the first spark of belonging to ourselves again. Yet for hope to take root, it must move from yearning into action, into the lived truth that we can shape our path from where we are. This is where agency awakens. Agency is hope embodied. It is the Orphan's next breath, the small step, the soft yes to life that says, *I am not powerless. I can choose how I meet this moment*.

The Awakening of Agency

"When there is nothing left to lose, we find the true self – the self that is whole, the self that is enough, the self that no longer looks to others for definition, or completion, or anything but companionship on the journey."
–Elizabeth Lesser

The Orphan's healing relies on the return of agency. Agency is the living memory of choice, which is the felt sense that even in pain, one can respond. It is the capacity and desire to assert one's self-authority over actions and circumstances, to choose one's path and take aligned action. It begins with recognition: *I have a choice. My actions matter. I can move toward life and nurture my own well-being.*

For the child who learned that reaching out didn't work, having agency once felt dangerous. Withdrawal became safety. Silence became survival. Many of us learned early that to remain loved, we had to adapt, to please, to disappear, to read the room and become what was most pleasing or harmonious. In doing so, we lost touch with the inner compass that once pointed toward our own needs and longings. The ache of this loss runs deep. Without agency, we float, waiting for rescue, uncertain whether we have the right to steer our own course.

To feel agency again is to feel life awakening in the body, the subtle pulse of willingness to participate, to create, to belong. Agency is not the hard grasp of willpower or the illusion that we can bend life to our will. True agency is the embodied knowing that we are participants in a living world, co-weaving with forces seen and unseen. It is the Orphan's understanding that she is not only shaped by life; she also shapes it.

Each small act of agency rewires the story of helplessness into one of presence. It might be choosing to breathe when the body tenses, stepping outside for air, making a nourishing meal, or speaking a boundary aloud. These gestures, though simple, are sacred. They whisper to the nervous system: *I am here. I can choose.*

Agency grows through self-trust. As the Orphan begins to exercise her ability to make choices, take responsibility, and meet what arises, she reclaims the authorship of her own life. From this place, she responds to circumstances rather than reacting to them. The more she listens inwardly and acts from truth, the stronger her sense of inner authority becomes.

This is the alchemy of agency: every time you choose action over passivity, honesty over habit, movement over paralysis, you weave a new story. The Orphan reminds you that you are not the child who was left behind. You are the woman who refuses to abandon herself by being steady, responsive, and free.

Agency begins as a seed, like trust. It grows each time we turn inward and choose to meet what is true. Taking responsibility does not mean blaming ourselves or our mothers; it means remembering that our healing unfolds through participation. Even small choices become strands of strength woven through the Orphan's ache. Over time, these strands form the foundation of inner trust. From this place, a felt sense of belonging rises from within.

My true healing began through cultivating agency. Only after I took responsibility for my life—all of it—did my transformation root. After years of therapy spent reliving my childhood pain through the lens of the Wounded Child, I remained stuck. It felt like I was bandaging my pain rather than actually healing it. Then, a teacher asked me a question that changed everything: "Why did you choose those parents?"

Good question. Over time, this became a koan,[13] a mystery to live into. When I began to embody it as truth, something in me broke open. By taking responsibility for my path, my agency was restored. Ask yourself: Why did you choose your parents? Why did you choose your mother? Play with this question. Dance with it. Somewhere within it lies a truth that can lift you from the ache of adaptation into the freedom of authorship.

The Journey from Soft Belly to Long, Slow, Deep Breathing

Each breath is an act of agency, a reminder that choice begins here in the body and in the willingness to remain with what is real.

In the first chapter, we practiced soft belly breathing, the natural rhythm of a newborn, with the belly rising and falling with ease and the breath

13 A koan is a Zen meditation technique, an unanswerable question used in satori work.

moving naturally. This breath reconnects us to the innocence of our beginning, when being was enough.

But innocence is disrupted. When safety and connection break, the child feels orphaned from her mother's presence. Longing for closeness, she learns to brace, to hold her breath, to wait. To heal these moments, a new kind of breath is needed, one that rebuilds trust from within.

Long, slow, deep breathing is a practice of conscious regulation. Unlike the effortless rhythm of soft belly breathing, this breath invites participation. We extend the inhale, after filling the belly and chest, we pause; and release the exhale completely, drawing the navel back in, and again pause. The rhythm is steady, deliberate.

Both breaths soothe the nervous system and activate the body's natural capacity to restore balance. Yet their quality differs. Soft belly breathing is receptive and feels like being held. Long, slow, deep breathing is intentional and feels like learning to hold oneself. For the Orphan, this shift marks a turning point: from innocence to agency, from being carried to carrying oneself, from depending on another's steadiness to discovering one's own.

This breath does not replace the first; it builds upon it. First, we remember the innocence of being held. Then, we embody the strength of holding ourselves. Each breath becomes a thread of trust in life and in one's own rhythm.

Experiential Practice: Long Slow Deep Breathing

For more than a decade, I have practiced Kundalini Yoga almost daily. When time is short, I often turn to this simple breath. Its rhythm of expansion, pause, release, pause, steadies me, bringing clarity and presence. Eleven minutes a day is enough to deepen awareness, regulate emotion, and restore faith in the life force that moves through me.

This is the breath I now invite you to explore. It builds on the softness you've cultivated and invites a deeper strength. With each inhale, draw in nourishment and life and pause. With each exhale, release tension, expectation and again pause. Each pause, both on the inhale and exhale creates a moment of stillness within that is essential to your healing. Gradually, the breath becomes a sacred container that holds both your ache and your emerging trust.

Begin by finding a comfortable seat in sukhasana, cross-legged on a cushion, or in a firm chair, feet connected to the ground. Keep your spine tall, shoulders relaxed, and chin slightly tucked. Rest your hands on your knees in gyan mudra, thumb and index finger touching.

Sitting in sukhasana, with hands resting on the knees in gyan mudra with the thumb and index finger touching lightly, the remaining fingers extended, the body becomes an instrument of inner wisdom. The chin is softly tucked, shoulders relaxed, heart lifted, and spine aligned from tailbone to crown. This posture stabilizes the energy through the central channel and supports the awakening of self-trust at the sacred center.

Focus on your belly. Breathe in deeply and slowly, allowing your abdomen to expand like a balloon filling with air. Exhale gently, pulling your navel toward your spine, until it is completely empty. Pause briefly at the top of each inhale and exhale, noticing the stillness. This is the space where life gathers before moving again.

Long, slow, deep breathing calms the nervous system, regulates emotions, strengthens awareness, enhances vitality, and cultivates trust.

Practice daily, even a few minutes is enough to get started. Practicing for eleven minutes a day is a wonderful resource for self. Over time, this breath will remind you: *I am here. I can hold myself. I belong*.

The Orphan's Return to Trust

The Solace of Aloneness

Each breath is an act of agency, a simple declaration of life: *I am here. I can choose*. Through long slow deep breath, the Orphan begins to trust her capacity to meet herself. From this steadiness, she is ready to explore the deeper terrain of her ache. This is the movement from loneliness to aloneness.

As we meet the Orphan archetype as an inner energy, it is natural to encounter and focus on the ache of loneliness. This is the mother ache in its purest form, the echo of unmet needs, of being unseen or abandoned. Yet within this same ache lies the seed of profound growth. The Orphan is a bearer of sorrow and also a guide toward strength.

The journey from loneliness to aloneness is an initiation to embrace. Loneliness is the wound, the hollow shaped by what was missing. Aloneness, by contrast, is an inner sanctuary, a state of trust in one's own presence.

In this chapter, aloneness is not the same as loneliness, nor is it the same as solitude. Loneliness is the pain of disconnection, the ache that arises when a child reaches for contact and finds no one there. Solitude is a chosen state, often nourishing, in which one steps away from others to rest, reflect, or restore. Aloneness, as I am using it here, names something different and deeper. It is the moment when reaching outward stops and presence turns inward. It is the realization that no one else can take this healing journey for you, and that you have the capacity to stay with yourself without collapsing or abandoning your own experience. Aloneness is not isolation or resignation. It is a developmental and spiritual threshold. When the Orphan learns to inhabit aloneness, she does not become separate from life. She becomes rooted in herself. From this ground, agency, trust, and true self connection become possible.

Feeling lonely is painful because our earliest survival depends on connection. We are wired to belong. Loneliness reflects a rupture in that belonging—a disconnection from self, from mother, from tribe. We might try to ease this pain by reaching out toward a partner, friends, getting lost in a crowd. Yet even among other people, loneliness can persist. This is because loneliness is not healed by proximity; it is healed by intimacy, by being seen without masks. Our adaptive patterns, once meant to keep us safe, now keep us from true intimacy. They help us fit in, but at the cost of being truly known.

When we recognize these patterns and begin to lay them down, something miraculous happens: we meet ourselves. And in that meeting, we realize that our aloneness is a wellspring of self-connection. Aloneness is not the absence of others. It is the presence of oneself. It is the felt sense of wholeness that cannot be filled outside of ourselves. What we seek in another must first be found within our own beings.

In the landscape of the mother ache, this shift is pivotal. When we release our expectations of our mothers, we free ourselves from the endless ache of longing for what is not. Cutting that cord of longing does not sever love; it restores balance. In accepting what our mothers could not give, we open to what we can now give ourselves by embracing our aloneness.

Through agency, the Orphan learns self-trust. Through self-trust, she discovers that she can meet her own needs with presence and care. As this inner steadiness grows, the hunger for external validation softens. She no longer reaches outward to fill an inner void.

Over time, loneliness begins to transform. Loneliness is the ache of unmet needs reaching for someone else to fulfill them. Aloneness is the experience of being with oneself in wholeness. When the Orphan feels safe inside her own company, aloneness becomes a source of nourishment rather than fear.

This is sacred ground. Aloneness becomes the place where her fullness lives, where she no longer abandons herself or seeks love through self-betrayal. When she stands on this ground, relationships change. Connection becomes authentic because she is no longer manipulating for closeness or bargaining for belonging. Love arises from freedom, not need.

This reframes the Orphan as a teacher of self-sovereignty. Just as soaked fibers become pliable and ready for weaving, the experience of loneliness—tenderly held and allowed—prepares the heart to weave a new pattern of resilience and authentic connection with oneself. Aloneness becomes a practice of trust, a celebration of the strength that emerges when we are fully present with ourselves.

The truth is both simple and profound: we are born alone, and we die alone. To realize this is to begin to awaken. No one else can carry the weight of our life, not our mothers, nor the mothers we wished for. The Orphan Archetype embodies this clarity. She knows that aloneness is the return to our own selves and the freedom to walk beside ourselves with grace. Your aloneness is your truth.

Mother Ache Healing in the World:

The Woman Who Found Her Lineage

Genevieve was born when her mother was already carrying too much. Two sons filled the home with competing needs. Their father, older and often unwell, required constant attention. By the time Genevieve arrived, her mother was stretched between too much responsibility and fear. Genevieve felt this long before she could name it.

Her memories of early childhood come in fragments: the smell of cooking, the sound of her mother chopping vegetables, a sense of movement without rest. Her mother offered comfort only after crisis had already unfolded. When her father's temper rose or his heart became unstable, Genevieve was gathered into her mother's arms. The comfort was real, but it was infused with anxiety. The house itself seemed to hold its breath.

As she grew older, the warmth she longed for often turned into intrusion. Her mother read through her journals, pressed her friends with questions, and crossed boundaries that Genevieve did not yet know how to protect. Love felt suffocating. She felt like a misfit, an orphan really, and she wondered why she was stuck in this family that she did not relate to at all.

During adolescence, embarrassment settled into her body. Her mother's large, aging figure, her loud voice, her constant need for control became overwhelming. Genevieve turned her discomfort inward and began to fear becoming like her mother. She pushed away, then reached back. She wanted closeness, yet closeness felt smothering. These early patterns shaped her adult relationships for many years.

In adulthood, Genevieve became a mother herself. She was determined to create a different pattern for her two daughters, one that offered boundaries and warmth rather than intrusion or collapse, and she succeeded. When her own mother's health declined and she moved to be near her, Genevieve stepped into the role of caretaker. For three years she managed hospice care, medical decisions, and the steady unraveling of her mother's life. She wanted to help. She also felt resentment as she helped. Beneath both lived a longing for the kind of mother who could comfort her authentically.

Her mother's energetic patterns touched Genevieve's patterns, shaped by her mother's story and her grandmothers before her. Although she vowed not to repeat these patterns, she often felt pulled into them. As her mother neared the end of her life, Genevieve found herself exhausted and unsure how to make peace with the tangled strands of love and hurt.

After her mother died, she reached out to me. We began working together at the point when grief was raw, and the stories of her childhood felt heavy in her body. She wanted clarity, relief, and a way to trust the world again. Together we explored the cling–flee rhythm that had shaped her since childhood. The part that reached for love wanted belonging because she felt lonely. The part that pulled away wanted independence, freedom, to be herself. She wanted to embrace her aloneness. Neither was wrong. Each had protected her in its own way.

As she practiced holding both impulses with curiosity rather than judgment, something in her began to settle. She learned to sense when she was leaving herself and when she was collapsing into old roles. Little by little, she discovered an inner space that felt steady enough to hold her longing for belonging and her need for freedom.

A significant part of her healing came from exploring her lineage. She became curious about the women who came before her, including her grandmother, who had abandoned her mother to a children's home for more than a year. Understanding this history did not excuse the pain, but it helped her see the human story beneath the generations of fear and survival. With this clarity, forgiveness arose as a natural softening.

Over time Genevieve began to feel her deceased mother and grandmother near her, no longer as sources of ache but as witnesses on her path, supporting her. Through our facilitated Compassionate Inquiry work together, finding her musical voice, prayer, nature, and the growing trust inside her own body, she found her way back to the lineage she once felt disconnected from. She traveled to Italy and met her maternal family there and was welcomed with open arms. She realized that she had never been truly alone. The roots of her family had always been there, waiting for her to reclaim them.

Now she no longer feels like the Orphan Child in her story. She feels rooted, connected, and held. The love she longed for lives in her own being and comes from her own lineage, handed down through time immemorial.

Journal Reflections: Reweaving Trust

As you move through these reflections, pause whenever your body asks you to. The Orphan Child carries both resilience and ache, both courage and longing. Let each prompt be an invitation to listen without rushing, to honor the part of you that learned to go on when love felt uncertain.

Endowed and Entrusted to Heal

How does the idea that you are entrusted with a piece of the world's healing reshape your relationship with your mother ache?
How does it feel to imagine your healing as an offering to the whole?
Where do you sense the strength within you to embrace what you have been given to heal?
How might you show compassion to the part of you that hesitates or resists?

Tears as Prayer

How did it feel to watch the sad movie and invite tears to flow rather than try to hold them back?
What do your tears want you to know?
What part of you feels seen or softened when you allow yourself to cry?
When was the last time you felt safe enough to cry with another person?
If your tears are a prayer, what is that prayer asking for or offering?
Tears are not weakness. They are devotion made visible, the soul's way of speaking in water and light. Explore this.

Letting Go of Expectations

You explored this experientially within the chapter. These reflections offer a way to deepen that process.
How did it feel in my body to release the expectations I have carried toward my mother?
What emotions surfaced as I loosened the old belief that things should have been different?
Where do I sense spaciousness or relief from letting go, even slightly?
How might I continue softening expectations so that openness and presence can guide me rather than my past early needs?

Awakening Self-Agency

Where in my life have I felt unseen, dismissed, or without choice?
How did I protect myself when I had no power to change what was happening?
What helps me sense my own strength and autonomy now?

How might I begin to make choices that honor my truth and my needs?
What does agency feel like in my body? How can I practice the posture of agency?
Why did I choose these parents? This mother?

Long, Slow Deep Breathing—Trusting Your Own Rhythm

When I practiced this breath, how did it change my inner state?
Where in my life am I still waiting to be carried instead of carrying myself?
What shifts in me when I choose to breathe fully, with intention and presence?
How does this breath remind me that I belong to life, and life belongs to me?

From Loneliness to Aloneness

As you reflect, let yourself feel the difference between the ache of loneliness and the sacred nature of aloneness:
When do I feel most lonely?
Do I try to fill this sense of loneliness through other people or things?
What happens in my body when I turn toward myself instead of seeking comfort outside?
Can I remember a time when being alone felt peaceful, creative, or nourishing?
How might I begin to experience my aloneness as companionship with myself, as a sanctuary rather than a void?

Genieve's Story

What felt familiar to me in Genevieve's experience of being overwhelmed by her mother, caring for her mother or losing her mother?
How did her reconnection with her European lineage and ancestral roots affect my understanding of healing or belonging?
Do I see ways in which trusting her aloneness guided Genevieve forward, and how might that guide my own experience of realizing I was never truly alone?

Take one more breath before closing your journal. The Orphan Child within you has traveled far. As you reflect on these prompts, notice any softening or new clarity that emerged. Healing this archetype acknowledges our feelings of loneliness, and at the same time we are learning to embrace our essential intrinsic aloneness, which is the path to self-fulfillment.

Conclusion: Honoring Our Inner Orphan's Trust

Tears, breath, and surrender have softened the fibers of our stories. In the tender work of the Orphan, we have learned to release what could not be and to open to our own agency. Loneliness has been a teacher, as we begin to remember that we are never truly alone. We are held by our ancestors and the same life that breathes through all things. Our aloneness is our gateway to the very fulfillment we are seeking outside of ourselves and when we pivot from this energetic pull and turn inward, we find that very fulfillment within our own beings. This recognition is the bridge that carries us forward, where the longing of the Orphan ripens into the acceptance that the Maiden within us teaches.

Part I: Closing Reflection

Pause now, and feel the breath in your belly, soft and warm, rising and falling like a gentle tide. Sense the Innocent Child within you, fragile and luminous, and let her natural awareness remind you of this capacity within you. Feel the Magical Child gathering the strands of your story, curious and unafraid, letting each memory, each painful experience, be set out to reweave into your basket of healing. Invite the Wounded Child to move beside them, sorting with curiosity while the Orphan Child watches, holding the trust and freedom of letting go of expectation. Water the seed within you that the Great Mother has entrusted you with this healing journey and endowed you with the capacity to embark upon it fully.

Feel your feet on the earth. Remember the rhythms of shaking, dancing, and breathing that loosen what no longer serves you. All these children, these archetypes, these practices, are yours. The basket is ready to weave. The strands are yours, and the hands that weave them are your own.

Part II: Weaving the Basket of Healing

The strands of your healing basket have been gathered and softened; now it is time to weave. In Part II, we shift from preparation to creation. The healing basket begins to take shape, crafted with intention and care.

In the following chapters, we'll encounter new archetypes: The Maiden teaches acceptance of what is. The Seeker reminds us of our connection to self. The Weaver of Life brings understanding to the patterns of the mind. The Healer embodies empathy, guiding us to authentic emotion.

As you enter this next phase, imagine yourself seated before your basket. Each weave honors both past and present. This is your sacred work, creating a vessel uniquely yours, crafted by the one who has always been entrusted with its making: you.

Chapter Five:

The Maiden and Weaving the Ground of Acceptance

"The curious paradox is that when I accept myself just as I am, then I can change."

—Carl Rogers

After releasing expectations about your mother in the previous chapter, you now face what remains—your own healing journey. The Orphan taught you to let go of what could not be given and to stand in the truth of your aloneness. Now, the Maiden steps forward, inviting you to begin again by meeting what is here, rather than chasing what was lost. Her path is one of inner courage: to trust the ground beneath her, to allow new possibilities to open, and to begin weaving with the materials already in her hands.

The Maiden is the archetype of renewal. Though her outer season may have passed, she remains within you as an inner energy: fresh, hopeful, and willing to open to life again. She is not limited to youth; she is the part of you that still has the capacity to imagine a different future. The girl who once longed to be seen grows into the woman who now sees herself with the potential for growth, expansion, healing.

Traditionally, the Maiden belongs to the ancient Maiden, Mother, Crone triad, representing youth and the first unfolding of life. While this lineage is honored here, in our work of healing the mother ache, the Maiden is not confined to understanding our past, she is within us still under all the layers of our later years of experience and we call on her energetic power as an ally here now.

She may appear to you as the girl you once were, leaving home, falling in love, moving into your first apartment, or stepping into your first job. Yet she also reflects the part of you within that is still willing to try, still willing to learn, still willing to trust that change is possible. Her offering on this path is the willingness to meet her life with *acceptance* or the gentle allowing of what is here, as it is, in this moment.

For women carrying the mother ache, the Maiden bears scars. She holds the ache of being unseen, unsupported, or shamed during childhood. Instead of freedom, she may carry fear. Instead of delight she may carry shame. Instead of confidence, doubt. Acceptance is the first thread she must weave because only by embracing her truth can she transform these wounds into strength.

As we move through the later stages of our lives, we often forget her. Yet she remains essential, because it is during the Maiden years that the early mother ache begins to manifest in our lives. The early meanings formed in childhood shape our choices: the partners we select, the friendships we invest in, and the dreams we pursue or abandon. The events of our childhood that we did not have the capacity to process deeply influence the Maiden's choices as she steps out on her own.

To heal the mother ache, we return to the Maiden to reconnect with the part of ourselves that first tried to make a new life despite our early pain. She reveals how the ache lived in our longing, our self-doubt, our patterns of seeking and striving. Meeting her with compassion becomes an act of reclaiming the healthy life she needed.

Acceptance, through the Maiden's lens is a clear-sighted willingness to stop struggling against what was and to turn toward what is. Acceptance becomes an inner initiation, a way of opening the heart without collapsing into the past. The Maiden's acceptance is distinct from the broader, more seasoned acceptance that emerges in the mature feminine. In many traditions, this deeper acceptance is associated with the Mother or the Crone, archetypes who hold life with perspective and wisdom shaped by time. The Maiden stands in a different place. She offers the first, trembling willingness to meet reality as it is, before understanding fully arrives.

Her acceptance is an initiation: the moment you stop fighting the past and turn toward the life that is yours to inhabit. As you journey through this book, you will meet archetypes such as the Healer, the Weaver of Life, the Mystic, and the Priestess. Each of these archetypes carries a more spacious, integrated expression of acceptance. The Maiden prepares the ground for them. She opens the door. Her acceptance is the brave beginning that allows the later feminine wisdom to take root.

Acceptance is not approval or resignation. It does not excuse or erase the past. Acceptance is facing reality with presence. It means ending the struggle with what was and starting to weave with the materials you have received. In doing so, the Maiden grounds your healing in what has been waiting for your remembrance, your embrace.

The Maiden weaves the base of the basket, laying each strand with care as she begins her initiation into healing. Acceptance guides her hands: the readiness to start from what is real and build from there. With every crossing of fibers, she places her trust in the ground that steadies her. These first circles become the foundation of her healing basket—acceptance makes it strong enough to hold the weaving that will follow.

Weaving the Ground of Belonging

Every basket begins at its base. The first step is to lay down the rods that form its core and structure. Basket makers call this the slath: the crossing that holds everything else in place. Around it, a single strand is twined in a spiral, binding each piece together and catching each stake in turn. As the spiral expands, the base becomes strong enough to support the basket's sides. The base must be stable, for it will carry the weight of everything that follows.

Similarly, in healing, acceptance forms the foundation of your inner basket. Without it, the energetic structure of your healing basket cannot hold.

A Personal Story from the Maiden Years

I nearly didn't graduate from high school. At the beginning of senior year, living with my mother, I fell into a deep depression. My best friend had gone back to boarding school; I felt disconnected from myself and from life. For over three weeks, I stayed in bed, unable to get up to go to school.

A more stable part of me finally understood I needed structure. I moved back into my father's house and went back to class. It was excruciating. I had to catch up on weeks of work, and my grades were poor. With a therapist's help, I started to see my depression not as a personal failure but as an illness I could address with care. Her steadiness became a small thread of hope.

After graduation, I took a job at a ski shop, rented a tiny apartment, and watched my friends leave for college. The shame and loneliness ran deep. Yet, something unexpected grew as I found connection with others at work and a modest sense of pride in my job. I was good at something. That was my maiden's entry. Though it was not glamorous, it was real.

Had I remained in resentment and depression, the story might have ended there. Instead, I accepted that I was responsible for my own life and began to gather myself. I saved money and set my sights on college. A year later, I walked into the University of Colorado Boulder admissions office with my application, having previously been rejected when I applied my senior year due to poor grades. "Admissions are closed," the woman at the desk said. The old ache rose, but my Maiden refused to leave. I told the admissions officer I was working full-time and planned to pay my way through college. Perhaps sensing my determination, she kindly invited me to sit down and asked to see the paperwork I had brought, my application, SAT score and essay. After reviewing these and asking me a few questions, she disappeared into the back, returned, and said, "You have a place."

That moment changed everything. I worked my way through school and finished my degree. It wasn't easy; depression shadowed me throughout those years and achievement became one of the ways I tried to outrun the ache. But the Maiden—the part willing to try, no matter how hopeless it all seemed—carried me forward.

Looking back, that depression had many roots. One was living with a mother who couldn't mother me. During my sophomore year of high school I had moved back in with my mother, who had relocated from Dallas, which had seemed like a dream come true because in her absence I had romanticized my mother as being perfect. Our time together had been based on holidays, weekends, celebrations, eating out, shopping. I thought she was quite glamorous with her closet full of stylish clothes and her cool personality.

Hence the dream come true was short lived. Living together on a daily basis was a whole other meeting of ourselves as both daughter and mother. We shared a house but without clear boundaries or structure. My mother was often absent or else enmeshed with me. My fourteen- and fifteen-year-old self floundered; our dynamic rippled with the unease of two roommates with completely different needs and expectations. My Wounded Child ached for care. One night, about a year before I collapsed into depression, during an argument, I cried, "I need my mother!" She thought I was being dramatic. My honest plea sounded like hysteria and went unheard. What I wanted was simple: to be seen, to be held, to feel that she was there *as my mom*.

When that didn't happen, my Maiden learned a different truth: I could stand firm even when love was uncertain. I could start over, even from pain.

That season taught me my first lesson in acceptance. I couldn't change my mother or undo what was lost. I could choose how to face what was in front of me. Each small act—getting out of bed, asking for help, walking into that admissions office—became a thread of self-trust gained through accepting what was true.

Acceptance is not a single moment; it's a practice. It begins when we stop waiting for rescue and turn toward the life that is ours to live. The Maiden's path begins here: facing reality as it is, not as we wish it to be, and laying the first strong rods of the basket we are meant to weave.

What We Truly Needed

As the Maiden begins to weave the base of her basket, she gathers the raw fibers of memory and the strands of what she truly needed to feel safe, loved, and whole. These are the foundational strands of a secure bond between mother and child, the consistent qualities that build trust, belonging, and a stable sense of self.

While working with clients on healing the mother wound and writing this book, I have developed my own understanding of seven essential needs that every child brings into the world. These needs are not abstract concepts; they are the living strands that make up a child's inner world. When these needs are met, they foster resilience, self-worth, and the ability to form genuine connections. When they are unmet, the mother ache takes hold.

Understanding what was missing isn't about blaming our mothers. It's about gaining clarity and compassion. Each of our mothers was shaped by her own story and limitations, just like us. By recognizing unmet needs, we illuminate the root of our ache and open the door to meeting those needs now, from within.

As you read the seven needs that follow, allow yourself to witness rather than judge. Notice which ones were woven into your early years, even if imperfectly, and which were frayed or missing. Let your awareness be gentle and curious. This isn't about fault or failure; it's about truth. The Maiden's task is to see clearly, to gather what was given, and to name what wasn't with acceptance so she can start weaving the strong foundation her adult self now needs.

Presence

The first need of every child is to be seen and held. Presence refers to the mother's physical and emotional availability, the tangible feeling that she is there. Through her gaze, her voice, and her touch, the child learns, *I exist. I matter*. When presence is absent, the child feels unsure whether her needs will be met. *Is she there? Will I be fed?*

Safety

The second need is safety, protection from unpredictability and harm. Safety allows the child to relax into her body and trust her surroundings.

Without it, fear and hypervigilance take over her nervous system. She begins to scan for danger instead of feeling at ease.

Nurturance

Nurturance is the steady flow of care, both physical and emotional. It refers to a mother's ability to respond consistently and kindly to her child's needs. When nurturance is lacking or inconsistent, the child learns to fend for herself and may come to believe that love must be bargained for or earned through performance.

Guidance

Through the mother's guidance, the daughter learns how to navigate the world. Guidance provides structure, boundaries, and reassurance. It helps the child feel safe exploring life beyond her mother's arms. Without it, she may feel lost, overwhelmed, or uncertain of her own direction.

Acceptance

Acceptance is the mother's unconditional acknowledgment of her child as she is. It teaches that love does not depend on pleasing or performing. When acceptance is missing, the child molds herself into shapes that will be approved of, hiding her true self behind masks of adaptation.

Encouragement of Autonomy

Every child needs space to try, to fail, and to begin again. Encouragement of autonomy lets the child test her independence while still feeling supported. Without it, she may cling to others for direction or swing to the opposite extreme, rebelling in search of freedom she does not yet trust.

Validation of Feelings

The final need is for the child's emotions to be acknowledged and respected. Validation teaches that feelings are real, appropriate, and safe to express. When this is missing, the child learns to suppress her feelings, doubt her perceptions, or overcompensate to stay connected to a parent who cannot mirror her inner world.

Taken together, these seven needs form the foundation of a healthy mother-daughter bond. When they are met, they weave trust, confidence, and belonging into the child's being. When they are frayed or missing, the mother ache takes hold. By naming what was present and what was not, you begin the delicate work of reclaiming these strands and weaving the strong base your healing requires.

Experiential Invitation: The Seven Basic Needs

Before you begin, take a slow, grounding breath. This is an invitation to honor your own needs and to recognize that every child arrives with these same essential needs for love, safety, and belonging. Some were met and some were not. I suggest you pull out your journal to explore these. As you write, let tenderness accompany your remembering.

What does it feel like to acknowledge that I had these seven needs as a child?
Which of these needs were met for me, even partially?
Which needs were not met, and how do I carry that ache now?
How do I feel in my body as I accept that some of my needs were missed?
What messages did I receive about whether my needs were important or not?
How have I learned to meet these needs for myself as an adult?
How might I meet these needs for myself in the future?

When you finish, take a moment to rest your hands on your heart or navel and breathe. Each realization is a thread in your basket of healing. To name a need is to honor it.

The Three Centers of Intelligence

"I said to my body, softly, 'I want to be your friend.' It took a long breath and replied, 'I have been waiting my whole life for this."

—Nayyirah Waheed

As you start to understand your true needs, you might notice how challenging it is to stay connected with what you feel. You try to observe what is present, and suddenly the mind intervenes. It prefers to explain or distract. This is a form of protection. The mind learned long ago to guide you away from what once felt unbearable.

Accepting the truth about what was needed and what was missing during childhood can bring pain. To survive, many of us learned to retreat into our minds and distance ourselves from the body's deeper knowing. Over time, this disconnection became a way of life. The mind began to dominate, and the body's wisdom faded.

However, humans are not meant to rely on the mind alone. We live and know through three centers of intelligence: the navel, the heart, and the mind. Each one is sacred, and each offers a distinct way of understanding ourselves and the world.

The navel center is our foundation. It governs vitality, agency, and the felt sense of inner ground. From here we know when something is right or wrong for us through instinct and embodied strength. When this center is compromised, we may feel untethered, overly driven, or unable to trust ourselves.

The heart center is the seat of feeling and relational knowing. Through the heart we experience love, grief, longing, empathy, and connection. The heart allows us to feel with depth while remaining connected to ourselves. When the heart is protected or constricted, emotion may feel overwhelming, distant, or difficult to access.

The mind is the center of meaning-making. It interprets experience, forms stories, and helps us orient in the world. The mind is a powerful ally that brings clarity and understanding when it works in relationship with the navel and heart centers. When disconnected from these centers the mind can be a vortex of never-ending narratives always focused on either the past or future. Never here, now.

When these three centers are in relationship—grounded in the navel, open in the heart, and clear in the mind—we experience balance and coherence. Healing in this work unfolds through restoring conversation among these three ways of knowing.

When these three work together, we feel balanced and whole. When they are divided, we experience a disconnect within ourselves. The mind, accustomed to leading, often becomes the protector. It pulls us away from sensation and spins stories to make experience feel safer. These stories, although well-meaning, create the energetic patterns that once helped us survive but now keep us circling in thought, unable to relax in our bodies or trust our hearts.

There is, however, another capacity available to us, an inner awareness that simply observes. This spacious presence does not judge or analyze; it witnesses with steadiness and clarity. In this book, we call this the sacred center. For the sacred center of awareness to flourish, we must learn the anchoring strength of the navel. Here, at this center, the Maiden begins to root, reconnecting with the calm, steady guidance at her core.

The Navel as a Foundation for True Acceptance

To begin weaving the basket at the navel is to anchor our healing where life itself started. Here we were first nourished. Here we were connected to our mothers unconditionally. Before thought, before language, we knew the rhythm of our mother, the steady beat of her heart, and her energetic state through our navel wisdom.

Acceptance cannot be achieved through our mind's effort. Acceptance means relaxing into what is real, moment by moment, without turning away. The reason it's so hard to command the mind to stop thinking this or that and accept what's present is because the early meaning patterns of the mind are imprinted in our bodies. The result is that when we're disconnected from our bodies the mind speeds up, the emotions spiral, and we become disconnected from our inner wisdom. By dropping below thought into the body's navel center, we connect with our inner strength. True acceptance arises here. It is born from the navel, where our life-force energy began.

The navel center is located just below the belly button, acting as a lighthouse inside the body. Ancient yogis taught that seventy-two energy meridians originate from this center, branching into seventy-two thousand energy channels that carry prana, the life force, throughout the body. Here, at the navel, prana and apana, the forces of nourishment and release, have the potential to be balanced within. This balance is important for maintaining physical health as well as healing.

The navel as an intelligence center has been forgotten. We allude to it in brief moments when we say: "Trust your gut," or "I have a gut feeling." But we have ignored the deeper significance these phrases suggest. We are rarely taught to respect our navel as a true intelligence center of its own. Our culture emphasizes learning through the mind, and our minds become the core of our identities. The navel is left untended.

When I moved back into my father's home, finished high school, and went to the admissions office to ask for a spot at the university, these weren't acts of the mind. My thoughts said: *You can't, You'll fail, You don't belong*. Yet something deeper pushed through. That was navel intelligence, the instinctual courage that moves us forward despite our habitual early meaning thoughts, patterns.

Reclaiming this center restores our sense of belonging. The navel connects us to the Great Mother, the living web of creation. Rooted here, we feel the pulse of Earth beneath us and the breath of the cosmos above. Acceptance becomes a felt sense of alignment with life, an understanding that we are part of something larger than our stories. Strengthening this connection allows us to stand tall in our bodies and move with confidence.

When we reconnect with the navel, we create a strong foundation for our healing basket. Acceptance shifts from being just a concept to becoming a lived experience. Here, intention turns into action. Each breath, each choice made from the center, is a step toward home.

Navel Awareness and the Maiden's Path of Acceptance

Practicing the long, slow, deep breathing exercises we explored earlier is essential. Even when not explicitly practicing, remind yourself to breathe deeply, letting your breath reach the navel whenever you remember. The more you do this, the more it becomes second nature. Our pain led us to adapt, and part of that adaptation was shallow breathing. By intentionally recalling our deep breathing, we nurture the fire of vitality that dwells in the navel center. This subtle flame guides us on our path. Staying mindful of this center throughout the day is an act of devotion. It's how we remember that we can find peace with our childhoods, learn from them, and genuinely heal.

Our connection to our navel also deepens when we tend to our fundamental needs for nourishment, rest, and movement. While what these three essential self-care elements look like for each of us may vary, as part of your healing journey, they must be woven into the base of your healing basket.

When it comes to food, consider both the physical quality of what you eat and its energetic imprint. Notice which foods support you and which drain your energy or leave you feeling sluggish. For me, simple, natural foods like fruits, nuts, vegetables, and whole grains carry the clarity of the earth and feel like self-care. Sometimes, comfort foods are necessary, such as mashed potatoes; other times, a chocolate bar tastes like pure joy. Practicing moderation and finding balance work well for me. Paying attention and discovering what works for you will strengthen your navel connection. Remember, this isn't about dieting to change your physical form; it's about inviting awareness and acceptance to enhance your navel center's intelligence.

Sleep is another essential pillar of stability. When we are well-rested, we are more receptive, less reactive, and better equipped to handle life's challenges. If sleep is difficult for you, seek support. Deep rest is not a luxury; it is part of the rhythm that allows energy to flow through the navel and keeps you grounded in your body.

Daily chores like washing dishes, tending the garden, sweeping, and laundry can become sacred practices. These simple tasks, done mindfully and with deep breathing, strengthen your core connection. As you move, notice how effort generates warmth in the belly, building resilience. This is how grit is born, through conscious engagement in the everyday moments of life.

Throughout the day, gently bring your awareness back to your navel. At first, it might require effort, but over time it becomes second nature and starts to feel like the steady glow of an inner sun. When your attention wanders, simply redirect it, as if tending to a small flame. This consistent awareness builds trust in your own energy and your connection to the larger rhythm of life.

When we lose touch with the navel, we lose connection to that rhythm including the living presence of the sun, moon, stars, and Earth's breath, all embodied in the Great Mother. We become like a flower growing in the shade, unable to reach the light. Reconnecting with the navel reopens our inner channel to the vitality around us. It awakens the fire of purpose and the easeful joy of belonging to the natural order.

Tending to the body is the Maiden's task. Through her body, she learns acceptance—not as surrender or passivity, but as participation. She accepts what is and chooses to engage with it through breath, nourishment, movement, and attention.

> *"To be beautiful means to be yourself. You don't need to be accepted by others. You need to accept yourself."*
>
> —Thích Nhất Hạnh

Living from the navel center means orienting yourself from the deepest point of physical stability. The navel center is the place where strength, breath, and instinct meet. When this center is engaged, the body naturally aligns: the legs and pelvis root you below; the heart center opens above, allowing emotional intelligence to flow; and with this support, the mind center can then remain clearer. The navel center is the root of your sacred center. When you inhabit this grounded core, you nourish the very foundation from which the subtle neutral mind—the blossom of the sacred center—can emerge. Without this rootedness, the sacred center struggles to bloom. The Maiden learns this through embodiment by aligning her posture as she sits, stands, or walks, she strengthens the ground from which clarity, steadiness, and inner neutrality naturally arise. Let's explore how this feels in your own body.

Experiential Practice: The Postures of Wholeness—Sitting, Standing, and Walking

Come into a seated sukhasana pose, as we learned together earlier: lifting your sit bones, sitting on the edge of a cushion and crossing your legs. Use a firm chair with feet firmly planted on the ground if sukhasana does not work for you. Settle into your body and gently lengthen your spine by drawing your pelvic floor up and in. When you do this, your belly should naturally pull inward toward your spine. Lift your heart slightly, allowing the chest to open. Let your shoulders soften down and back. Rest your hands on your knees, palms facing up, with your thumb touching your index finger and your other three fingers extended outward in gyan mudra, the wisdom seal. Tuck your chin slightly so the crown of your head aligns over your spine, maintaining a straight vertical line that is balanced, neither leaning forward nor backward. Breathe slowly, directing each breath toward your navel. Feel the strength that grows as you sit upright in this ancient posture of ease, all supported by your navel.

When you're ready, maintain this internal structure and connection as you transition into *tadasana* or mountain pose. Stand with your feet hip-width apart and firmly planted. Distribute your weight across both legs. Gently lift through your spine, as if a thread is pulling you upward from the crown. Keep your heart lifted, shoulders relaxed down, and chin slightly tucked. Let your arms hang naturally by your sides with palms facing inward. Notice how this simple posture radiates both stability and openness. This is the stance of acceptance, grounded and strong.

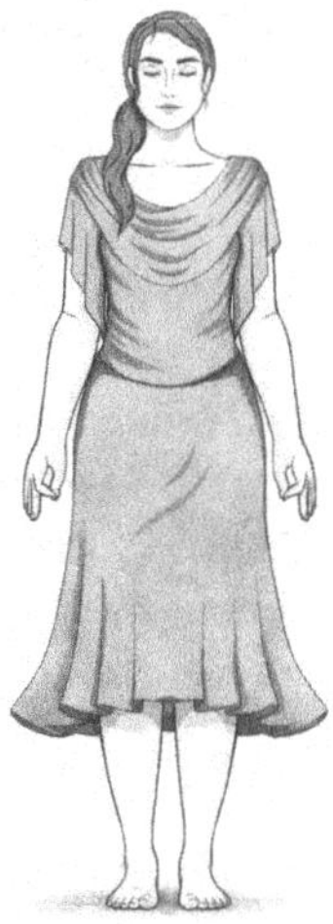

Standing in tadasana, the feet press evenly into the earth, grounding the body's weight through the four corners of each foot. The legs are engaged but not tense. The spine rises tall from the tailbone through the crown of the head, the chin slightly tucked, shoulders relaxed, and the heart lifted. The arms rest softly by the sides, palms facing inward or in gyan mudra. This posture establishes stability and receptivity.

Start to walk slowly and mindfully from this point, turning your steps into a living meditation. Let your arms swing gently and bring your hands into gyan mudra, with your thumb and index finger lightly touching. Keep your awareness at the navel, sensing it as the focal point from which your movement originates. Allow each step to start from this center, moving your body forward with balance. Walk at a steady rhythm. Feel your feet connect with the earth, keep your spine tall, and let your breath flow naturally. As you walk, remind yourself that you move from your center.

From mountain pose, the Maiden steps forward slowly, maintaining alignment and inner steadiness. Each step begins from the navel center and moves outward through the limbs. The gaze remains soft and forward, the breath smooth and even. Walking becomes a meditation: strength in motion, the body remembering its harmony. This practice supports the navel connection and translates acceptance into movement and flow.

Practice these navel awareness postures daily while sitting, standing, or walking. Each time you remember to realign your posture and connect with your navel, you strengthen your connection to life's rhythm. Over time, this awareness becomes effortless, a natural way of being present. Doing a twenty-minute walk each day and practicing this will support your healing in many ways and help you get outside into nature. It's a healing practice that's simple, accessible, and free.

Courage: The Fire of the Navel

You have now named what was needed, including the touch, safety, mirroring, and gentle presence that might have been absent in childhood. Recognizing these truths can evoke grief, longing, and anger. It is tender work to remain fully aware of what was missing. You might feel the urge to turn away, to move quickly toward forgiveness, or to excuse what could not be given. Stay present with yourself here. This is where the deeper work begins.

To face what was absent requires courage. It requires strength to look steadily at what once caused pain and admit, *I needed more than I received.* Courage is not the absence of fear but the willingness to stay present with it. Each time you breathe into the truth instead of hiding from it, you ignite the subtle fire in your navel, the inner flame that steadies you through discomfort and draws you back to your center.

This is not symbolic. The navel is the physical seat of courage. It is where life force gathers and moves, where instinct and resilience dwell. When awareness takes root here, the body remembers its strength. This courage is a willingness to stay present in the body, to keep breathing, and to meet what is real. It increases each time you bring attention back to the navel during moments of doubt or fear.

Courage born here acts as a bridge between grief and grace. It lets you honor what was lost while opening to what is now possible. With this courage, you begin to trust yourself to stand where you once collapsed, to breathe where you once held your breath, and to stay open where you once shut down.

Let this courage guide you. Each breath drawn from the navel is a vow to stay with yourself, to choose presence over avoidance, and to trust that love can flow again in new ways. This is acceptance: to open your hands, to open your heart, and to remain in the warmth of your own center. Each breath that returns you to your navel strengthens courage and prepares you to open again.

From this grounded center, something ancient stirs. Beneath the rhythm of your own breath, another pulse begins to move, steady, timeless, and vast. It is the rhythm that moves the tides, opens the petals of a flower, and whispers through all things: *you belong*. The same current that sustains your life also sustains the stars. What you feel as courage in your belly is the first shimmer of this larger love rising to meet you.

As this current deepens, courage ripens into connection. What begins as personal strength reveals itself as part of a greater web of life, a maternal presence that has always held you. This is the pulse of the Divine Mother moving through your own body, reminding you that courage and love are not separate. I like to think of the Divine Mother as the first daughter of the

Great Mother, a gift from her to help us in a form that we can understand and envision.

Experiential Practice: Breath of Fire—Awakening Courage at the Navel

Courage, in this work, is not force or bravado. It is the willingness to feel life moving through us and to meet what arises without collapsing or turning away. In many wisdom traditions, this courage lives in the navel center which represents the seat of vitality, intuition, and inner strength.

This short practice uses Breath of Fire to awaken that center and gently kindle the fire of presence.

To begin:

Come into prayer pose, as introduced in Chapter Three. Sit upright with the spine tall and relaxed. Press the palms together with steady, comfortable pressure to create stability through the upper body.

Close the eyes and gently roll them upward toward the brow point. Let the shoulders soften and the chest remain relaxed.

The breath:

Breath of Fire is a rhythmic, active breath that engages the navel. The inhale and exhale are equal in strength, with the emphasis on creating a steady, even rhythm, not breathing too forcefully. On each exhale, the navel draws gently inward. On the inhale, it releases naturally.

To find the rhythm, you may begin by sticking your tongue out and lightly panting like a dog. When the rhythm feels natural, draw the tongue in and continue the same breath through the nose. Let the belly do the work by using it to pump your breath; keep the face and chest soft.

Begin with one minute, focusing on steadiness rather than intensity. If the breath feels supportive and regulating, you may continue for up to three minutes.

To complete the breathwork, let the breath return to its natural rhythm. Keep the eyes closed for a few moments and notice sensations in the navel, the heart, and the body as a whole. You might experience more vitality, warmth, steadiness, or a subtle sense of confidence.

This practice is not about pushing hard. It is about remembering the quiet strength that lives in the belly and tapping into it in a very short time.

If at any point you feel dizzy, anxious, or overwhelmed, stop and return to long, slow, natural breathing. As with all practices in this book, listen to your body and choose what supports regulation rather than activation.

The Divine Mother and Our Seven Needs

When we connect with the Divine Mother, we are not denying the love of our human mothers. We are inviting a deeper source of love, vast enough to hold both our ache and our being. Through the navel, we receive her life-force, the same energy that animates the stars and nourishes the Earth.

We have already named the seven qualities every child needed from her mother to thrive. Most of us received only some of these. Our mothers, shaped by their own experiences, couldn't always provide what we needed. Expecting any human mother to fulfill every need is unrealistic. That's why the Maiden's path is a journey of learning acceptance. Why, then, do we arrive with needs so vast that no human mother could ever fully meet them? Maybe because these longings, this very ache, serves as a bridge to our spiritual awakening. By recognizing what was missing, we open ourselves to the deeper love that is the essence of being human. The Divine Mother is that bridge. She is the presence who holds what human mothers cannot, and she invites us to begin fulfilling these needs from within.

The Divine Mother is the first expression of the Great Mother. Throughout history and across cultures, she appears in many forms: Tara, Mary, Pachamama, Isis, Durga, Kuan Yin, and Kali. She is both fierce and tender. She does not abandon. She has entrusted you with your life and healing. Even when your personal mother could not provide what you needed, you have always belonged to Her, the eternal source of mothering that nourishes the roots of all women through time. The Divine Mother is the soil beneath your feet, the pulse within your belly, and the vast love that continues to hold you now.

The Divine Mother rises from the lineage of the Great Mother. She is the first daughter, the infinite embodied into recognizable form. In her stillness, the Maiden recognizes the mirror of her own becoming: to be both created and creating, both held and holding. She is the embodiment of acceptance made divine—the human heart remembering its sacred origin.

The Divine Mother reminds us that what was once unmet can still be fulfilled. In her presence, we are seen and held. In her arms, we feel safe enough to rest. She nourishes us with unwavering love. She guides us with steady wisdom. She accepts us wholly, without condition. She encourages our independence, reminding us that we are never alone. She validates our feelings, reminding us that no part of us is wrong. In her embrace, every need finds its answer. Through her, the Maiden learns that acceptance can become the firm base of her basket.

Over time, the Divine Mother helps us embody what she models. Her presence anchors us in the body. Her safety teaches us to set boundaries that protect what matters. Her nurturance inspires rest, nourishment, and kindness. Her guidance awakens inner wisdom. Her acceptance invites us to embrace every part of ourselves. Her encouragement fosters trust in our capacity to grow. Her validation affirms that our emotions belong. What she offers to each of us we then learn to give to ourselves.

As you recognize the gap between what you needed and what you received, the base of your basket becomes stronger. Naming each acknowledgment: *this is what I needed, this is what I received*, is a strand firmly placed. The pain of the wound and the comfort of the Divine Mother's presence weave together, forming a foundation that can support the full truth of your story.

Acceptance here is both personal and archetypal. You honor your human story while resting in the embrace of the Mother who has always held you. The awareness that our mothers were imperfect, and yet we are still held, strengthens the spiral of healing and completes the foundation of our basket.

Experiential Invitation: A Circle of Return to the Divine Mother

Before entering this practice, it may help to understand its purpose. I first learned a form of this guided meditation process years ago from an elder therapist during my own early healing. Later, I began using it in my work with clients healing the mother ache. I have seen how powerful it is for illuminating the true shape of the mother ache. It can be difficult to name what was missing in our early lives until we can also see, with clarity and tenderness, what our inner children are still longing for, which is the presence, protection, attunement, or love they never received. This practice creates space for that recognition. It helps gather your younger inner children, your earthly mother, and the Divine Mother into a single circle of witnessing, so you can feel both the truth of your story and the blessing available now. It is a ceremony of witnessing by honoring the truth of what was, receiving the blessing of what is, and anchoring your healing in both.

Give yourself a generous amount of time, at least an hour, at your altar for this meditation. Light a candle. Burn some incense. Close the door. You might want to set up real chairs or just close your eyes and picture this circle forming around you.

Begin at the Center

Sit comfortably and imagine yourself as the Maiden in this chapter, the one starting fresh, setting the first stakes for her healing basket. You are seated in the center, surrounded by empty chairs, each waiting to be filled. Start by taking long, slow, deep breaths for several minutes, letting the rhythm of your breath bring you into the present moment.

Invite Your Inner Guests

Begin filling the circle with the inner figures you've met on this journey. Invite the Innocent Child, who holds your hope and intention. The Magical Child, who gathers your story with curiosity. The Wounded Child, who carries ache and grief with trust. The Orphan Child, who accepts responsibility and releases expectations.

See each one taking its place in the circle. Notice what arises as you become surrounded by your inner children, the ones you have been reclaiming within yourself. Allow yourself to feel their presence. Offer awareness, curiosity, and acceptance to all.

Invite Your Mother

Now, bring your human mother into the circle. Watch her take a seat before you. As she arrives, observe how each of your younger selves react to her. How do your inner children feel in her presence?

Allow each voice that wishes to speak a moment to be heard. Some may soften, others may resist or blame. All responses are valid. There is no need to fix or control. You are simply witnessing. How do your inner children respond? Does the Innocent Child feel seen? Does the Magical Child feel welcome? Does the Wounded Child feel safe? Does the Orphan Child feel wanted?

Invite the Divine Mother

Now imagine the Divine Mother joining your circle. She may appear as Tara, Pachamama, Mary, Durga, Guadalupe, Kali, or another luminous form that feels true to you. See her radiant presence taking her place in the circle.

Notice her qualities. What emanates from her: warmth, strength, tenderness, fierce protection, deep compassion? How do your inner children respond? Do the Innocent, Magical, Wounded and Orphan Children within you feel as if their essence is welcome and held in reverence?

Gently ask yourself, what would it have been like to have her as my mother in the past? Then, what is it like to know she is with me now?

Sit in the Circle of Truth and Love

Bring your awareness to your navel as you sit within this sacred circle. See clearly the truth of your human mother and recognize how impossible it was for her to embody all that the Divine Mother holds. Whisper softly, *this is what I received, this is what I needed.* Both truths belong. And I am still held, always, in the love of both my mother and the Divine Mother.

What you needed is also what your mother needed, and what she needed was what her mother needed before her. The ache didn't start with you, and the healing won't end with you. It flows both backward and forward through time, touching everyone who came before and everyone who will come after.

Take this in deeply. Feel the Divine Mother's love for you, your mother, her mother, and all the women who have lived this ache. The absence is being rewoven. The pattern is being restored through you.

Breathe this into your navel. Feel the spiral tightening, the base of your basket becoming strong enough to hold not only your healing, but the healing of your lineage.

Weaving from the Center by Strengthening the Navel

You have sat in the circle of truth and love, holding both the ache of what was and the blessing of what remains. You have witnessed your mother, your lineage, and yourself with honesty and grace. Staying present in this space takes courage. It demands both an open heart and a grounded body. After experiencing such depth, it's natural to feel tender or unmoored. Healing of this magnitude calls for balance, a gentle way to return gently to the ground of your being.

This is where the navel calls you home. In the earlier postures: seated in sukhasana, standing tall in mountain pose, and walking from your navel, you began to explore this center as the axis of presence. Now, intentionally strengthening it helps integrate the heart's insights into lived experience. The navel translates awareness into action and anchors your energy in the present moment. Through breath, movement, and attention, it becomes the hearth where healing takes form.

Strengthening the navel is primarily in service of integration, not fitness (though fitness is a beneficial byproduct.) The acceptance, trust, honesty, and awareness we have been cultivating must take root in the body to become lived truth. This occurs at the navel center. A strong navel stabilizes the nervous system and fosters emotional balance. It enables you to approach life from your center rather than from reaction.

There are many ways to strengthen this center. Choose what feels nourishing and sustainable. Yoga, Pilates, dance, martial arts, or even mindful engagement in daily chores all awaken the intelligence of the navel. Each conscious movement builds stability into your basket of healing.

You may also try breathwork and meditations that activate energy at the navel, helping to release stored emotion or fatigue. Over time, this center starts to feel like a compass, guiding you toward clarity and inner knowing.

No matter what form your practice takes, consistency is more important than intensity. Return to the navel often and with purpose. The more you connect and strengthen it, the more its intelligence reveals itself. Over time, acceptance stops being just an idea and becomes a living rhythm, a steady pulse rising from the fire at your core.

The Maiden's Initiation: Then and Now

As this inner fire grows stronger, it prepares the Maiden for the next threshold: the call to start shaping her own life. I was recently invited to create a ceremony for a young woman beginning her first moon, or menstrual bleed, which made me reflect on how rarely such initiations are honored today. In modern Western culture, the Maiden's initiation often takes the form of leaving home, starting college, moving into a first apartment, or beginning a first job. She tests her wings, free from her mother's rules or curfews. She may fall in love, make mistakes, and start to hear her own voice.

This stage can be both exhilarating and tender. When the mother ache is strong, the Maiden may feel guilty about her independence, ashamed of her sexuality, or unsteady without recognition of her growth. These first steps into adulthood can seem unsupported or invisible, and in their absence, the mother ache often emerges most clearly. Even if her mother's voice is no longer present, its echo still shapes her choices and her sense of self.

For many of our ancestors, the Maiden's passage was marked with reverence. Across cultures, a young woman's transition into adulthood was honored through ceremony. For example, in Navajo tradition, the Kinaaldá Ceremony blessed a girl's emerging womanhood through a four-day rite of passage, guided by her mother, grandmothers, and aunties, combining teaching, ritual, movement, and embodied care, initiating the young women into adulthood and honoring this symbolic transformation. In early Celtic and Scottish traditions, young women were often blessed at the first fruits festivals, receiving protection charms and guidance from elder women; and in pre-Christian Norse communities, a girl's entrance into womanhood was publicly acknowledged through gift-giving, feasting, and the bestowal of a woman's keys, which were symbols of adulthood and household authority. Whether held in deserts, forests, longhouses, or villages, these rites shared one essential truth: the Maiden was recognized, supported, and celebrated as she crossed the threshold into womanhood.[14]

In Western society, we have lost much of this recognition. Menarche and the other thresholds of womanhood are rarely celebrated; more often, they are hidden, dismissed, or shamed. As a result, many women carry a subtle sense of incompleteness, a missing thread in their tapestry of becoming.

Healing the mother ache encourages us to reconnect with the Maiden within and give her the initiation she never received. This involves honoring her courage, her choices, and her determination to keep walking, even when the path was steep and rocky.

For me, this has meant remembering the girl I once was, the one who stayed in this body, who found her way through the ache, who refused to give up. I thank the Maiden within me for choosing life and trying her best.

If it feels right, take a moment to remember your own Maiden self. See her clearly. Honor her resilience. She carried you here. Close your eyes and bring her image to your heart. Let her know she is no longer alone. Every breath you take now is a continuation of her courage. In honoring her, you strengthen the base of your healing basket and open the way for the woman you are becoming.

---

14 For readers interested in broader cross-cultural understandings of women's initiation rites, accessible overviews can be found in Carol P. Christ and Judith Plaskow, *Weaving the Visions* (San Francisco: Harper & Row, 1989), which gathers feminist, historical, and spiritual perspectives from diverse traditions, and Ronald Hutton, *The Stations of the Sun* (Oxford: Oxford University Press, 1996), which surveys seasonal and coming-of-age customs in British and Celtic cultures. For a more detailed account of the Navajo Kinaaldá ceremony, see Charlotte J. Frisbie, *Kinaaldá: A Study of the Navaho Girl's Puberty Ceremony* (New York: Irvington Publishers, 1967). These works offer accessible entry points into many of the ceremonial traditions referenced here.

The Maiden and The Sacred Trilogy Within

In recognizing the maiden's initiation as a rite of passage, we also want to honor the other passages all women share. Across cultures and centuries, the journey of womanhood has often been described through three sacred faces: Maiden, Mother, and Crone. Together, they form an ancient trinity: three movements in the symphony of a woman's life, three flames that live within every woman, regardless of age or circumstance.

The Maiden is the dawn. She carries innocence, curiosity, and the courage of beginnings. She reminds us of hope, trust, and the beauty of first steps. The Mother is the noon. She embodies creation, devotion, and the capacity to nurture life, whether through children, art, relationships, or work. The Crone is the twilight. She is wisdom ripened through time, the keeper of memory, and the guide who knows the value of endings and renewal.

Across the world, women have honored these transitions with ritual and reverence. In ancient Greece, Artemis, Demeter, and Hecate reflected this cycle of maiden, mother, and wise one. In the Celtic lands, Brigid, Danu, and Cerridwen held similar power. Indigenous traditions, too, have long recognized the woman's life as an eternal spiral from first blood, to bearing life, to becoming elder, and finally ancestor, only to begin the weave again. In the Navajo tradition, for example, the Kinaaldá Ceremony honors a girl's first menstruation as the beginning of a lifelong unfolding of duty and care, with later rituals marking motherhood and elderhood as further turns in the sacred cycle.[15] Indigenous peoples for millennia have honored these cycles of womanhood with ceremony and ritual.[16] How is it that we have forgotten and become disconnected from ourselves in this way?

These archetypes are not only seasons we pass through. They are living presences within. The Maiden still breathes inside every Crone while the Mother nurtures within the Maiden. Each holds the others, as the moon

---

15 Charlotte J. Frisbie, *Kinaaldá: A Study of the Navaho Girl's Puberty Ceremony* (New York: Irvington Publishers, 1967). The Kinaaldá ceremony takes place over four days, and during this time the Maiden is educated by her mother, aunties, grandmothers on the "knowledge necessary to assume an adult role in the society." The Navajo believe that these four days determine the Maiden's future.

16 Carolyn Niethammer, *Daughters of the Earth* (New York: Macmillan, 1977). A deeply researched and respectful study of Native American women's lives, tracing feminine rites of passage, daily labor, and spiritual roles across the arc of maidenhood, motherhood, and elderhood.

holds its phases. To our eye it is waxing, full, and waning, yet its cosmic body is always whole.

And beneath them all moves the Divine Mother with her essence flowing through every form. She is the field that contains the Maiden's dreams, the Mother's love, and the Crone's wisdom. When we attune to her, we remember that these phases are not linear stages but expressions of one sacred source continually revealing itself through us. The Divine Mother is the still point at the center of the turning wheel, the pulse of creation that reminds us we are never separate from her or from one another.

Now, at sixty, I find myself standing in the Crone's light, looking back with tenderness on my Maiden's dreams and my Mother's devotion. I see how each has shaped me and how each continues to guide me. The Maiden reminds me to stay curious and try new things. The Mother reminds me to give with love. The Crone reminds me to rest in wisdom and trust the turning of the wheel.

As you continue your healing journey, may you feel these three women alive within you—Maiden, Mother, and Crone—each offering her gift, each one held in the embrace of the Divine Mother.

Mother Ache Healing in the World:

The Maiden Who Learned to Choose Herself

Maggie came to me in her early thirties, outwardly accomplished and inwardly uncertain. She had done all the *right* things, including education, relationships, and steady work, and yet she carried a quiet, persistent feeling that her life did not quite belong to her. When asked what she wanted, her body hesitated. When asked how she felt, she often looked outward, as if waiting for the right response to appear between us.

She spoke of her mother with affection and loyalty. Her mother had been present in every way a child might hope for, leading Girl Scouts and soccer, volunteering at school, creating a home that appeared warm and attentive. Maggie described a childhood filled with involvement, structure, and care. There was no obvious neglect and no overt harm. And yet, something in her nervous system had learned to stay careful, attuned, and quietly constrained.

As Maggie entered adolescence, the relationship subtly shifted. Her mother began sharing more than a daughter could metabolize, confessions of regret, stories of an abortion she had never fully grieved, reflections on mistakes and missed chances. Maggie became the steady one, the confidant. Without being named as such, she was initiated into a role that required emotional maturity far beyond her years.

In our sessions, Maggie came to understand that because of this she learned, somatically, not to err. She learned that closeness depended on sameness. She learned that separation carried the risk of hurting someone she loved.

By the time Maggie arrived at my practice, her body carried the cost of this early intimacy. Her belly was tight, her breath shallow, her voice gentle to the point of self-erasure. Anger lived somewhere deep within her, but it had never been given permission to move. To feel it seemed dangerous like an act that might fracture love itself.

Our work together unfolded slowly. Through mother ache–informed inquiry, breathwork, active meditations with cathartic elements,[17] and somatic practices, we listened for sensations, for the places in Maggie's body that still held vigilance, loyalty, and restraint. Again and again, the work brought us to her navel center, the seat of courage, strength, and instinctual truth.

As Maggie learned to breathe into her belly and ground her feet, something long suppressed began to surface. At first it came as subtle tremors, then heat, then tears. And finally, unmistakably, anger.

This anger was not cruel or destructive. It was clean. Clarifying. Protective. It spoke of boundaries that had never been drawn, of a Maiden who had not been allowed to stumble, experiment, or discover herself through trial and error. As Maggie stayed with these sensations without judgment, without apology her posture changed. Her breath deepened. Her voice grew steadier.

For the first time, she could feel the grief beneath the anger caused by the mask of her forced goodness. Eventually, Maggie made a choice that felt

---

17 Osho Dynamic Meditation is a widely practiced active meditation, designed to engage the body and nervous system before entering stillness. The practice unfolds in five stages, including vigorous chaotic breathing, cathartic expression, movement and mantra-based navel-center activation, followed by stillness and celebration. Practiced regularly, often in a daily sequence of seven or twenty-one days, it can support emotional release, increased vitality, and deeper states of presence and self-awareness. Super helpful for those of us unable to access our anger.

radical within her family system: she called a time out. Not a rejection, not a rupture, but a pause. She needed space to feel into who she was without the constant pull of relational gravity. Her family was confused and concerned. Some believed she had lost her way. From the outside, it looked like rebellion but from the inside, it was initiation.

In this space, Maggie began asking new questions. Instead of *What is expected of me?* She began to ask: *What do I enjoy? What do I desire? What feels true in my body?* These questions did not arrive with immediate answers. And that, too, was part of the healing. The Maiden does not emerge fully formed. She discovers herself through curiosity, misstep, and listening inward.

Maggie's story reminds us that the mother ache does not always come from absence or harm. Sometimes it grows from love without boundaries, from intimacy without differentiation. In these cases, the Maiden must undertake a courageous and often misunderstood journey toward self-sovereignty. In loosening the first weave of her life, Maggie learned something essential: that anger can be sacred and that becoming oneself is an act of love not betrayal.

Journal Reflections: Reweaving Acceptance

The reflections that follow invite you to soften and return to the part of you that is learning how to meet life from your center, with acceptance. As you work with these reflections, let yourself slow down. This is your space to pause, to breathe, and to remember who you are beneath the habits that once kept you moving.

The Three Centers of Intelligence

How do I recognize each center's way of knowing in my daily life? How do I experience the intelligence of my navel, heart, and mind?
Write about the qualities of each within.
Which center feels most familiar or dominant, and which feels less accessible?

The Navel as a Foundation for True Acceptance

What helps me feel rooted in my body, especially when I face emotional discomfort?

How does connecting to my navel center affect the way I meet what is true in my life?
Where do I notice resistance softening when I connect to my navel?

Navel Awareness and the Maiden's Path of Acceptance

What becomes possible when I stop fighting what I cannot change?
How does navel awareness support me in embracing my own story without denial or collapse?
Where do I sense roots of acceptance taking form in my body?

Long, Slow, Deep Breathing

How did my body respond to the long, slow, deep breathing practice?
What emotions or sensations rose when I slowed down long enough to notice myself?

The Postures of Wholeness

When I sit, stand, or walk intentionally connecting to my navel, what changes inside me?
Where do I collapse or tense, and what might that reveal about old patterns?
How does a balanced posture strengthen my capacity to stay present?

Courage: The Fire of the Navel

Where in my life am I being asked to be brave?
How does courage feel in my body? Is it subtle, fiery, or insistent?
What small act of courage is calling to me now?

Breath of Fire

After practicing Breath of Fire, what sensations did I notice in my belly or navel area? How did pumping the navel affect my sense of energy, strength, or presence?
What shifted in my body, mood, or inner state after this practice? Did I notice any change in clarity, confidence, or steadiness?
If the navel is a center of intuition and courage, what might be asking to awaken or move in my life right now?

The Divine Mother and Our Seven Needs

Which of the seven needs still feel tender or unmet within me?

How do I imagine the Divine Mother responding to those needs now?
What compassion arises as I acknowledge the child I once was?

A Circle of Return

What arose when I imagined myself being held by my earthly mother, the Divine Mother, and my own inner world?
How did my cast of inner children respond to both my mother and the Divine Mother? What did I learn about myself from this?
Which part of the circle felt most difficult or most comforting?
What truth emerged about what I still long for or what I am finally ready to release?

Weaving from the Center

What stabilizes me when I feel scattered or overwhelmed?
Which practices help me return to my sacred center?
How might strengthening my navel center change the way I move through the world?

The Maiden's Initiation: Then and Now

What memories of my youth feel like moments when I crossed into a new phase of becoming?
How was I received by the world in the maiden season of my life?
What Maiden qualities do I long to reclaim, such as openness, aliveness, courage, creativity, desire?
How does recognizing her now support my healing and the acceptance I am cultivating?

Maggie's Story

How did Maggie's story resonate with me?
In what ways have I learned to be a good daughter by minimizing, editing, or shaping myself to preserve connection? What parts of me learned that separation might cause harm?
Where do I sense unexpressed anger or frustration in my body? What might this anger be protecting or asking for if I listened without judgment?
What would it mean to give myself permission to separate with honesty and care? What small step toward autonomy or self-definition feels possible right now?

Take a final breath and rest your hands over your navel and heart. The Maiden within you is alive each time you begin again, each time you meet your truth with acceptance. Let these reflections deepen your relationship with your inner initiator, your companion in renewal, and the one who teaches you to stand on the ground of your own becoming.

Conclusion: Coming Home to the Center

The work of our inner Maiden creates the base of our healing. Through remembering the intelligence of the navel center, we learn how to stay with what is true without fleeing or trying to force change. Practicing acceptance becomes grounding. A way of standing on the earth of our own lives with courage and presence.

By learning to listen inwardly, we discover that belonging does not come from being chosen or rescued. It arises when we are willing to meet ourselves as we are. Each return to the navel strengthens our capacity to remain present with uncertainty and ache. This is the initiation of acceptance. It is a rhythm that we must continually practice. A practice of coming back to center when the world pulls us outward. Remembering that our navel holds courage and this inner fire knows how to guide us.

From this grounded place, something new becomes possible. When acceptance has taken root, the Maiden within us notices patterns. We begin to see how our bodies hold the key to our healing. This is where the next chapter begins.

Chapter Six:

The Seeker and Coming Home Through the Body

"But if you travel far enough, one day you will recognize yourself coming down the road to meet yourself. And you will say—YES."

—Marion Woodman

Within each of us lives a Seeker, a traveler who dares to step beyond the safety of the familiar to discover the treasures of healing and wisdom waiting in the wilderness within. In myths and legends, she is the adventurer, the heroine who crosses thresholds, faces trials, and gathers treasure. Yet her truest pilgrimage is not measured in miles. Her true journey unfolds as she turns inward to the terrain of her own body, where each breath becomes a compass and each sensation is a signpost home.

In mythopoetic traditions, this initiation has often been described as the Hero's Journey, which is a path marked by separation, conquest, and return. Yet as Maureen Murdock articulates in *The Heroine's Journey*, the feminine path follows a different arc altogether.[18] Rather than requiring the feminine to prove herself in the world, the heroine's journey begins with a rupture

18 Maureen Murdock, *The Heroine's Journey: Woman's Quest for Wholeness* (Boston: Shambhala Publications, 1990). This is a rich and accessible work for readers wishing to explore how the feminine journey of transformation differs from the traditional hero's path, emphasizing return, reconnection, and wholeness.

from the feminine and unfolds as a slow return to it. In contrast to the masculine journey oriented toward conquest and victory, the heroine's journey unfolds as a return to her feminine nature through reconnection with the body, the inner world, nurturance.

Hence, in this chapter, the Seeker steps forward to continue the work started by her younger selves. She builds on the Maiden's reemerging navel wisdom. She recognizes the patterns that once shaped her mother ache, such as unmet needs, survival strategies, and the early meanings that limited her sense of self and now gathers them as materials for transformation.

The Seeker's journey begins with *connection*. She learns to listen to the subtle currents of life-force moving through her body by tuning into the guidance of her own being. Through sensing and witnessing, she reestablishes a connection to herself, and as this connection deepens within her, she experiences genuine connection to others and eventually to all existence.

The Seeker bends close to her work, weaving the foundational coils of her healing basket. Awareness, curiosity, honesty, trust, and acceptance become the keys that guide her inward. As fiber crosses fiber, she learns that agency arises from within and that belonging begins with connection to self.

Her basket weaving task is to thread this new awareness of connection into the initial rows of her healing basket. The strands she works with are the lived qualities she has already been practicing: awareness, curiosity, honesty, trust, and acceptance. These become the keys with which she learns to map her inner world, guiding her attention as she turns inward and stays present with what arises. With each strand placed consciously, she discovers that the journey she has been seeking was never meant to be found outside herself. It has always been an inward path, revealed through the steady act of self-connection.

Returning to the Body

As we work to heal our mother ache, we often discover how far we've drifted from our own bodies. Growing up, many of us learned to survive by aligning with our mothers' moods, needs, and expectations. In doing so, we ignored our bodies' signals, trading instinct for belonging, and self-attunement for approval. Now, the Seeker turns inward to trace the strands within her own body, feel where the weave has grown thin, and learn a new language of connection that begins with herself.

I lost connection with my body early in life. When my mother moved away to Texas during my kindergarten year, I coped by shutting down. I went numb, and hiding became my survival mechanism. I spoke so little that I was placed in speech therapy in first and second grades, a terrifying experience that only deepened my early meaning that something was wrong with me. Beneath that inability to speak, there was a deep disconnection, a dissociation that protected me from feeling the pain of abandonment.

Yet paradoxically, as a child, my body was also my sanctuary. It carried me into nature, helped me run, climb, and float down the creek near my childhood home. In those moments of riding my bike for hours, feeling the wind and sunlight, I felt free. My body knew how to bring me back to life long before my mind did.

Over the years, finding my way back to a unified mind-body sense of self has been its own pilgrimage. Every path I've walked, whether meditation, therapy, plant medicine, yoga, or breathwork, has led me home to the same sacred vessel I once left behind. I understand that reconnecting with my body has always been the true foundation of my healing.

Knowing through the mind alone is not enough; healing happens through the body. Healing happens in breath, sensation, in the tender willingness to feel again. Let this next practice guide you toward that lived sense of home within yourself by gently connecting to your body.

Experiential Invitation: The First Return

Find a place where you can sit or lie down without interruption. Let your body rest in whatever position feels most natural.

Take a few slow, deep breaths, feeling the rise and fall of your belly. After a few steady breaths, as you exhale, imagine your breath traveling down through your body, from the top of your head, down softening the space at your heart center, down through your navel, your hips, into your legs, and all the way to the tips of your toes.

Gently bring awareness to the points where your body meets the ground. Let your attention rest there, as though the earth itself were holding you, because it is. You don't have to force presence. Allow it.

If you notice a sense of blankness or distance, there's no need to alter it. That, too, is part of your experience. Whisper silently to your body, *thank you for being my sacred temple in this life*. Feel what happens when you take a moment to acknowledge your body as the miracle that it truly is and express gratitude to it.

Now place one hand on your heart and the other on your belly. Feel the warmth under your palms, the gentle pulse of life that continues even when your awareness drifts away. Let your breath move between your hands, connecting your heart and belly, your feeling and intuitive knowing.

Stay here, resting in the rhythm of this sacred connection. When you're ready, open your eyes. Notice again how the earth supports you and how the air feels on your skin.

You are here. You have always been here. This body is your sacred vessel for this life. It holds you steadfast and is constantly trying to communicate with you. *Listen*. Each time you do this it reinforces your bridge home to you.

The Body Remembers

Modern trauma research confirms what ancient wisdom keepers have always known: our lived experiences are stored in our body's tissues as energy patterns. Somatic pioneers remind us that healing begins by feeling what the body remembers. Peter Levine[19] teaches that trauma is not caused by the event itself but by the nervous system's unresolved responses to the event. Until these are released, the body remains on alert, bracing for what has already passed to happen again.

Contemporary women writers and somatic practitioners are reclaiming a more relational and compassionate understanding of how the body holds experience. Rather than framing the body as a passive container of trauma, they invite us to recognize it as intelligent, adaptive, and responsive. Judith Herman[20] reminds us that healing cannot occur in isolation, but requires safety, connection, and the restoration of trust. When these are established, the body becomes capable of revealing the hurt it has been carrying.

Hillary McBride[21] writes of the body as a source of wisdom, communicating through sensation, emotion, and impulse when we learn how to listen. Suzanne Scurlock-Durana[22] emphasizes full-bodied presence, reminding us that healing unfolds through attuned awareness and nervous system regulation rather than analytical insight. Sophie Strand[23] questions the notion that the body "keeps the score," offering instead the image of the body as a living doorway; one that adapts, remembers, and speaks in the language of sensation, inviting relationship rather than blame.

Together, these voices echo what ancient wisdom keepers have always known: healing begins when we enter into conversation with the body, honoring its signals as guidance rather than pathology.

Returning to the body is like returning home to oneself. It gives what was once fragmented the chance to become whole again. The Seeker's true terrain is the close, personal wilderness within rather than distant lands without. With each step she takes inward, she weaves another strand of connection, guiding her back to the steady ground of her own being.

---

19 Peter A. Levine, *Waking the Tiger: Healing Trauma* (Berkeley, CA: North Atlantic Books, 1997).

20 Judith Lewis Herman, *Trauma and Recovery: The Aftermath of Violence—from Domestic Abuse to Political Terror* (New York: Basic Books, 1992).

21 Hillary L. McBride, *The Wisdom of Your Body: Finding Healing, Wholeness, and Connection through Embodied Living*(Grand Rapids, MI: Brazos Press, 2021).

22 Suzanne Scurlock-Durana, *Full-Body Presence: Learning to Listen to Your Body's Wisdom* (Louisville, CO: Sounds True, 2018).

23 Sophie Strand, "The Body is a Doorway," *Make Me Good Soil* (Substack), May 6, 2022, https://sophiestrand.substack.com/p/the-body-is-a-doorway

The Seeker's work is embodiment itself: observing sensations without judgment, relearning how to fully inhabit the body, and rebuilding a trusting relationship with its intelligence. When we reconnect in this way, we harness the body's wisdom and incorporate it into our basket of healing. Only by honoring the body as the foundation of healing can the basket hold the strands that we are weaving.

Creating an Anchor in the Present

To reconnect with the body is a journey in and of itself. Hence, our inner Seeker needs an anchor within the body, a place to return to when the currents of sensation and memory start to pull us under. Without this internal anchor, exploration can feel unmoored or overwhelming. An anchor helps us stay present with discomfort. We can't heal the past without one foot in the present. The anchor is what stabilizes that foot. It is a felt sense of grounding that keeps awareness from drifting into fear or dissociation.

My first experience with this anchoring happened during a craniosacral session at the beginning of my healing journey with Arpita, a therapist I deeply admired. I arrived nervous, unsure, with my mind full of stories it believed were important. Instead of starting a conversation, she simply asked me to close my eyes and breathe into my body. I was surprised and also relieved. As I followed her instruction, I felt a fluttering heat rise in my chest. Arpita asked gently, "What do you need?"

The answer came instantly from somewhere deeper than thought: "I need safety." And I knew this longing wasn't just about that moment; it was the echo of a lifetime. After further exploration, together, we found a posture with my hands cradling my face that allowed a wave of calm to spread through me. This became my anchor: a physical gesture that told my nervous system, *I'm here. I'm safe. I can stay.* Since then, I've returned to this posture repeatedly. It is a somatic antidote to the endless narratives of my mind, a touchstone that pulls me back into presence. Our bodies remember what our minds forget: that our true experience of life exists not in words but in sensation.

Experiential Invitation: Finding An Inner Anchor

The Seeker's next step is to discover her own anchor: a posture that helps the body feel supported and held. Each body will find this differently. The invitation is to notice what allows a sense of safety to emerge.

Try resting your hands on your heart or belly, crossing your arms so your palms touch your upper arms or shoulders, or gently cradling your face. Feel how each gesture shifts your inner state. Choose one that feels natural, neither rigid nor collapsed, both soft and steady. You might add gentle rocking or swaying movements that mirror the rhythm of being held. These simple motions help regulate the nervous system, signaling safety and belonging.

When you find the posture that feels true, let it become your living anchor. This is the place you can always return to whenever the waves of life rise. Here, at the intersection of breath, body, and awareness, the initial strands of deep connection begin to weave themselves back together.

How the Mother Ache Lives in the Body

The body is our first home, yet it is so constant, so intimate, that we often forget it until it cries out through pain, fatigue, or illness. For many daughters, that home becomes a battleground. The mother ache shapes a woman's relationship with her body in enduring ways, through her mother's modeling, her words, and the expectations woven into daily life. The body then becomes something to be managed, controlled, and criticized through dieting, comparison, and self-surveillance. Dissociation and mistrust replace a sense of belonging. Guilt, shame, and performance replace ease and joy.

We cut, starve, overeat, overwork, criticize, and numb ourselves to avoid the pain lurking beneath the surface. Meanwhile, we carefully shape the outer image—hair, makeup, clothing—as if polishing a shell could protect the tender life within.

Research confirms what many of us have felt all along: a mother's relationship with her own body deeply influences her daughter's. Studies show that when mothers make critical comments, engage in fat talk, or focus on controlling appearance around food and weight, daughters are more likely to adopt body dissatisfaction and conditional self-worth. Conversely, when mothers demonstrate self-acceptance and autonomy rather than control, daughters tend to develop body confidence and self-trust. The mother is the first mirror in which a daughter sees herself. How she inhabits her own body, how she eats, dresses, moves, or speaks about herself forms part of that reflection.[24]

When appearance pressure is normalized within a family, the daughter's body often becomes a space for comparison rather than connection. Over time, she learns to watch herself, to see her body as an object instead of an ally. The desire to feel alive through movement, pleasure, or sensuality then conflicts with inherited shame and fear, leaving the body both desired and mistrusted.

This divide often extends into sexuality and creativity. Both depend on a sense of belonging in one's body. When the body feels unsafe or burdened by expectation, desire becomes performance, and creativity narrows. The life force that animates both intimacy and imagination can only flow when the body is experienced as a safe home.

The Seeker's path is to reclaim this sacred relationship. Through reconnecting, we learn to listen again to our body's own language of sensation and rhythm. This language is ancient and honest, whispering the truth of our experience in each moment. As we listen, self-judgment begins to loosen, and self-appreciation awakens. The spiral turns inward, reminding us that our body was never the enemy. Our body is and always has been our original and most powerful ally, waiting to be inhabited as the sacred vessel of our healing journey.

---

24 See M. Elizabeth Frisén and Phyllis C. Katz, "The Influence of Mothers' Body Dissatisfaction on Their Daughters' Body Image," *Journal of Child Psychology and Psychiatry* 50, no. 3 (2009): 326–334; Renee Engeln, *Beauty Sick: How the Cultural Obsession with Appearance Hurts Girls and Women* (New York: Harper, 2017); and Dara Greenwood et al., "Body Talk: Maternal Fat Talk and Body Dissatisfaction in Young Women," *Body Image* 7, no. 3 (2010): 213–219.

Listening to the Body: Felt Sense and Somatic Experiencing

Reconnecting with our bodies begins through sensation. The body remembers every thread of unhealed mother ache. Our Seeker's most essential tool is the *felt sense,* which is the subtle awareness of what is happening in the body right now. By pausing, observing, and naming sensations without judgment, we begin to revive an inner dialogue that has long been silenced.

The felt sense, a term introduced by Eugene Gendlin,[25] describes our bodies' perception of our experience in the moment. The felt sense is a physical awareness of sensation that carries meaning but no words. It is the body's inner knowing, and this intelligence is not derived from our minds or emotions. When we learn to listen to the felt sense, we step out of the mind's narratives, which live in the past or future, and arrive in the truth of the present. This is where healing can take root in our beings.

The body's sensations are nonverbal cues, such as warmth and cold, tightening and softening, pulsing, trembling, hollowness, and fullness. These sensations are the signals that guide the Seeker back into direct relationship with her body.

For a woman healing the mother ache, attuning to this bodily language is essential. It restores self-connection where adaptation once required self-abandonment. The Seeker learns to listen inwardly and notice warmth or coolness, heaviness or spaciousness, constriction or flow. Each sensation is a messenger inviting her to return to her natural state of self-connection. Sensations are the body's language and learning to listen to and understand these inner signals is key.

Dr. Peter Levine's work expounds upon this practice. Levine found that the actual triggering event itself doesn't cause trauma. Instead, trauma happens after the event if the body cannot release the survival energy of fight, freeze, or flight it generates. He explains that in nature, animals instinctively shake, tremble, or stretch once danger is gone, completing the nervous

25 Eugene T. Gendlin, *Focusing* (New York: Bantam Books, 1982).

system cycle and releasing residual trauma from their bodies.[26] Humans, however, are often required to suppress these impulses. Many daughters burdened with the mother ache learned early to stay small, still, and quiet to maintain connection. Their bodies held what they couldn't verbally or physically express because of this survival need.

Levine's Somatic Experiencing offers a map for releasing this stored energy and restoring natural flow. It teaches us to listen with compassion and to move between activation and calm without fear.

The practice involves using simple principles that support embodiment. These are:

Resourcing

We begin with what feels stable now: the breath, the ground, a hand on your heart. These remind the body that it is safe to explore. The anchoring posture we explored above is an excellent resource.

Tracking

Next, we notice sensations. Tightness, fluttering, warmth, pressure.

Titration

Once we are able to stay with sensation, we work in small doses. We touch the edge of experience without overwhelming the system, then pause. Healing unfolds through gradual contact, not through force or flooding.

Pendulation

Pendulation is the rhythm of moving between activation and rest, tension and ease. We allow sensation to rise, then intentionally return to safety or neutrality. This back-and-forth teaches the body that feeling can happen without danger.

---

26 Peter A. Levine, *Waking the Tiger: Healing Trauma* (Berkeley, CA: North Atlantic Books, 1997); and Peter A. Levine, *In an Unspoken Voice: How the Body Releases Trauma and Restores Goodness* (Berkeley, CA: North Atlantic Books, 2010). Both of these books offer accessible introductions to understanding the science of how the body and nervous system hold, express, and heal lived experience.

Completion

As safety grows, we want to allow spontaneous movements, such as sighs, stretches, or trembles, to arise naturally. This is the body completing what was once interrupted. Through this process, the Seeker learns that healing is about reclaiming the present. Each gentle return to sensation is a thread of trust, weaving body and awareness back together.

The following experiential invitations are meant to help you feel this return directly. They offer simple ways to meet the wisdom of your body through sensation with curiosity. Here you are invited to learn the subtle language of your body so you can listen with greater ease and reconnect to this inherent wisdom. Begin gently and let each practice guide you one step deeper into yourself.

Experiential Practice: Noticing Body Sensation (Felt Sense)

Find a nurturing space where you won't be disturbed. Let your body settle. Breathe into your navel and feel the ground beneath you.

Ask softly, *How am I right now*? and wait for your body to answer, focusing on any sensation in the body: tightness, warmth, pulsing, pressure, or tingling.

Stay with it, breathing gently. You don't need to fix or name it.

Thank your body for speaking.

The Seeker listens with awareness, curiosity, and acceptance. Practice this throughout your day as it feels right. When you reach a place where the felt sense is starting to become familiar, then you can build on this by using some of the Somatic Experiencing principles we explored above.

Experiential Invitation: Mini Somatic Experiencing Self-Session

Set aside thirty minutes in a tranquil space. Begin by grounding yourself through your anchoring posture we discussed earlier or using another resource such as breathwork (soft belly breathing, for instance). When you feel resourced and ready, shift your attention to your body and notice any sensations. Find the one that is speaking loudest and stay with it for a few breaths. If the intensity increases, return to your resource. Move slowly between the two; this gentle rhythm is called pendulation. Allow any natural impulse to move, sigh, stretch, or tremble. Finish by resting in your resource again, letting calm flow through your body.

If self-guided sessions feel challenging or if deep trauma emerges, consider working with a trained Somatic Experiencing practitioner. A few supported sessions can be transformative, providing safety, attunement, and guidance as you begin to reconnect with your body and it learns to release what it once held.

Other Ways to Reconnect

As you tune into sensation and track the subtle shifts of your inner landscape, you begin to build the foundation of self-connection one felt moment at a time. From here, it can be helpful to introduce simple external supports that deepen this reconnection. These gentle tools offer the body a sense of warmth and reassurance, especially when old patterns of vigilance or collapse begin to stir.

The body holds the stories of our mother ache, and sometimes the safest way to invite release is through grounding, rhythmic touch. The following two exercises, adapted from Peter Levine's *Waking the Tiger*,[27] use warm, steady contact to help the nervous system soften protective patterns and remember safety. They are simple, accessible ways to rebuild body connection through the soothing rhythm of touch.

Tapping

Using your hand, softly tap or pat different parts of your body. As you do, name them aloud and say: "This is my arm, I welcome you back. This is my shoulder, I welcome you back." This rhythmic contact reawakens presence and reclaims ownership of your body.

---

27 Peter A. Levine, *Waking the Tiger: Healing Trauma* (Berkeley, CA: North Atlantic Books, 1997), 63.

The Showerhead Technique

In the shower, using a hand-held shower head, with warm water, slowly move the pulsing water over your body. Bring your attention to the sensation of the water as it moves across your skin. Trace its path over your shoulders, arms, back, chest, and legs. Name each body part as you feel it and say: "I welcome you back." If you don't have a handheld showerhead, you can simply place each part of your body under the water's stream. Let the water's touch become a gentle blessing.

These practices may seem simple, but their effect is profound. They reestablish the conversation between mind and body, helping you feel anchored and alive *in your body*. When you feel scattered or tense, they serve as grounding rituals, meaningful ways to come home through sensation.

Relearning Safe Touch

As this reconnection deepens, another layer of healing begins to unfold. For many daughters carrying the mother ache, touch itself carries a tender history. When warmth, consistency, or attuned contact were absent or distorted early in life, the body learned to brace. Muscles tightened, breath shortened, and touch began to feel risky. Physical touch itself could register as unsafe.

Relearning safe touch is therefore a sacred part of the Seeker's journey. It unfolds slowly, through choice and agency, allowing the body to experience contact without overwhelm. This may include the techniques above, and it also includes modalities such as massage, Reiki, acupuncture, or other healing modalities where touch is offered with attunement and clear boundaries. It may also be as simple as resting a hand on your heart, massaging your own feet, holding your face gently.

Each of these gestures communicates a truth to the body: you belong to yourself. They offer experiences of contact that are paced, consensual, and kind, experiences that may have been missing earlier in life. Over time, these moments begin to rewire the nervous system's expectations, replacing the bracing with softening and fear with choice.

Nature, too, offers its own form of safe touch. Bare feet on the ground, a tree supporting your back, sunlight warming your skin. Nature restores trust in connection without demand. Animals and pets teach the same lesson through presence alone: the steady rhythm of breath, the warmth of fur, the comfort of shared connection. Movement becomes another language of touch. Yoga, dance, tai chi, or gentle stretching reminds the body that it is both boundary and bridge; the place where your spirit meets form in this precious life that you inhabit. This is how connection is rebuilt. Slowly. Kindly. One sensation at a time.

The Three Centers of Connection

The Seeker's journey is a journey to reunite what was once divided. Her protective patterns are ancient guardians of safety. As she honors them, they soften, allowing new pathways of connection to form. The body's three centers of intelligence—the navel, heart, and mind—begin to communicate again. The navel grounds her in stability. The heart opens her to feeling. The mind grows calm, becoming a neutral witness. When these three move together, a harmony emerges, creating a rhythm of self-connection, where instinct, emotion, and awareness flow as one living intelligence.

Experiential Practice: Humming Meditation to Reconnect the Body and Voice

To deepen the harmony between your navel, heart, and mind, I invite you to a simple practice that connects these centers through breath and vibration. Humming links the body and voice, awakening the body's wisdom beyond words. The sound starts in the belly, where life-force awakens. It rises to the heart, softening and opening, and settles the mind, encouraging stillness. As these centers find a rhythm together through the humming, the inner spiral of connection begins to return through the vibration.

To begin, sit comfortably in sukhasana, keeping your spine tall yet relaxed. Close your eyes and start humming aloud, allowing the sound vibrations to travel along your spine, as if through a hollow bamboo flute. Inhale deeply through your nose and let the hum vibrate naturally as you exhale. With each deep hum, imagine the vibration rising from your navel, flowing through your heart, and reaching the top of your head. Continue for about eleven minutes, staying present with the movement of sound and the subtle harmony it creates within.

If you like, play soft background music such as Tibetan bowls, chimes, or gentle nature sounds to support your focus. Let the soundscape hold you as the hum carries you inward, awakening your voice as an instrument of connection and healing.

If humming feels nourishing and you'd like to explore it more deeply, consider Osho's Nadabrahma Meditation. This one-hour practice begins with humming and transitions into slow, graceful hand movements of giving and receiving. It harmonizes the body and mind, easing inner conflict and restoring natural peace. The soundtrack for this is available on all streaming platforms. I often return to this meditation during times of transition or grief; it helps me recenter in the heart and remember the rhythm of wholeness.

While practicing this meditation, you weave strands of sound into the lower part of your healing basket. Each vibration begins to sync your navel, heart, and mind into a single flowing current. This is how the Seeker learns to listen from within, which opens the door to moving, feeling, and thinking as one integrated being.

Edges that Hold the Whole

Another aspect of self-connection is knowing when to step back. Boundaries are what make connection feel safe. They protect what is tender and provide space for what is growing. The Seeker is weaving the lower part of the basket now, and each strand needs room. If they are crowded or pulled too tight, the weave loses its shape. Similarly, boundaries create space for your healing to hold.

The first step is listening to your felt sense as we practiced earlier. Your body will tell you what feels safe, nourishing, or overwhelming. These are signals. Boundaries are how you honor these signals. They are bridges that keep you connected to yourself. Without them, old patterns tend to return. With them, your nervous system can settle as you explore new options. When the body is calm, the heart and mind can follow.

Boundaries matter profoundly in your relationship with your mother. This can be one of the hardest places to set them and also one of the most necessary. The first step is to focus on what you need right now: not what you needed before, not what you wish she could give, but what supports you in the present. Notice what feels safe, what feels overwhelming, and what feels draining.

Boundaries with your mother can take many forms. They might involve taking time away from the relationship to breathe, limiting how often you communicate, or choosing which topics to discuss. They could also mean ending a visit when criticism arises or reshaping the relationship by changing how you show up. The goal remains the same: to protect your well-being so that healing can continue.

By creating healthy boundaries, you are reclaiming yourself and recognizing your needs. Boundaries create space for love to grow in truth. Just as the Seeker weaves the basket's lower walls steady and strong, you weave your life by shaping where connection is maintained and where it needs to pause. Boundaries enable both you and your mother to relate more honestly.

You can even practice this physically. Stand tall. Extend one arm forward, palm facing out. The body recognizes this gesture as *Stop. Enough. No.* Feel this posture's strength and steadiness. You may never use this gesture outwardly, but you can carry its energy. When you feel pulled into a yes that isn't true, pause. Breathe. Remember this posture. Boundaries hold the weave steady; they enable your healing to deepen, strand by strand.

Experiential Invitation: Boundaries with Your Mother

Find a quiet space. Sit in stillness. Breathe into your body. Notice if you feel settled or where you feel tight. If there is any tightness breath into that before continuing, acknowledging its presence kindly.

Bring your mother to mind without forcing images or stories. Simply notice what arises. Pay attention to your body and any sensations that arise.

Ask yourself: What do I need right now in this relationship? Not what you wish she could give, but what supports you in this moment.

Let one boundary form clearly. It may be simple: less time together, no phone calls at night, no tolerance for criticism. Trust the clarity that comes.

Speak the boundary out loud to yourself: "I need..." or "I will..." Feel how your body responds when you claim it.

Decide how to hold it. Some boundaries are spoken while others are shaped through consistent action. Write this boundary down and place it somewhere you will see it if needed, such as on your bathroom mirror, your nightstand. This will serve as a gentle reminder that you have choice, agency.

Healing in Relationship

Although this work is internal, it does not have to be done alone. Healing also occurs through relationships. Wounds caused by a lack of connection can be healed through connection, especially when the ache began in our earliest bonds. Working with a trusted guide, therapist, or circle of compassionate witnesses helps restore the safety and presence that may have been missing, supporting you as you work with the materials in this book.

A skilled therapist or healing practitioner can provide a steady, attuned presence that helps calm your nervous system as past emotions surface. Their grounded empathy creates a new imprint that reassures you: you are safe, you are seen, and your feelings are valid. Over time, this consistent presence repairs the internal pattern shaped by early experiences of lacking attunement.

Healing can also happen in sacred companionship with other women, through women's circles or intentional gatherings. When shared with a friend or peer walking a similar path, the journey becomes a living practice of connection. In these sacred sisterhoods, the focus is on witnessing with the heart by listening deeply, reflecting back as mirrors, and honoring each other's pace. It's best to avoid giving advice or interpreting each other's experiences, as tempting as that might be. You might meet weekly to read a passage of this book together or share the journal reflections.

What matters most is the quality of presence. Bringing these aspects of ourselves we have been exploring—awareness, curiosity, honesty, trust, and acceptance—into relationships creates a safe container and is good practice. And it's just as helpful to notice when these qualities are not present so we can weave them into the mix with intention. Humor is always good medicine for healing work.

Whether with a therapist, a small group, or a trusted friend, conscious connection weaves a new sense of belonging. It reminds you that you don't have to carry your healing alone.

If your mother ache stems from emotional neglect or inconsistency, these relationships become living teachers. They model what consistent care feels like and assist you in internalizing the experience of being met with empathy and respect. Each safe exchange is a strand that strengthens the weave of your healing basket.

In this way, healing becomes both personal and communal. You learn to connect internally and to accept support outwardly, reestablishing genuine self connection.

What follows is the story of a woman whose search for connection led her inward through the body, through safe touch, and through the slow remembering that belonging begins within.

The Woman Who Relearned Connection

"To love a woman, one must love her flesh, her breath, her being. To love oneself is to do the same."

—Clarissa Pinkola Estés

Electra remembers her early childhood as being normal and happy. Riding on the back of her parents' bicycle, her mother's body warm against her cheek. The smell of fresh-baked bread drifting through the kitchen. On the surface, her basic needs were met and life appeared steady. Yet emotional warmth was carefully rationed, as though tenderness required permission. Her mother was capable and efficient, always doing, always managing. Comfort was offered sparingly, the physical comfort of touch rare.

Electra learned this quickly. At three and a half, when she was dropped at her grandparents' house, tears rose in her throat, but she swallowed them back. Composure felt safer than crying. Later, when her mother accidentally set the kitchen on fire, Electra hid silently in her closet, fear contained and unseen. Already she knew not to reach out to be held. In her family, emotion followed rules. Her father led. Her mother managed. The children cooperated. Electra became the good girl, the helper, the one who caused no trouble. Without words, she absorbed the lesson: love requires self-control and self-containment.

As her body began to change in puberty, these patterns deepened. Her gorgeous curves resulted in a sense of shame within her. A critical remark from her mother about her maturing body lodged itself deeply. When Electra asked to wear a bikini at fourteen, she was refused. The message settled into her bones: your body is dangerous, your beauty is a liability, your sensuality cannot be trusted. In church, purity was praised and pleasure viewed with suspicion. At nineteen, when she sought birth control, her mother scolded her sharply. Years later, during a heartbreak in London, her mother sided with the man who left her. Emotional support was unreliable. The ache of that absence followed her into adulthood.

From these experiences, Electra formed an unspoken creed: *you are lovable only when you contain yourself and meet expectations*. Her body became something to manage and hide. Her longing for connection went underground. She strove to achieve in her outer world, and she did, achieving an MBA and a career on the international stage. What she did not yet know was that the doorway back to herself would come through something much simpler and intrinsic with warmth, safety, and touch.

This conditioning did not begin with her mother. Electra's grandmother carried her own inheritance of fear and propriety. Once, when Electra was young, her grandmother saw a woman on the street and remarked sharply that the woman needed a bra. In a single moment, Electra learned that bodies were to be confined and hidden. A lineage of self-surveillance and shame passed into her keeping.

In adulthood, the life Electra had carefully constructed began to fracture. Corporate success no longer sustained her. The strategies that once helped her belong now left her isolated. Something in her was calling for a deeper kind of connection, one that her familiar ways of coping could not reach.

This unraveling marked the beginning of her reweaving.

In her late thirties, after attending a Path of Love Retreat, Electra moved to Brazil. Distance softened her allegiance to old patterns. There, she formed a close friendship with a Brazilian woman whose presence embodied warmth without condition. Through her, Electra encountered a feminine lineage in which sensuality, touch, and embodied presence were not sources of shame, but living birthrights woven into the fabric of every close relationship.

This steady, non-demanding touchy-feely closeness unsettled her at first. Slowly, though, it began to thaw places in her that had been guarded for decades. Being held, touched, with simple feminine warmth, allowed her nervous system to experience her own self-connection in a new way.

Her body, once treated as a liability, became her teacher. Through breath, movement, and conscious touch, she began to experience herself as whole rather than broken. Tantra entered her life as a reclamation of sensuality and a profound presence. Sensation became a language of belonging rather than shame. Through the steady support of other women, she learned that touch could be safe, attuned, and healing.

Returning from Brazil, Electra continues to explore the difference between living from habitual self-monitoring and living from a natural state of connection to herself. In our work together, we have explored that when familiar thoughts arise: *you're not enough* or *your body is bad,* she can pause, soften and reframe. *What does my body feel right now? What is this sensation asking for?* This subtle shift creates space. Old beliefs continued to loosen their grip. What once felt like truth reveals itself as the barrier to truth.

And her life now reflects this. Over time, Electra has stopped seeking herself through approval or achievement. Connection no longer requires effort or erasure. It arises naturally as she returns to her body again and again, trusting its intelligence. What had once been a source of shame is now a source of wisdom.

Today, as a Tantra teacher, Electra guides other women in this same remembering. She teaches them how to reconnect with their bodies, and how to listen to the signals that lead home. Each connective remembrance is a strand in the basket she now carries, not only for herself but also for her sisters on the path.

She understands now that her body was never the problem. It was the doorway back to herself. Through connection and the courage to release her early conditioning, she rewove her life with gentleness and strength. This is the Seeker's path: discovering that the body holds the key, and that healing unfolds through relationship and connection with oneself.

As you sit with Electra's story, allow it to settle within you. What follows is an invitation to turn inward and listen to how this same path is already unfolding in your own body and life.

Journal Reflections: Reweaving Connection

Returning to the Body

What sensations or emotions did I notice as I returned to my body in this intentional way?
Did I feel resistance, numbness, or distance, and how did I meet it?
Is there a part of me that believes my body is not safe?
What would it be like to slow down and connect with my body as a daily practice?
What does my body need from me right now?

Finding an Anchor in the Body

What place, sensation, or rhythm in my body feels steady or safe?
How does my body signal when I am connected to this anchor?
How might I gently return here when I feel overwhelmed or disconnected?

Reclaiming the Sacred Body

What messages did I receive from my mother about my body, beauty, food, or appearance?
How did I witness my mother relating to her own body?
In what ways have I tried to control, punish, or manage my body to feel loved or accepted?
How might my relationship with my body change if I honored it as the sacred temple of my life?
What would reverence for my body look like in small, everyday ways?

Listening to the Body Through Felt Sense and SE

What sensations do I notice when I turn inward?
What helps me feel steady or supported as I listen?
Does my body want to move, sigh, rest, or release anything?
What message or truth might my body be offering me today?
What happens when I trust sensation more than thought?

Reflections on Safe Touch

What kinds of touch feel safe to me right now?
Where do I notice hesitation, fear, or tightening around touch?
How do I feel when I place my own hand on my body with care?

Who in my life offers touch that feels nourishing and trustworthy?
What small step can I take to invite safe touch back into my life?

Reflections on Humming as Meditation

What do I notice when I hum and feel vibration in my body?
Can I sense the vibration moving through my spine?
Can I imagine this vibration as a connective cord between my navel, heart, and mind?
How does humming affect my mood and sense of presence?
How might I bring humming into my daily life as a tool for self-connection?

Honoring Boundaries

What boundaries do I need with my mother right now to feel safe and supported?
What signals does my body give when a boundary is needed?
What small shift could help protect my healing?
What does a loving boundary feel like in my body?

Reflections on Electra's Story

What moved me in Electra's story?
Which parts resonated with my own experience of the mother ache?
Where do I recognize similar patterns in my life?
What possibilities for healing or reweaving does her story awaken in me?

Conclusion: A Blessing for the Lineage

"When you come back to the body, you come back to life."
—Resmaa Menakem

As you return to your body, a wider story comes into view. The burdens you carried did not begin with you. Your mother carried her own forms of disconnection, and her mother did as well. Each woman learned how to survive with what she had, often at the cost of touch, comfort, attunement. When you heal by meeting what was honestly, you are not turning away from them. You are loosening an inherited knot and choosing a new kind of connection that allows your body to be honored as the sacred vessel that it is. In this way, the Seeker gathers the fibers she inherited with care, reweaving them into a basket that can hold self-connection without repeating the old patterns of disconnection.

Step outside and let the earth remind you of the original connection that transcends time. Every inhale is given, every exhale received. Feel your feet on the ground, one hand on your navel, the other on your heart. Remember the Great Mother and the Divine Mother whom you are intrinsically connected to, who feed you through your very breath, and through the earth, and sky. And so, the Seeker rests, knowing that what she sought has always been within her and within all things.

Chapter Seven:

The Weaver of Life and the Patterns of the Mind

"Your task is not to seek for love, but to seek and find all the barriers within yourself that you have built against it."

—Jalaluddin Rumi

As the Seeker continues her inward journey of self-connection, another archetypal energy begins to emerge: the Weaver of Life. The Weaver, one of the oldest feminine archetypes, is found across cultures and lineages worldwide. In ancient societies, weaving was a sacred art, a way of bringing the visible and invisible into relationship. From Andean traditions to ancient Egypt to the Greek Fates, weaving has long symbolized the power of feminine wisdom, integrating experiences, creating meaning, and shaping life by connecting each strand to a greater whole through *understanding*.

When I speak of understanding, I am referring to *hikmah*, an inner wisdom that emerges when we move from the sacred center rather than from the periphery mind. The word hikmah is used widely in Sufi traditions to describe a wisdom that arises from our subtle minds, rather than our more familiar intellectual minds. This is a knowing that is embodied and revealed through presence. In the context of our journey together to heal the mother ache, hikmah is what unfolds when awareness softens into curiosity and is held by trust through inner connection. From this intrinsic state within us, deeper understanding arises. This allows us to see our inner thought patterns kindly and with enough spaciousness that they can begin to shift into healthier ones.

Our minds are full of thoughts, which we can think of as energy patterns. The Weaver values all of these patterns. Even the tangled places, the knots, every inner voice and reaction that arises is a strand waiting to be rewoven into coherence. Understanding deepens when we realize that we are not these inner voices, these thought patterns, and transformation occurs as we learn to gently disidentify from them by tracing them back to where they originated within us and recognizing the purpose they once served.

For those of us healing the mother ache, many of the mind's patterns began in our early relationships with our mothers. Her presence or absence and her attunement shaped what our young minds learned to believe about ourselves. Our Weaver now returns to these early patterns with steady hands, so they can be rewoven into something supportive rather than constricting.

This chapter invites you to follow your own Weaver's hands, to look at the patterns, narratives, and early meanings that reappear often and without invitation in your mind. Instead of seeing them as painful truths about *who you are*, you begin to recognize them as strands that can be intentionally rewoven through understanding into new more supportive patterns. Healing occurs as each strand is welcomed through awareness and tended to with care. The Weaver shows that your history and heartache, once understood, become the very materials of your inner strength.

In this chapter, I invite you to see how your protective patterns took shape and still echo inside your mind, and how these influence your life. As you bring awareness to these inner movements, they begin to settle into a new pattern that honors your past while making space for who you truly are. In this coherence, your sense of self grows strong enough to hold both the ache you've carried and healing work you are doing.

The Weaver weaves the basket's mid-section with patterns. Her hands move in a steady rhythm. Here, she learns the art of relationship to these patterns—tension balanced with ease, structure with flow. As the basket grows, so does her understanding that life itself is a weave of energies brought into coherence, and her hands are the meeting place.

The Basket of the Mind

"The soul always knows what to do to heal itself. The challenge is to silence the mind."

—Caroline Myss

The Weaver of Life's task is to craft a basket that can hold new patterns of being, and to do this, she must first see the old ones clearly. Imagine your mind as a basket. The conscious mind is the visible pattern on the surface, our familiar thought patterns. Beneath the surface lies the unconscious mind: the hidden crossings at the base of the basket and the inner unseen weave that gives the basket its shape. It is here that early experiences and unspoken beliefs are embedded. Though invisible, they shape the entire form. The mother ache resides in these hidden strands: the ache of unmet needs and unfinished love. It rests in the unconscious mind, guiding the weave from inside. Unless brought into awareness, it continues to shape the basket of our lives.

This is why the Weaver must look closely within. Understanding begins when we recognize both the visible pattern and the hidden structure. Most of what influences us does not come from the surface mind at all, but from the deeper weave beneath it. We are not just the thoughts on the surface. We are also not the ache woven into the hidden places. We are the Weaver of our own lives. We can bring old patterns to light, recognize the purpose they once served, and gradually create a basket strong and spacious enough to hold who we truly are.

The Mind's Original Function

Our minds began with a simple, sacred purpose: to help us make meaning of our experience. The mind is the storyteller of the psyche. Since we were born, the mind has been weaving together sensations, emotions, and memories, creating an inner narrative that then defines our identities.

When we first came into the world, we did not yet have language. We had only our bodies and experienced ourselves through hunger, touch, and our other early physical sensations. Gradually, the mind developed around these early experiences of what was soothing, what was frightening, and what signaled safety.

Much of this early meaning-making occurred through our connection with our mothers. Her warmth or coldness, her consistency or unpredictability, her ability or inability to soothe us shaped the earliest patterns our minds formed about our safety, worthiness and belonging.

These early interpretations were not logical or deliberate. They were formed as survival maps. Before language, the nervous system tracked experience: what brought comfort, what triggered fear, what helped preserve connection. Without words, the body and mind organized these impressions into patterns that supported safety. These patterns became programs if you will, for the mind to follow to secure safety. The mind learned to connect these patterns into a protective structure. Over time, these became our mind's programming: ways of thinking, anticipating, reaching, guarding, or pulling away. This programming continues unabated until we bring conscious awareness and understanding to it. This is because the mind doesn't update its programing as we age. It does not realize that our present is far safer than the past from which these patterns emerged, because we are no longer completely dependent on our caregivers to survive.

Much of what we call self-doubt, self-criticism, overthinking, or emotional reactivity arises from these early patterns the mind formed when we were still dependent on our caregivers. These responses are protective energy patterns (PEPs), old energetic movements that once helped us navigate and interpret our early environments.[28] They still come forward whenever the mind senses even a trace of discomfort or danger.

Imagine your inner world as a woven basket. At the very center is your sacred center, which is the still point, the place of understanding. From this center, the weave expands outward in spirals, taking on shape as the strands cross and anchor into one another.

The outer basket, exposed to the world, is where the weave tightens. This is where your protective energy patterns live. These are the voices we hear in our minds repeatedly. *You can't. Don't do that. You're so stupid.* They adapted to the emotional weather of your early home just as a basket adapts to its outer environment: faded if left in the sun, tattered if left in the wind. Now, as an adult, these protective energy patterns still live and work along the outer rim of your mind. They move quickly and are so habitual that we are not even aware that they have shifted into gear. They respond instantly to any perceived disturbance: a tone of voice, a shift in someone's expression, a pause in a conversation, or an unmet expectation. They are an echo of our earliest experiences, long gone.

Protective energy patterns are movements at the edge. They arise from the periphery mind. They try to help, but they constrict rather than support. They literally don't realize that we are no longer the helpless child who must maintain connection to survive. Healing is about learning to loosen the tension of our protective energy patterns by weaving these outer strands into the present with coherence so the entire basket can breathe again.

When we begin to understand the periphery mind as a young guardian shaped by early relationships, something inside softens. We become less

---

28 The term *protective energy patterns* is my own, developed through years of somatic practice and observation. It refers to the subtle energetic ways the body and mind organize themselves to stay safe in response to early relational wounds.

afraid of its movements and more curious about what they reveal. Instead of reacting to the mind's protective energy patterns, we can begin to ask: What story is this energy trying to tell? What hurt is it trying to protect me from? What pattern was once necessary but no longer belongs in the weave of my adult life?

So we start here, remembering the mind's original intent. The mind was simply trying to help us survive by creating energetic patterns to do so. Its earliest movements were woven in service of connection and safety. When we honor this, the weave loosens, and the possibility for a new relationship emerges, one based on understanding and choice.

The Periphery Mind

As we begin to understand the protective energy patterns that formed in our early years, it becomes clear that these movements, though intimate and familiar, are not our true selves. They belong to the periphery mind: the outer band of consciousness shaped by our earliest experiences of connection and rupture.

The periphery mind is where protective energy patterns arise. It stays alert, attuned to potential disappointment or disconnection, and tries to anticipate what might go wrong so we can stay safe. It organizes experience around old maps of belonging and threat. This vigilance once helped us survive, yet now it can keep us circling the edges of our lives instead of inhabiting them.

When we live from the periphery mind, we are living either in the past or future. We brace for what has not yet happened, or retreat into what already did. The mind spins faster at the outer edges, and we lose touch with the steadier ground we long for, which can only be experienced in the present.

Beneath this spinning rim lies the sacred center, the still place within each of us that is not drowning in past pain or future worry. It does not need to analyze or strive; it simply knows. While the periphery reacts, the center remains spacious and responsive. When we pause and turn our attention inward, we begin to feel this core: the pulse of our inner being that has never been hurt. From here, we can meet our protective energy patterns with clarity and warmth rather than identify with them.

Before we explore the periphery more deeply, it helps to first sense the sacred center. The sacred center is not something you must create; it is a place that has always been within you. Earlier, in the Maiden chapter, you learned to connect with the navel center of intelligence, your inner anchor. Here, we expand that awareness by inviting you to experience the subtle neutral mind, the space within that does not react or defend. These two—your navel center and the subtle neutral mind—together form the sacred center. When we rest here, even briefly, we can meet the movements of the periphery without identifying. The journey of understanding invites us to move between these two layers of awareness. This is where hikmah, our inner understanding, arises from the steady center illuminating the patterns at the rim.

Before we explore how the periphery mind moves in its familiar protective patterns, it helps to connect to the place within you that is not swept into their momentum: the sacred center. This inner still point is always available, even when the mind is noisy or reactive. To approach it, we begin with a meditation practice that trains our minds to witness the mind's periphery dance, creating a degree of separation. Vipassana offers this possibility. Through clear seeing, you learn to meet the movements of the mind with understanding rather than identification.

Experiential Practice: Vipassana Meditation

Vipassana, often translated as "clear seeing," is a practice of witnessing the mind rather than entering its movements. This clarity is the Weaver's gift: the ability to observe patterns as energy rather than identity, to see the mind without becoming entangled in it.

To practice set aside eleven minutes in a space where you will not be disturbed. Come into sukhasana. Sit comfortably with your spine tall yet relaxed. Rest your hands on your lap or in gyan mudra, with index and thumb touching, and other fingers extended. Allow your breath to lengthen and soften until it feels unhurried and steady.

Let your awareness rest on the simple rise and fall of the breath. Soon the periphery mind will appear, thoughts, memories, judgments, planning, and commentary. Instead of following them, gently acknowledge each movement with a simple name such as *thinking*, *remembering*, or *planning*, and then return to the breath. Nothing needs to be pushed away. Nothing needs to be improved. You are learning to see clearly.

If emotions arise, let them appear as passing weather. You are not training yourself to suppress anything; you are learning to witness without merging. This is the Weaver's stance: spacious, discerning, steady.

Remain anchored in the body, softened in the heart, and guided by the breath. In this simple act of sitting and seeing, the Weaver strengthens her capacity to hold the mind's activity without becoming woven into it. Over time, this witnessing becomes inner stability, a subtle hum of being.

When the practice ends, take a few deeper breaths. Notice the space around your thoughts, the clarity that remains even after the meditation is complete. This is the mind returning to its sacred center.

Practicing an eleven-minute meditation like this each day is a profound gift. Each time you sit, you reinforce the natural strand of awareness that runs through every narrative in your mind. Even on days when the mind is noisy, the choice to sit and witness becomes the weave of healing itself.

Over time, this daily meditation builds an inner sense of clarity. It teaches you to notice the mind without identification, to watch patterns rise and fall, and to rest in the spaciousness beneath them. This is the healing.

Befriending Our Mind's Patterns

As we begin to meet the mind's patterns without identification, something remarkable happens: the inner landscape begins to relax What we once labeled as overreaction or self-sabotage starts to feel less disempowering and more understandable. We start to see that these inner voices are not irrational. They are expressions of protective energy patterns trying to keep us safe in very old, familiar ways.

Every inner voice, whether protective, anxious, striving, critical, or discouraging has something it is trying to convey. Some speak loudly because they are used to not being heard. Some whisper because they learned it wasn't safe to take up space. Some repeat old warnings because that was once the only way to stay connected. Some try to manage everything because they fear what will happen if they let go. Rather than treating these voices as problems, we can begin to meet them as young friends within us, each carrying a piece of our story that is seeking understanding. For instance:

A protective voice might say, *don't trust them*. Beneath that voice lies an old fear of being hurt again.

A critical voice might press, *you should do better*. Beneath it may live a belief that worth must be earned.

A perfectionistic voice might insist, *you have to get this right*. Beneath it rests the old memory of how painful it once was to be shamed or misunderstood.

When we meet these voices with curiosity instead of resistance, something inside softens. The voices stop fighting for dominance and begin to reveal their purpose. We can ask: What are you trying to protect? When did you learn to speak this way? What are you afraid might happen if you stepped back? What do you need from me in this moment?

These questions help unweave the tangled nature of our minds. They show us the intention behind the pattern, and the care and concern beneath voices that may appear harsh or abrasive on the surface. We learn to listen long enough to understand the intention they carry, without *identifying* with them.

When the mind feels heard, it no longer needs to shout. When we acknowledge its purpose, it no longer needs to brace. When we offer warmth, the mind becomes more willing to soften these old patterns.

In this way, befriending the mind becomes a practice of inner repair, a slow, steady reweaving of relationship to self. We learn to differentiate between the protective energy patterns of the past and the presence available to us now. We learn to offer reassurance instead of reaction. We create a spaciousness around our inner world that did not exist in childhood. And perhaps most profoundly, we learn that we do not have to merge with every voice that arises. We can listen from the sacred center, where understanding lives.

The Four Movements of Protective Energy

As we begin to see our protective energy patterns with more clarity, we also notice that they tend to move in recognizable directions. Across the years, working with women healing the mother ache, I've observed that no matter the story or shape of a protective energy patterns, its energy often organizes itself in one of four distinct movements.[29]

These movements are stubborn and powerful. They are mind-energy in motion, shaped long ago when the psyche was learning how to stay safe. They reveal the ways the mind attempts to protect us from the pain or confusion that once felt overwhelming or beyond our capacity to make sense of.

Here are the four primary directions of energy that protective energy patterns often take within the periphery mind. I call these directions movements.

Reaching

The instinct to move outward in search of reassurance, closeness, approval, or connection. When this movement takes over, the mind scans for signs that love is available and tries to secure it.

Guarding

The instinct to tighten, brace, or prepare for hurt. This movement creates hypervigilance by anticipating criticism, rejection, or conflict before it arrives. It shields the heart by preparing for the worst.

Judging

The instinct to push away. Judgment can feel harsh or righteous, but beneath it often lies fear. This movement distances us from vulnerability by evaluating, criticizing, or withdrawing into superiority or self-protection.

Collapsing

The instinct to fold inward. When this movement appears, energy sinks. We feel small, powerless, overwhelmed, or disconnected from our inner strength. It is the psyche's way of saying, *this is too much.* Although we experience these energy movements as thoughts and reactions, they are really just energetic signatures formed long ago. They begin in the felt sense and emotional heart center and then quickly move into the mind and ripple outward from there. This is why we can begin to recognize them through sensation: a tightening in the chest, a sinking in the belly, i.e., our felt sense, rather than by the message they convey through words.

---

29 These four movements of protective energy emerged through years of my own study, somatic inquiry, and observation in therapeutic work. They echo familiar adaptive archetypes—such as the perfectionist, pleaser, martyr, or victim—but are presented here in their simplest, most embodied form. This particular framework of reaching, guarding, judging, and collapsing is my own synthesis, offered to help readers sense these patterns in the body rather than view them only as psychological labels.

The journey of understanding invites us to see these movements without merging with them. To witness the momentum without letting it carry us away. To see the energetic pattern and remain rooted in the body.

These four movements are the language of the periphery mind; the ways it organizes our experience when it senses old pain stirring. When we can observe them with understanding, we begin to see the intelligence beneath them. And from the sacred center, we can begin the work of reweaving. Let's take a closer look.

Movement One: Reaching

Reaching is the inner energetic movement of seeking outside of ourselves: closeness, reassurance, signs that love is available and that we are not alone. This movement rises when the periphery mind senses even the slightest possibility of disconnection. It pulls our attention outward, scanning for cues, watching faces, interpreting tone, trying to make sure we still belong.

Reaching often forms in early childhood when connection felt unpredictable or uneven. If a mother's attention came in waves, sometimes warm, sometimes distant, the young psyche learned to reach toward her, hoping to catch the next moment of closeness. If love felt conditional, the child's nervous system became organized around securing it. A look, a sigh, a shift in tone could send the system searching for ways to restore harmony.

As adults, reaching can show up in subtle ways. We might wait for someone's response and feel unsettled until it arrives. We might over-apologize to keep the peace, soften our needs to maintain harmony, or adjust ourselves to prevent rejection. We might monitor conversations carefully, hoping not to say the wrong thing. These behaviors are not neediness; they are remnants of a time when connection was necessary for survival.

The energetic signature of reaching is upward and outward. The body leans slightly forward. The breath hovers high in the chest. Attention moves away from the self and onto the other. Emotionally, reaching feels like needing, hoping, yearning, anticipating. The mind becomes alert, interpreting cues to determine whether we are safe and accepted.

When reaching takes over, we lose touch with our center. We look to another person to steady us, forgetting that the steadiness we seek is within us.

Through understanding we begin to learn to observe this movement. Reaching does not mean we are weak or dependent. It means our system learned early that connection required effort and vigilance. By recognizing this, we soften. We begin to differentiate between the instinct to reach and the deeper truth that we no longer need to secure love with outside efforts.

When we feel the impulse to reach, we can pause and notice: What does this movement believe I must do to be loved? We can let our attention return to the body, the breath, to the inner ground of our navel center that does not shift with someone else's presence. Slowly, the reaching softens. The energy that once moved outward returns inward. We feel ourselves again.

Movement Two: Guarding

Guarding is the inner energetic movement of bracing: tightening around the heart, anticipating hurt, preparing for impact before anything has actually happened. It is the periphery mind's way of saying: *Be careful. Something could go wrong*. At its core, guarding is an attempt to be safe by staying prepared.

This movement often develops when a child grows up in an environment that feels unpredictable, emotionally volatile, or unsafe. If a mother's mood shifted quickly or if she felt overwhelmed, irritable, withdrawn, or burdened, the young nervous system learned to stay on alert. It learned to read micro-shifts in tone or expression as early warning signs. The child became a watcher, a tracker, scanning for cues that something might be amiss.

In adulthood, guarding can appear as hypervigilance, mistrust, tension, or emotional distance. We may keep people at arm's length or assume the worst before the moment arrives. We may prepare for rejection in advance, rehearse conversations to prevent being misunderstood, or brace for disappointment. Guarding makes closeness with others challenging, and relaxation might feel uncomfortable.

The energetic signature of guarding is tightening and containment. The body holds itself together, our throats and shoulders tighten, the breath becomes shallow. Emotionally, guarding feels like scanning, assessing. The mind becomes fast and strategic, trying to prevent the hurt it once could not escape.

Guarding disconnects us from the present moment because it is oriented toward what might go wrong in the future. Even when life is calm, this movement prepares for rupture. It is an old survival posture and does not reflect our current reality.

Understanding invites us to approach this movement with patience. Guarding is not cynicism. It is a child's wisdom carried into adulthood. It is a protective instinct that once kept us safe. When we recognize this, the tension eases. Guarding stops feeling like a character flaw and begins to feel like an understandable response to early unpredictability.

When guarding arises, we can gently turn inward and ask: *What am I bracing for? What am I afraid might happen? What does this part of me believe it must protect?*

These questions open a small chink in the guarding armor through understanding. They help us feel the vulnerability beneath the vigilance. From the sacred center, we remind ourselves that we do not have to anticipate danger at every turn. We breathe into the tight places and invite the body to soften, even slightly. We begin to trust our own capacity to meet whatever arises. The world does not feel as dangerous. We do not feel as alone inside it.

When guarding softens, what remains is discernment, a clear, calm ability to sense what is true without fear or tension. This is the gift waiting within the energetic movement, revealed only when we meet it with presence.

Movement Three: Judging

Judging is the energetic movement of pushing away by creating distance through evaluation: criticism, competing, comparison. When the periphery mind senses vulnerability or threat, judgment becomes a shield. It places us above and apart from others. At its core, judgment is a way of protecting the heart by creating space between ourselves and others.

This movement often takes root in childhood when closeness felt confusing or unpredictable. If a mother's presence was inconsistent, sometimes loving, sometimes withdrawn, sometimes intrusive, the young psyche learned to protect its tenderness by stepping back internally. It learned that staying close might expose it to hurt, and so it created a buffer: a layer of mental distance that could keep the heart from feeling pain.

Judging takes many forms: the inner critic, the moral evaluator, the perfectionist, and they all arise through projection. Projection is judgment turned outward. It is a way the mind protects us from feeling what lives within by relocating its source to someone else. When we project, we are not seeing the other clearly; we are seeing the places inside us that still ache. We in essence blame or shame others for our own inner misery.

As adults, judging shows up in nuanced, familiar ways. We might critique others quickly, feel irritated by their choices, or compare ourselves to them. We might even turn judgment inward, evaluating ourselves harshly in an attempt to stay in control. Though judgment can appear sharp or confident on the surface, it often hides a soft, scared place underneath. When we judge others, it is a reflection of our own inner worth.

The energetic signature of judging is outward and defensive. The chest subtly lifts; the jaw tightens. Emotionally, judging feels like distancing. The mind becomes quick and precise, driven by reactivity and fear rather than clarity.

Judging pulls us away from the sacred center because it assumes and reinforces separation. It says, *I must stand apart to stay safe*. Understanding that this movement is not a moral failure is important. Judging ourselves for being judgmental can become a never-ending mind dance. We must learn to see it as a protective energy pattern learned long ago that has run amok. When seen through understanding, judgment softens without effort.

When judgment arises, toward ourselves or others, we can pause and ask gently: *What feels threatened in me right now? What pain or fear is this judgment protecting me from feeling?*

These questions reveal the truth beneath the sharpness. They help us notice the vulnerability that judgment is guarding. From the sacred center, we can meet this movement with warmth, acknowledging its purpose and then consciously drop it.

Judgment softens through recognition. When we acknowledge that it is trying to keep us from feeling exposed or hurt, the edge lessens. The distance closes. We return to ourselves, and in doing so, we begin to see others more clearly through the lens of presence.

With understanding, judgment transforms into discernment, which is the ability to see clearly without reactivity. Discernment arises from the center, not the periphery. It allows us to honor our boundaries without severing connection, and to stay true to ourselves. When judgment softens, the heart opens naturally.

Movement Four: Collapsing

Collapsing is the inner energetic movement of folding inward: the moment when the system loses its sense of strength and agency. It is the periphery mind's way of saying, *this is too much*. When collapsing arises, energy sinks. The body softens or slumps. The breath becomes shallow. We feel small, powerless, overwhelmed.

This movement often forms in early environments where a child did not have the protection or support needed to process fear or frustration. If a mother was emotionally unavailable or dismissive of feelings, the child's nervous system learned to retreat inward. Collapsing became a way to survive by becoming invisible or by not needing too much. The child's system concluded, often without words: *It's not safe to try* or *I must disappear to stay safe*. In adulthood, collapsing can show up in moments when life asks more of us than our system feels able to give. It may appear as hopelessness, self-doubt, confusion, emotional shutdown, or a sense of inadequacy. We might abandon tasks that matter to us, avoid difficult conversations, or withdraw from connection, not because we don't care, but because our system feels unable to engage.

The energetic signature of collapsing is downward and inward. The spine rounds, the chest softens, the gaze lowers. Emotionally, collapsing feels like an inward sinking marked by hopelessness, smallness, or the ache of believing that nothing you do will make a difference.

This movement is often accompanied by a familiar narrative: *I can't do this. I'm not enough. I should not even try.* These thoughts are not truths; they are echoes from a time when the child truly could not do more because she lacked capacity and the support her system needed.

Understanding invites us to meet collapsing with profound gentleness. This movement is not laziness, weakness, or avoidance. It is a survival reflex. The system is attempting to protect us from emotional overwhelm by retreating to the smallest possible expression of self. When seen through the eyes of understanding, collapsing becomes a doorway to self-understanding.

When collapsing arises, we can ask ourselves softly: *What feels too big right now? What part of me believes it can't do this? What support is missing in this moment? What does this movement need in order to lift even slightly?*

These questions create a small opening in the heaviness. They help us feel the tenderness beneath the shutdown. And from the sacred center, we can respond by offering presence to the part of us that has folded.

Collapsing softens by receiving inner self support: deep breathing, grounding, gentle awareness, warmth. As the sacred center grows stronger, the impulse to collapse becomes less overwhelming.

When collapsing loosens, what emerges is humility and resilience. We start to feel the ground beneath our feet again. The body lifts naturally. The breath returns. A sense of *I can do this* flickers back to life. This movement, once so painful, becomes a teacher, reminding us that our deepest tenderness is also our doorway back to the center.

Protective Energy Patterns: When Relief Becomes Compulsion

What we often call addiction or compulsion is not a flaw in character or will. It is the nervous system doing its best to survive. When early meanings carry more ache than can be felt at once, the system organizes around protection. It reaches for relief, guards what soothes, collapses into numbness, or turns against itself through judgment. These movements are not failures. They are protections shaped in relationship.

Seen this way, addiction is not separate from the patterns we have already named. It is an intensified expression of them. Reaching seeks something outside the self that promises relief or completion. Guarding protects the strategy that makes survival possible, often through secrecy or rigidity. Collapsing quietens what feels unbearable, dimming sensation and aliveness. Judging follows close behind, tightening the loop through shame and self-blame. What appears compulsive on the surface often began as care. The body found something that helped it breathe, settle, or feel safe when other forms of support were not available.

Healing does not begin by taking these strategies away. It begins by listening to what they have been carrying. As presence grows and early meanings soften, the same energy that once needed to reach, guard, collapse, or judge can gradually reorganize. In this reorganization, choice can begin to emerge as a possibility to build upon.

Experiential invitation: Listening to Protective Strategies

Take a moment to settle your body. Feel the support beneath you. Become aware of your breath.

Notice whether there are any habits, substances, or patterns you turn toward when things feel overwhelming, lonely, or too much. There is no need to label these as problems. Simply notice what comes to mind.

If one does, sense into how it moves in you. Does it feel like reaching for relief or connection? Guarding something that helps you cope? Collapsing into quiet or numbness? Or judging yourself before or after? There may be more than one. Let your body show you.

Ask gently: *What does this strategy give me when I reach for it? Relief, quiet, connection, energy, comfort, disappearance?*

Place a hand on your navel or heart. Let your body know you are not here to take anything away. You are here to listen. These protective movements formed very early, shaped by what was needed to survive before you had language or choice. The work here is tending the deeper place that learned to rely on it.

Write a few words about what this pattern may have helped you carry or endure. Stop when you feel complete.

Postures of Protection: How the Body Reveals Our Patterns

The movements of our protective energy patterns do not live only in the mind. They also appear in the subtle ways we hold ourselves, the postures we return to without even realizing it. These shapes are the body's memory, the way the nervous system once learned to shield the child we were.

Over years of teaching meditation, movement, and breath, I have come to see how posture becomes a doorway into our earliest adaptations. The body tells the truth long before the mind does. Hunched shoulders, a lifted chin, a lowered gaze: each reveals a story the child once carried about safety, love, and belonging.

When a protective energy pattern moves through us, the body responds instinctively. Reaching may lean us forward or widen our eyes in search of connection. Guarding may firm the jaw or stiffen the spine into subtle armor. Judging may lift the chest, tighten the jaw, the brow scowls. Collapsing may lower the gaze or sink the belly as energy withdraws inward.

These shapes are signs of intelligence, formed long before we had words. When we meet them with understanding, something begins to soften. We feel the younger selves who learned these postures and the fears that shaped them. Understanding takes root in the living body. Not in the thinking mind.

Experiential Invitation: Sensing Your Protective Postures

Let's explore this further through our own experience of our protective energy patterns in our bodies. Understanding arises more truthfully through sensation than through analysis. By taking these postures yourself, even briefly, you can feel how each pattern lives in you, how it protects, and how it softens when met with awareness.

Allow at least 30 minutes for this experiential exercise. Find a place where you can sit comfortably. Let your breath slow. Allow the weight of your body to settle.

Begin in sukhasana or on your firm chair in your meditative posture: spine erect, shoulders relaxed, heart slightly lifted, chin gently tucked, allow your breath to be easy and unforced. This is your home base, the place where presence begins.

From here, you will gently explore the somatic expressions of the four movements of the periphery mind. Move slowly, with curiosity.

Reaching—The Forward-Leaning Posture

Lean forward the slightest amount. Let the chin lift or the eyes reach outward, as though scanning for approval or connection. Feel the subtle urgency, the pull toward doing or pleasing. Exaggerate this posture so you really start to fill it as an energy movement within you. Pause, breathe, and return to center.

Guarding—The Armored Posture

Let your shoulders tense. Engage your jaw. Notice the impulse to clench your hands, tighten your belly, or hold your breath. Feel how the heart area becomes subtly guarded, closed. Sense the readiness beneath this shape, the vigilance, the alertness. Exaggerate this posture so you really start to fill it as an energy movement within you. Pause, breathe, and return to center.

Judging—The Contracted Posture

Lift your chest slightly and tighten through the shoulders. Firm the jaw and narrow the eyes. Feel the belly brace and the body become upright and tense, as if your certainty is holding you in place. Notice the emotional tone of this shape. Does something feel smaller, protected, hidden? Exaggerate this posture so you really start to fill it as an energy movement within you. Pause, breathe, and return to center.

Collapsing—The Folding Posture

Allow your shoulders to roll inward. Let your gaze drift down or away. Feel the emotional resonance: the smallness, the retreat, the desire to disappear or be unseen. Exaggerate this posture so you really start to fill it as an energy movement within you. Pause, breathe, and return to center.

Each posture is a shape your body learned to take when it needed protection. Each one reflects a protective energy pattern, an early movement that helped you stay connected. Notice which postures feel most familiar to your body, that have worked the hardest to keep you safe.

By exploring these shapes with presence, you begin to loosen these old energy movements within and strengthen your connection to your sacred center by weaving new energetic pathways of awareness simply by changing your posture. Your body has been telling the truth of your story for years. Now, through awareness, it begins to tell the truth of your healing.

Working with the Four Movements of Protective Energy

Once we begin to recognize reaching, guarding, judging, and collapsing as the four movements of the periphery mind, we can start to see how they literally color our everyday experience. These movements arise quickly, usually before we have time to think. They are the body's first response to a perceived shift in safety or belonging, long before the mind builds a story around what is happening.

In ordinary moments, these movements may appear so subtly that we do not notice them. A friend takes too long to reply, and the body leans forward in reaching. A partner's tone sounds slightly different, and guarding steps in. A stranger behaves unexpectedly, and judgment rises to create distance. A challenge appears and collapsing folds our energy inward. Recognizing the movements begins by noticing what happens in the body. Each movement has its own signature.

The mind then follows these energetic cues, often without our awareness. A critical thought arises. A self-protective interpretation. A harsh judgment about a friend. We assume these thoughts are us, when in truth they are the mind's attempt to make sense of the body's reaction.

Over time, we begin to recognize the earliest signs of each movement. The slight lean forward. The bracing in the shoulders. The lifted chest and tightening jaw. The downward gaze and soft collapse in the chest. With familiarity, the movements become less overwhelming. We no longer fuse with them. We no longer assume they are the truth about who we are or what is happening.

From the sacred center, we hold the movements the way a Weaver holds strands of fiber gently, intentionally. We begin to see that each movement contains wisdom. Reaching reveals where we yearn for connection. Guarding shows where we feel vulnerable. Judging reveals where boundaries or tenderness are needed. Collapsing shows where we are in need of support or care.

When we work with the movements in this way, the periphery mind slowly relaxes. It no longer needs to shout or brace. It begins to trust that there is an inner steadiness to meet the moment.

This is healing. Clarity. Understanding the mind. Simply by learning to observe these energetic patterns with presence. In this space of awareness, the movements become woven into a healthier pattern, one that honors where we have been and creates space for our true selves.

Reweaving Thought with Body Awareness

As we begin to understand the mind's protective movements, the next step is bringing those movements back into relationship with the body real time. The mind learned long ago to anticipate, interpret, and protect, but the body lives only in the present moment. When thought and sensation are disconnected within us, the mind spins its old stories unchecked. When they are reconnected within us, something softens.

You already know how to listen to sensation, as we practiced in Chapter Six through our inner Seeker archetype. Now the Weaver invites you to bring that same awareness to the movements of the mind. When a familiar pattern stirs, pause for a breath and feel the body alongside the thought. Notice which of the four energy movements is arising in your body. Sensation reveals what is true now, while the thought often reveals what was once true long ago. When we move from the story back to the body and its truth, understanding ripens into wisdom.

This is the heart of hikmah: an inner knowing that arises when the periphery mind is softened and we are then able to access our sacred center. Thought steadies. Emotion clarifies. The old weave loosens enough for a new one to form. What once felt fixed begins to move. What once felt overwhelming becomes workable. And the mind, feeling your steadiness, begins to trust you.

The story that follows offers a glimpse of this reweaving in motion.

Mother Ache Healing in the World:

The Girl Who Learned to Slow Her Inner World

Maleea was born into a home already shaped by grief. Before she arrived, her mother had lost a baby girl to SIDS, a loss that left fear and vigilance woven into daily life. Soon after, a daughter with special needs was born, and her mother's attention became organized around fear and protection. Love was delivered through this lens, shaped more by vigilance than attunement.

When Maleea arrived eighteen months later, healthy and bright, she was well cared for on a practical level, but her emotional world was often left unattended amid her sister's more pressing needs. Maleea's feedings were hurried. Touch was efficient, not warm. Wanting to ensure she drank quickly, her mother cut the tip of the bottle so the milk would flow faster, resulting in Maleea being unable to keep her formula down. Maleea's body learned its first lesson early: receive quickly or don't receive at all. Her nervous system adapted to speed as a survival tool. Slowing down did not feel safe.

This rhythm shaped her inner world. As a child, Maleea's energy moved into reaching. She learned to hurry toward what she needed, to anticipate others, to be useful before being asked. Reaching became a way to stay connected in a world that expected her to move fast.

Alongside this reaching, a quieter guarding took shape. She learned not to expect recognition, not to wait for appreciation, not to risk disappointment. Praise was rare due to her mother's fear that celebrating one child might wound another. Maleea adapted by succeeding without asking to be seen, guarding herself against the ache of unmet expectation.

By adolescence, these patterns had been braided together. Her system knew how to reach through pleasing and achievement, and how to guard by minimizing her own needs. When she said yes while wanting no, her body tightened. Her outer life appeared capable and composed, while her inner world remained organized around urgency and vigilance.

Her first doorway into understanding opened during her first of many silent Vipassana meditation retreats. As she sat in stillness, the habits of reaching and guarding loosened their grip. Tears surged forth in a relentless wave, deep, cathartic, and unstoppable. They poured out of her as a long-held urgency finally released. What had once felt like truth revealed itself as protection. In the quiet that followed, she discovered something new: her life did not require speed, and time could hold her.

This was the beginning of a new relationship with her mind.

Maleea initially came to work with me for integration support, yet it quickly became clear that we were standing in the hollowed ground of the mother ache. In our work together over the years, we returned to understanding and clear seeing. When old patterns tightened, Maleea practiced pausing. She learned to notice the moment energetic habits of reaching and guarding arose, and to name them gently rather than be swept up in their currents. Sacred plant medicines also supported this process, revealing how deeply the habit of rushing had shaped her sense of self and her relationship to time.

Gradually, her understanding widened. She began to see her mother with clearer eyes. Her mother had been living inside unprocessed grief and fear. The urgency that shaped their home was born from terror of loss, not indifference or lack of love. Recognizing this allowed Maleea to release the belief that she needed to hurry in order to be chosen.

Now, when the familiar tightening appears, she notices it. She pauses. She breathes into her chest. She watches the mind offer its old instructions and chooses not to follow. She meets the girl who once rushed to belong and offers her something new: time.

Understanding, for Maleea, is no longer passive. It is an active intention in her life. She remembers that her pace is sacred. She remembers that she does not need to earn love. She remembers that presence, not urgency, is what allows her to feel alive.

Through understanding her protective energy patterns, her mind learned to soften. Through witnessing, the old patterns of reaching and guarding lost their authority. And in the space that opened, Maleea discovered a new truth: she shines most brightly when she allows herself to move at the speed of her own breath.

Maleea's story opens a question many of us eventually face:

> *"I had to choose between the life of being and the life of doing, and I leapt at the latter like a trout to a fly. But each deed you do, each act, binds you to itself and to its consequences, and makes you act again and yet again. Then very seldom do you come upon a space, a time like this, between act and act, when you may stop and simply be. Or wonder who, after all, you are."*
>
> —Ursula K. Le Guin

Journal Reflections: Reweaving Understanding

Layers of the Mind

What surface thoughts repeat most often in the basket of my mind?
What hidden strands might be shaping these thoughts from below?
How do I sense the mother ache woven into these hidden patterns?
What would it mean to see myself as the Weaver who can choose new patterns?

The Mind's Original Function

As you reflect on this chapter, what is the first signal that tells you the periphery mind is active?
Describe the moment through the body sensations before the story forms.

Befriending Our Mind's Patterns

Which of the four movements of reaching, guarding, judging, or collapsing feels most familiar to you?
What recent experience helps you recognize it?
Choose one protective pattern you often rely on. In what early environment did this pattern first make sense?

The Periphery Mind

Bring to mind a recurring thought you have about yourself.
When you pause and sense your body, what feeling or sensation lives beneath that thought?
Notice what happens inside you when you shift attention from the story in your mind to the sensation in your body.
How does the experience change?

Experiential Invitation: Vipassana

What did I notice about the movements of my mind when I simply watched?
Which thoughts or emotions repeated themselves, and what might they be asking me to understand?
How did it feel in my body to witness rather than identify with what was arising?
What surprised me during this practice? What felt difficult? What felt easeful?

Did any moments of clarity, spaciousness, or stillness appear?
How might returning to this witnessing help me work with my protective patterns?
What did I learn about the difference between *the mind* and *myself*?

Addiction, Compulsion, and Protective Energy

When I notice a habit or pattern I return to for relief, what is happening in my body just before I reach for it?
Which protective energy feels most present in this pattern right now: reaching, guarding, collapsing, or judging? How do I recognize it in sensation or impulse rather than thought?
What does this strategy offer me in the moment? Relief, quiet, connection, comfort, steadiness, disappearance, something else?
If this pattern could speak, what might it say it has been trying to protect or carry for me?
Without analyzing or fixing, what early situation or feeling does this energy remind me of, even faintly?
Is there a way I can offer my body a small moment of presence or kindness right now, alongside this pattern, rather than against it?
What does choice feel like in my body, even in a very small way?

Postures Of Protection: How The Body Reveals Our Patterns

Reaching: What feeling arose in my body as I took the posture of reaching?
When in my life do I notice this reaching movement appear, and what is it hoping for?
Guarding: What tightened or braced inside me when I embodied guarding?
What situation or relationship in my life most often activates this movement of self-protection?
Judging: What thoughts or impulses surfaced as I entered the posture of judging?
When I sense this judging energy in daily life, what vulnerable feeling might lie beneath it?
Collapsing: What changed in my internal sense of self when I embodied collapsing?
Where in my life do I feel this movement arise, and what part of me is asking for support or safety?

If you let the Weaver within you speak, what understanding does she want you to have about your protective energy patterns?

Working With The Four Movements Of Protective Energy

In the flow of an ordinary day, when am I most likely to notice one of these movements arise, whether its reaching, guarding, judging, or collapsing?
What small pause or gesture of awareness could help me recognize a protective pattern and its movement in the moment, before it takes over?
How might my experience shift if, when a movement appears, I respond with curiosity instead of self-criticism?

Reweaving Thought With Body Awareness

What becomes possible in your inner world when your awareness returns to the body before the story takes hold and overtakes your entire system?

Maleea's Story

How did Maleea's story resonate with me? What moments or details stirred recognition in my own body or memory?
What would it mean to trust that my pace is sacred? How might my life feel different if I no longer needed to hurry in order to belong?

As you come to the end of these journaling explorations, notice what has shifted inside. Even the smallest recognition of a pattern creates understanding that begins to change the weave of the mind's patterns. The mind no longer works alone; its movements are met with the intelligence of the navel fire and subtle mind. Presence returns. Space opens. In this softening, a deeper intelligence begins to stir. This is healing.

Conclusion: From Recognition to Presence

As we begin to observe the movements of the periphery mind, we reclaim the clarity of the sacred center. From this place of awareness, we begin to sense that we are not our seemingly perpetual inner thoughts. We start to understand that we are the presence that can lovingly witness them and let them go. This recognition marks a profound turning point in the spiral of healing: the movement from identification to witnessing.

When we start to experience this space, the noise from the periphery softens. The vigilant mind loosens its grip, and something deeper begins to emerge from the gentle current of the sacred center. It waits for us always, patient and whole.

Our path together in the next chapters deepens this understanding. Having learned to recognize the patterns of the mind, we now shift toward the currents of the heart, which are the living waters flowing through the vessel of our beings. This is the journey we are on literally: from mind-driven survival to heart-centered presence.

The Weaver rests her hands. The mind grows calmer. And from that place, the heart takes up the sacred healing journey. Its movements are guided through feeling. Here, in the living current of emotion, love becomes the strands we are weaving together. Strands of survival become strands of strength; the weave remembers its original song.

The path of healing leads us inward, toward a deeper self that has always known wholeness. What wounds us early in life does not arrive by accident; it shapes the very doorway through which something greater seeks to awaken within us. When we turn away from our original ache, we turn away from the deep centering presence that lives inside it. When we listen instead, we discover that the wound itself carries the medicine we have been seeking.

This is where the Weaver guides you next, toward the place where truth lives in feeling. The mind weaves its stories. The heart weaves its truth. Understanding comes when the two are brought together in the sacred center.

Chapter Eight:

The Healer and the Wisdom of the Heart

"When you begin to touch your heart or let your heart be touched, you begin to discover that it's bottomless, that it doesn't have any resolution, that this heart is huge, vast, and limitless. You begin to discover how much warmth and gentleness is there, as well as how much space."

—Pema Chödrön

In the previous chapter, we met the mind's protective energy patterns that were created to keep us from overwhelming emotions in the past. Each one carries a story of our early experience and was born from necessity. Yet what once guarded the heart now prevents it from feeling our emotions. As we begin to recognize these patterns with kindness, the weave loosens. As light moves through the strands, we remember the heart's natural fluidity and our capacity to feel more fully.

This is an arduous journey from the head to the heart. To heal our mother ache, this is the path that each of us must walk. Here, the Healer archetype steps forward to support our efforts. The Healer within each of us knows that the body and heart are sacred spaces, and that true healing begins with the courage to feel with *empathy* in our hearts. Empathy is the ability to feel what arises, without needing to fix or change it.

The Healer archetype has ancient roots that women across cultures have carried for millennia. Long before formal medicine, women served as midwives, herbalists, bonesetters, and grief-tenders within their communities.[30] Anthropological records show that in many early societies, women were the primary keepers of plant medicine, birth rituals, and healing knowledge passed through oral tradition.[31]

The Healer within us understands that suffering often grows from what was never allowed to be felt, spoken, seen, or held. Healing, for her, is tending to the pain rather than seeking to remove it. This lineage lives in every woman still. To awaken the Healer within is to reclaim the sacred responsibility of tending your own heart.

As children, many of us learned that feeling was unsafe. Anger, pride, excitement, even joy, were often dismissed or shamed, especially when they brushed against a mother's discomfort. To be a good girl meant to be quiet, to comply, to hide the wild pulse of excitement. In that hiding, our essential nature also went underground. Along with our emotions, we buried courage, passion, and self-worth. What once preserved our safety now confines our becoming. Anger that could guard our healthy boundaries becomes shame. Grief that could soften the heart turns to numbness. Desire that could ignite creativity collapses into fear.

The Healer understands this and knows that these patterns that once carried the medicine she needed most no longer need to work so hard. Her task is to invite the suppressed feelings they guard to return home to be felt, honored, and released. Unfelt emotions live in the body like stagnant water dammed up in a river. Through empathy, the Healer helps them flow again.

Women are and have always been the healers healing themselves. They are the wounded healers. To be the healer healing oneself is to find the courage to meet the mother ache with empathy. Empathy is the ability to stay present with your own experience, feeling it through the heart without

---

30 Historically, the word *witch* was often used to persecute women who carried healing knowledge: midwives, herbalists, and those in direct relationship with the natural world and intuitive ways of knowing. Today, many healers reclaim the word as a form of remembrance and empowerment.

31 For readers interested in the cross-cultural history of women as healers, shamans, midwives, and ritual specialists, Barbara Tedlock's *The Woman in the Shaman's Body* (New York: Bantam, 2005) offers an accessible and illuminating exploration. It provides helpful historical and anthropological context for the Healer archetype referenced here. Also, Carolyn Niethammer, *Daughters of the Earth: The Lives and Legends of American Indian Women* (New York: Macmillan, 1977), a beautifully rendered work on the rites of passage of Indigenous women from birth through death, shaped by the wisdom and stories of the women elders of this land, has an amazing chapter on medicine women.

turning away. The wounded healer reminds us that our deepest wounds, once tended, become channels through which compassion and wisdom can then flow, first toward ourselves and then for the benefit of others. When a woman's pain is transformed into understanding, and her grief transcends into gratitude we all benefit. But the healing must first occur internally within each of us.

The Healer weaves the basket's upper rim, her gestures both precise and tender. She knows that the last layers hold the vessel's integrity, binding all that came before. In her touch is empathy: every wound, once tended, becomes a strand of strength. Her weaving is prayer and medicine, the patient act of turning ache into grace.

Understanding Emotion

"Without understanding how our feelings, thoughts, and behaviors work together, it's almost impossible to find our way back to ourselves and each other. When we don't understand how our emotions shape our thoughts and decisions we become disembodied from our own experiences and disconnected from each other."

—Brene Brown

Emotion is energy in motion. Each emotion carries its own wisdom, its own pulse within us. There are seven primary emotions that all humans experience:

Anger defends and ignites courage.

Excitement signals possibility, awakening the energy to move toward what feels life-giving.

Joy arises when we feel connected and present enough to receive the fullness of experience.

Sadness reveals love's depth and the need for tenderness.

Disgust teaches discernment and boundary.

Fear warns and protects.

Desire awakens pleasure, intimacy, and creativity.

The emotions we were taught to suppress do not disappear. When repressed, their energy fuels the periphery mind, weaving stories that keep us circling the same ache. They then manifest in the body at first with dis-ease—a sense of anxiety, uneasiness, depression—and often later as disease. When acknowledged, that same energy becomes vitality, creativity, and ease. Our true strength is in our natural state of emotional fluidity. What the mind calls emotion, the sacred center knows as fluid movement, energy longing to flow naturally within us.

When we resist these feelings, our heart center's shut down. When we allow them, in gentle increments, our heart's intelligence begins to flow again. This fluidity is what then allows our healing to unfold so that we can lead from our hearts authentically.

The Body as an Instrument of Feeling

"The best and most beautiful things in the world cannot be seen or even touched. They must be felt with the heart."

—Helen Keller

The Healer and the Wisdom of the Heart

Emotions are living sensations within the body that originate at the heart center. Our heart is our true compass with its own intelligence, guiding how we feel and relate. As little girls navigating the mother ache, when we shut this center down to avoid overwhelm or disconnection we also lost access to this intelligence. So, we must learn to reconnect here to heal our mother ache. When we listen inwardly, the heart becomes a guide, revealing healing truths the mind cannot reach.

When the heart is open, emotion moves as the elements move through the earth. Sadness falls like rain. Anger flares like a flame. Joy expands like sunlight through the ribs. Fear trembles and releases like wind through tall grass. Each feeling has a rhythm within the body. When we let these movements arise, we stay connected to the river of life.

When we block our emotions, our bodies respond intuitively. Our jaw tightens, our shoulders tense, our stomach aches because in suppressing this natural flow we have also interrupted that inner fluidity that then manifests in these holding patterns of discomfort. The energy of suppressed feeling becomes crystallized in our bodies as tension, fatigue, or numbness. It is essential to recognize that we closed our hearts out of a deep-seated, often subconscious drive for safety and survival. It is equally essential to recognize that as adults we no longer need to keep our hearts shut to survive. To evolve in our healing work, we want to reopen our hearts, and to do this we must remember its language.

The Healer within teaches this language through empathy. She listens for what lies beneath words in the more subtle and honest felt sense that we explored in Chapter Six. These sensations are the alphabet of feeling. When we attend to them with curiosity, we translate the body's wisdom into presence and rediscover trust in its messages about our true experience, here, now.

In this way, the heart becomes our guide. It shows us where the current of life is flowing and where we have lost this fluidity. It reminds us that wholeness is the capacity to stay present and to allow pain to be felt in manageable increments. The more we listen, the more we remember that the body is the gateway through which we heal and realize the sacred within us.

Perceptions Block Feelings and Flow

A key step in relearning to feel is distinguishing our perceptions from our emotions. Perceptions are the mind's immediate interpretations of our experiences. Interpretations are the thin veils of story that form over the raw sensations that form our emotions. For instance, if we see someone and our hearts feel a tug toward sadness, which is painful, to avoid this our periphery mind jumps in with an interpretation such as: *I feel rejected, I feel unsafe, I feel alone.* As soon as this thought appears we disconnect from the actual feeling beneath, the sadness. Indeed, just beneath these interpretations lie our true emotions: sadness, fear, anger, disgust, excitement, desire and joy, that we were conditioned to disregard as little ones. Again, these emotions don't go away when we avoid them, they remain in the body and manifest as tension, stuck energy, anxiety, depression, etc.

The periphery mind jumps in with our perceptions to make pain manageable, but in so doing it also pull us away from the immediacy of the truth of our actual experience. To reconnect with feeling, we must descend beneath the immediate perception into the raw current of feeling. The mind explains, the body experiences. The Healer invites us to pause before the explanation, to sense what lies beneath the words, and to experience it empathetically.

Experiential Invitation: From Perception to Feeling

We all have perceptions and often they are quite familiar. Identify a recurring perception that arises for you, such as *I was betrayed, I'm not seen, I feel disrespected.* Once you've identified a familiar perception, see if you can follow the spiral inward by tracking the following steps. This is an exercise that invites you to write the perception and the name of the emotion underneath to bring clarity.

Write down the perception: For example: *I often feel rejected.*

Ask gently: *What emotion lies beneath the perception?*

Notice the body's language: is there tightening, heat, trembling, ache, that accompanies this perception?

Name the emotion that lives beneath the perception: sadness, fear, anger, shame. Write the name of the emotion down below the perception. If you're unsure, review the seven emotions above and see if clarity emerges. This takes practice and patience because we are used to thinking of our perceptions as our feelings. They are not. They are our tools to avoid the feelings, which then stagnate and block our hearts fluidity. Once you are able to identify the feeling beneath the perception you can then softly ask yourself: *What quality of love hides within this?* For sadness, perhaps tenderness; for anger, protection; for fear, self-care. Now write this quality of love down below the perception.

Let yourself feel that original emotion, the authentic feeling beneath the perception, before it became a story without needing to define it. By simply noticing it, naming it and bringing empathy to it by recognizing its loving intention, you are inviting your heart center to find its natural fluidity again. Each time you follow the thread from perception to feeling, you are relearning your innate emotional intelligence. Being able to feel your feelings is the pathway guiding you home to you.

The Four R's of Emotional Alchemy

As we listen with empathy and begin to sort out our emotions from our surface perceptions, we might begin to see hidden patterns that reveal their rhythm within us. In the space of remembering our true feelings, what was once avoided as too much for us unfolds into fluidity, the healing process of recognition, release, and return. These rhythms often surface naturally as the body shows us how it has learned to brace, to regress, to repress, to react.

As we've explored, when we stifle our emotions, their energy doesn't disappear, it changes form. What we avoid, we act out. What we suppress, we carry forward in unhealthy ways. The work of healing invites us to notice how emotion moves through us and to transform our reflexive patterns into conscious choice. This is the essence of the *Four R's*: an alchemical sequence through which emotion evolves from contraction to coherence.[32] With empathy turned inward toward self, each R marks a potential turning of

---

32 Through my own healing journey and years of sitting with others to support their healing, I've come to recognize four common ways we turn away from feeling and can relearn feeling and I've named them the Four Rs.

the spiral inward: the mind softening into the body, the body yielding to the heart's expression of feeling, and this feeling returning us home to presence.

The Four R's arise within the protective energy patterns explored in the previous chapter. If those patterns describe how the mind organizes survival, the responses we explore here reveal how the heart manages once unsafe feelings. The Four R's provide a way for us to avoid pain short term by cutting off our emotions. They are as follows:

Resist

We tense against what's happening, armoring the heart and body to stay safe.

Regress

We slip into younger states, the child who freezes, pleases, or hides.

Repress

We push emotion underground, storing it as tension, fatigue, or illness.

React

We project feeling outward through blame, control, or withdrawal.

Each R is a form of protection that is trying to keep us from what once felt unbearable. Yet what protected us then constrains us now. When we meet these reflexes with awareness, the same energy begins to move again.

With presence, the Four R's transform into a new rhythm, four movements of emotional alchemy:

Recognize

Name what is here: This is sadness. This is anger. This is fear.

Release

Allow it to move through breath, sound, or tears, trusting its intelligence.

Reweave

Integrate what was felt through empathy, understanding how it shaped us in the past and perhaps no longer needs to in the present.

Respond

Act from presence rather than pattern, choosing alignment over reactivity.

This is the spiral of transformation from contraction to connection, from self-protection to self-trust. Each time you move from resistance to recognition, from regression to relating as an adult, from repression to release, from reactivity to responding, you are reweaving your being toward healing, wholeness.

Meeting Fear: The Guardian at the Threshold

"Change is frightening but where there's fear, there's power. If we learn to feel our fear without letting it stop us, fear can become an ally, a sign to tell us that something we have encountered can be transformed. Often our true strength is not in the things that represent what is familiar, comfortable, or positive but in our fear and even our resistance to change."

—Starhawk

The emotion of fear is the most common trigger, causing the pattern of the Four Rs to overtake our beings. Fear, whispers to us that safety lies in our familiar old worn ways, no matter how much suffering they cause. When we mistake fear for a bright red stop sign in our lives, we retreat and remain small. When we meet it as a threshold, it becomes a sacred invitation into becoming.

For many of us carrying the mother ache, fear is our body's first language. The fear of abandonment shaped us all, in one way or another. Long before words, we knew its signals: quickened pulse, shallow breath, clenched fingers, the urge to freeze or flee. These are ancient codes written in our DNA to help us survive. Now in our healing journey, the same instinct that once might have overwhelmed us asks to be met with presence.

In our lives, fear often unconsciously manifests as the four Rs: resistance, regression, repression, and reactivity. When you notice these, pause. Place one hand on your navel, one on your heart. Breathe softly. Whisper, *I am here. It's safe to take one small step*. Then take the next step by moving through the threshold. Light the candle. Do the breathwork. Open the journal. Take the walk in nature you don't think you have time for. Each small act retrains your nervous system to trust again and decreases the powerful energetic pull within us of these Four Rs.

When working with fear, it helps to remember that the things we avoid most fiercely, as if they are dragons from ancient myths and legends, often contain the truths we most need. What appears threatening may be guarding something precious within us. Bow to it. Let its fiery breath remind you that courage and fear dwell in the same navel center within you. When fear is met with empathy rather than avoidance or force, it changes shape, becoming like the rain after drought, softening the soil of our beings to new possibilities. As Joseph Campbell said, "The cave you fear to enter holds the treasure you seek."

Further, remember fear, when faced and acknowledged, does not vanish rather it transforms into courage. Each time you stay with fear rather than retreat into one of the Four Rs, you strengthen trust in your ability to heal by gently feeling what once felt unbearable. Through breath and tenderness, fear becomes the path that leads you home to yourself. Let's explore how we retreat with the Four Rs.

Resistance: The Hesitation Before the Doorway

Resistance says, *I can't*. It can manifest as fatigue, distraction, endless preparation, overthinking, or an inner voice repeating *not now*. Beneath resistance often lies fear of change and the uncertainty of who we will become when the old story ends. Resistance is the pause before the threshold, the instinct to stay put when something new begins to stir. Beneath every form of resistance is fear: fear of change, of loss, of stepping into unfamiliar territory, of failure. In its healthy form resistance is the body's way of saying, *please move slowly, be safe*. When it keeps us from our healing paths, however, it becomes a barrier that we need to recognize and then gently remove.

The first step is to notice how resistance manifests within you. Then, when you feel resistance arise, rather than forcing it aside, bring curiosity. Notice its texture. Is it heaviness in the limbs, a fog in the mind, a sudden urge to tidy the house or make tea? Each manifestation carries a message that we can become aware of with curiosity.

If you sense resistance, pause and breathe into your belly. Whisper: *It's okay to take one small step*. Then do something simple: light the candle, open your journal and write, place a hand on your heart and breath. Each small act teaches your nervous system that movement is safe. Over time, resistance softens into readiness. What once felt like a wall becomes a doorway that opens of its own accord. Resistance cannot be overcome by willpower; it must be listened to and respected. When you offer it respect, it reveals its hidden gift, the wisdom of timing.

Regression: The Child Who Still Resides Within

Regression says, *I won't*, pulling us backward into the wounded child's narrative: *I'm not ready; it's too hard*. These echoes reveal the parts of us still longing for reassurance. Regression is the echo of earlier fear when emotion felt too large for a small body to hold. It pulls you backward into younger states of being, the little one who freezes, hides, or pleases to survive. You may hear her voice whispering, *I'm not ready. It's too much. Please don't make me*.

It is best not to judge regression as weakness. Instead, think of it as a memory arising through sensation asking to be met in the present. The nervous system, loyal to what once kept you safe, momentarily forgets that you have grown.

When regression appears, do not argue with it. Meet it as you would a trembling child. Soften your shoulders. Bring a hand to your heart. Feel the warmth of your palm as reassurance. Whisper, *I'm here now. You are not alone. We can do this together.* The moment you choose to stay with and recognize a regressed state within you, courage begins to bloom. The adult self and the child self can then begin to breathe together again, weaving trust where there was once separation. In this tender meeting, the spiral turns once more. You discover that the wounded child within is not lost, nor is she in charge; she has been waiting for your simple recognition.

Repression: The Hidden Truth Beneath the Skin

Repression is the art of hiding our own feelings from ourselves. It often occurs unintentionally, as an ancient instinct of self-protection. When we learned that crying led to punishment, or that anger caused love to be withdrawn, we buried those feelings deep within the body. We locked them in our hearts, where they could not be seen or felt.

But nothing buried ever truly remains hidden. What is pressed down eventually manifests as physical or psychological symptoms, such as fatigue, anxiety, or illness. The body remembers everything, and what it cannot speak, it stores and eventually acts out. Repression is the body's prayer for safety; it whispers, *I will carry what you cannot bear to feel.*

The Healer within meets repression with gentle empathy. When you notice tension, exhaustion, or numbness in the body, place a hand over your heart with care. Breathe warmth into it. Name the sensation as you hold it gently. Practicing the sacred pause and mini self-inquiry that we will explore later in this chapter, over time will allow the repressed emotions to release in manageable increments.

In time, the body begins to gently release what it has silently carried for you. Tears come without story. Shivers move through like small storms. The dam softens and feeling returns. This is a release into the natural fluidity that we all long for. Repression becomes expression, the body remembering its song.

Reaction: The Fire That Wants to Be Seen

Reaction is the outward expression of unprocessed emotion. Like sparks from a campfire landing in dry grass on a windy day, it spreads quickly and without restraint. When feeling becomes too much to contain, we project it outward. Reaction is emotion seeking contact, aching to be witnessed.

When we react, we hand the power of our inner world over to our outer world and those in it. Someone else's tone, gesture, or absence becomes the match to ignite a waiting flame. Our periphery mind and its narratives take over, and we lose connection to the truth of our experience. For our healing journey, it is important to recognize that beneath every reaction lives a feeling that longs to be embodied so that it can be set free.

Working with our reactivity takes patience and honesty. We must learn to pause in the heat of the moment. Feel where the energy lives in our body. The jaw, the chest, the gut. Name the emotion softly: *This is anger. This is grief. This is fear.* Breathe. Let it move without directing it outward toward others. The flame that once burned destructively now has the potential to become a light of awareness, empathy, respect.

With practice, reaction turns to response when the heart takes the reins. You begin to see that anger can protect without harming, that grief can open without drowning, that passion can serve creation rather than be destructive.

As the Healer teaches, nothing in you is wrong. Every reaction is a messenger seeking its right place in the weave of your life. When met with breath and presence, this fire becomes empowerment.

Integration: The Courage to Stay

The Four R's we use to avoid feeling—Resist, Regress, Repress, React—mark the outer edges of the spiral of our healing baskets, and land in our periphery minds as truth. Each is a reflex born from love and the will to survive. As we bring awareness to them, they soften into their higher incarnations—Recognize, Release, Reweave, and Respond—allowing us to follow the spiral back inward toward our sacred centers.

This is the alchemy of healing: turning defense into devotion, survival into song. The very forces that once protected us become the weavers of our wholeness.

Every time you pause instead of resist, breathe into a feeling instead of repress it, stay with a strong emotional energy instead of regress, or take responsibility for your feelings instead of reacting, the healing basket of your being tightens and strengthens.

Fear, resistance, regression, repression, and reaction are not an obstacles on the path, they *are* the path we must walk to move from the head to the heart. Each carries a fragment of instinct, a guardian of timing and care and each should be treated with respect, honored for their roles in trying to keep you safe, so that they can be released.

When we meet them with awareness and empathy, they begin to reveal their deeper purpose. Resistance softens into readiness. Regression transforms into reunion with the inner child. Repression melts into release. Reaction turns into response. Each movement is a turning of the spiral back inward, and our mother ache and its contraction gives way to the fluidity that healing requires.

To stay present through these thresholds is to remember that safety is to stay with fear by harnessing empathy and courage. Healing does not ask you to transcend your humanness; it asks you to inhabit it fully. Every tremor, every pause, every breath that chooses staying over fleeing is an act of courage.

This is how courage matures, through the willingness to remain in small moments. Baby steps. The simple willingness to keep breathing. To keep feeling. To keep returning to the heart's steady rhythm that says, *I am here, now.*

Empathy Requires Attunement

To stay present through these thresholds requires attunement, which is the true foundation of empathy. It is the art of meeting your inner world at the same frequency with which it appears, just as you would naturally shift your tone when meeting a child, a friend, or a teacher. We attune to others instinctively, yet we often forget to offer this same presence to ourselves. Attunement is resonance. It is the way we meet our own feelings, sensations, and patterns at the same frequency, with the quality they are asking for: gentleness for fear, steadiness for grief, spaciousness for confusion, warmth for shame, rather than a different frequency such as rejection or dismissal. When we respond to our inner world with the same courtesy that we offer those we meet in our outer world, something begins to soften.

This is the Healer's way. She listens with empathy, presence. She meets anger with understanding, sorrow with warmth, numbness with patience, and fear with a steady hand. Empathy becomes possible only through this kind of attunement, this willingness to match the energetic signature of what is arising rather than trying to override it. Attunement restores coherence inside us; it brings the scattered pieces of our inner world into relationship again. As you learn to attune to yourself in this way, empathy stops being something you try to do. It becomes a natural extension of how you exist in your own presence.

Empathy Starts Within

As we reconnect and attune with our emotions, empathy begins to unfold naturally, just like water returning to its source. True empathy arises only when we are connected to our heart centers, our emotions. When the heart is closed, gestures of care become performance rather than presence. Many of us were taught this false empathy early on: *Don't cry. Be nice. Say you're sorry.* Such corrections trained us to manage emotions instead of feeling them, to perform kindness rather than embody compassion.

Real empathy begins in the body, in the tender willingness to stay with our own experience. When we meet our sadness, anger, fear, disgust, excitement without judgment, the heart relearns its own language. From this space, it begins to recognize the same notes in another.

When someone shares their pain, notice what stirs within you. Can you breathe with their sorrow while remaining anchored in your own? Can you feel-with rather than feel-for? This is the Healer's art of empathy, presence without merging, compassion without rescue.

Every act of internal empathy becomes a strand in the upper weave of your healing basket. The more you soften toward yourself, the more strength you have to hold others. This is how the heart matures, through honest feeling, rooted awareness, and the courage to stay open in the presence of what hurts and what heals alike. You cannot have genuine empathy for others without first having genuine empathy for yourself.

Feeling What Was Never Safe to Feel

At the top of the basket, we meet strands that may feel both fragile and sticky: the emotional bonds we formed with our mothers and the mother ache. From birth, we are wired to seek safety and connection with our mothers. When that connection felt uncertain, we adapted by mirroring moods, anticipating needs, and hiding parts of ourselves to preserve love.

This adaptation writes an inner loyalty script: If I feel anger, she might leave. If I cry, I'll lose love. The heart learns to censor and comply. As adults, we may apologize excessively, suppress emotion, or feel guilty for wanting what we need.

It's important to remember that this loyalty is not only personal to each of us and our relationship with our mother. This loyalty is also a part of our ancestral maternal lineage. Generations of women have suppressed emotion to maintain bonds and survive. This thread of adaptation flows through the maternal lineage, shaping what it means to be a daughter.

Healing asks us to untangle survival-based loyalty from genuine love. Feeling anger or sadness toward your mother does not betray her; it honors truth, and in that truth, we can access a more honest love. When we allow our true emotions to flow, we strengthen empathy for ourselves, for our mothers, and all who came before.

Ask yourself, which feelings did you hide from your mother? Anger, grief, excitement, fear, joy, desire? These hidden emotions carry an echo into our adult lives. They may appear in subtle ways: in the Four R's we explored above, and other ways such as holding back the truth, over-accommodating, or dimming enthusiasm. These are traces of the paths walked by our ancestors for survival. Awareness and empathy enable us to release them and choose new, more nurturing paths for ourselves.

As awareness deepens, empathy begins to weave itself back through the lineage. When you revisit your mother's story, you may begin to see the tender logic of her defenses and how her own childhood, fears, and cultural inheritance shaped the ways she could or could not feel her emotions. This seeing does not erase the pain. It simply makes space for both truths to coexist. She mothered you based on her experiences and the choices that ensued as a result, and you feel what you feel based on your experience of her as her daughter.

Each act of empathy toward yourself, your mother, and the women before you is a strand you can consciously weave into your own healing basket. This is our inner Healer's work: to gather what has been torn through time and rejoin it in the heart's basket. As you soften into this wider love, you start to sense that the ache itself was never against you. It was guiding you home to the wholeness that holds both ache and love as one.

Relating to Your Mother in the Present

Empathy invites relationship with what is real, not what we wish were true. By now, you have gathered your story and held it through the many lenses of your adult self. Your basket is strong enough to hold the truth: you cannot change your mother, but you can change how you relate to her.

Empathy softens the ache until discernment can arise. It teaches you when to open, when to hold steady, and when to step back. For some, this means creating clearer boundaries. For others, it may mean distance or simply a new kind of listening. Some find they can stay in connection without being consumed, standing before their mother and remembering: *I am me, and I am not responsible for her.*

Empathy does not erase pain or excuse harm. It widens the heart to include both her wounds and yours, allowing love to breathe between truth and acceptance.

Each encounter becomes a lesson to practice what we have been exploring in each chapter:

Awareness to meet the moment as it presents.
Curiosity to stay open without abandoning yourself.
Honesty to speak what is true.
Trust to stay rooted in your inner knowing.
Acceptance to honor who she is and who you are.
Connection to stay anchored in the body.
Empathy to hold what still aches with tenderness.

This is how the Healer works. She meets the moment as it is, weaving truth and love together, one breath at a time.

Common Detours on the Path of Empathy

As you open your heart and begin to meet your mother as she is you might be reminded that healing does not unfold in straight lines. The heart learns through opening, contracting, and softening again. When you notice yourself moving too quickly to forgive, tending to others before yourself, or rising into perceptions instead of feeling, pause. These are not missteps; they are invitations.

Every detour carries the trace of an old vow to stay safe, a part of you that once believed feeling was too much to bear. Now, with the steadiness you've cultivated, you can meet these patterns as guides, each one leading you back toward the pulse of self-empathy that is becoming your new rhythm. Some of the detours I have experienced in myself and those I work with are:

Premature Forgiveness

The idea of forgiveness can be very satisfying but when offered too soon, it becomes a shield against pain. We may rush to forgive to rise above our anger or grief, believing serenity is more spiritual than sorrow. Yet true forgiveness grows from feeling, not from fleeing from it. Before you forgive, let the ache speak. Let anger burn clean. Let tears fall. Wholeness is born from honesty. Forgiveness arises naturally, when your heart is ready to release.

Spiritual Bypassing

Sometimes we use spiritual ideas to avoid emotional truth by telling ourselves, *It's all perfectly in God's plan,* or *I chose this lesson*. While such words can hold wisdom, they can also minimize the feelings that need our care. Healing asks us to descend, not ascend. To find the sacred within the body, in the pulse of the heart, in the tears that finally flow.

Turning Empathy Outward First

It is often easier to feel compassion for others rather than for yourself. Especially for daughters shaped by caretaking, empathy flows outward by habit. But empathy that excludes you is incomplete. Each time you feel empathy toward another be sure to make sure you are also aware of what you are feeling, what you might need. The heart grows whole by circling inward.

Mistaking Insight for Feeling

Insight can illuminate the path, but it cannot replace embodiment. You might think, *I understand why she did that,* while your body still trembles. Insight is the mind's balm; feeling is the heart's true north. Let both have their place, but do not let insight become armor against the truth of emotion.

Each detour, when met with compassion, becomes a doorway home. When you notice one, breathe. Place a hand on your heart and whisper softly, *I'm here*. The path of empathy is about returning again and again to the living center of love that can hold it all.

A Living Example: Reweaving Connection with My Mother

To bring this teaching into lived experience, I want to share a personal story from my own journey of reconnecting with my mother. I mentioned earlier in this book that there was a time when I chose to have no contact with her for several years. When I felt ready, I finally reached out, and our first meeting took place in the presence of an elder therapist I had been working with. My mother came willingly. I could feel both her love and her pain, both her longing to be close and the hurt of having been cut off for such a long time.

In that space, I told her the truth: that her hurtful remarks had become too painful for me to keep absorbing. That her early abandonment of me had caused me great pain and deeply affected me. That her inability to parent me as a teen had been another equally painful abandonment. She listened quietly, then apologized with sincerity. "I know," she said. "I can't believe some of the things I said. I can't believe I abandoned you when you were so young. I wish I would have been more there for you as a teenager."

I accepted her apology and felt its sincerity with all of my heart. Together we created a new agreement. I told her I didn't need her to rescue or correct me—a gentle way of naming her fear-based reactions—but that what I most needed was her unconditional love and friendship. Somehow, she understood. I think it came as a relief. She was released from the burden of false responsibility for me and could simply love and be loved. It became a new kind of contract: one unburdened by the past and spacious enough for both of us to breathe.

Now, more than fifteen years later, we have kept that agreement. Our relationship is close and easy. We share lunches, browse thrift stores, and laugh together often. Since our religious and political views differ, we've agreed to honor those differences by keeping a clear boundary, a no-fly zone. Recently, when she began to speak about politics, I smiled and said softly, "Let's not go there." She nodded, and we returned to enjoying our lunch together.

Today, at eighty, my mother is a bright spirit who is warm, generous, and steadfast in her Christian faith. I'm grateful for the woman she is and for the relationship we've woven together, one based on honesty and the joy of simply being with each other.

And I love her. I have always loved her. I will always love her. It is woven into my being like a fiber, and no matter how much ache I have carried through her as my mother, that love remains an intrinsic part of me. I am grateful for it.

Your path with your mother will look different. What matters is not the form it takes, but the clarity, compassion, and courage with which you walk it. Empathy and boundaries can coexist. Together, they make love sustainable.

Reconnecting Through Feeling

"The Sacred Pause is a moment of remembering—remembering to be here, to be kind, to be free."

—Tara Brach

As we have learned throughout this chapter, the Healer teaches empathy through embodiment. She reminds us that wholeness is the willingness to stay present with pain. We strengthen our heart centers by encouraging this fluidity that teaches us to stay open. With this openness we find that we become supple enough to bend without breaking.

To reclaim the heart's intelligence, we practice pausing, sensing, and naming what arises. Relearning to feel safely requires both gentleness and structure. The Sacred Pause, as taught by Tara Brach in *Radical Acceptance*,[33] provides just such a container, a simple meditative practice that invites our emotions to be seen and felt. I read this book just a year ago for the first time, and I was so moved by it that I invited a group of women friends

33 Tara Brach, *Radical Acceptance: Embracing Your Life with the Heart of a Buddha* (New York: Bantam, 2003).

to explore its teachings together. Ever since, the Sacred Pause has been one of my most treasured daily weaving practices.

Experiential Invitation: The Sacred Pause

This mini meditation requires only a few minutes to complete and can be done anywhere. Sit comfortably and breathe slowly, softening your belly. Bring awareness to the body. What sensations are here: warmth, pressure, fluttering, or heaviness? Now think of a situation that is up for you, perhaps a troubling interaction at work or with a loved one, one of the four Rs we explored, or perhaps something related to your mother.

Ask inwardly, *What is here?*

If a perception arises, such as, *I feel rejected*, look beneath it. As we practiced above, rejection is a perception; the feeling underneath might be sadness or fear. Name it gently: *This is sadness. This is anger.*

Stay with it. Breathe. As you do so it will move through. As the emotion flows, notice how it shifts, softens, and releases, like water returning to its source. If the mind insists on its story, whisper inwardly, *I hear you, beloved mind. You feel betrayed. This is your way of naming sadness.* Treat whatever arises with honesty, without needing to change it.

Each pause loosens the knots of suppression and releases the life-force energy that was once trapped in holding these feelings. That same energy becomes available again for creativity, connection, and love.

The Sacred Pause is a rhythm and a form of presence that deepens with each remembrance. To bring this meditative practice into your life, start small. Choose one or two times each day to pause for just a few minutes. You might practice while waiting for the kettle to boil in the morning, before turning on your phone, or as you transition from one activity to another. Practice it as you shift from your desk to household tasks, before leaving the house, or before stepping into the next moment of your day.

Over time, the pause will guide you to remember the language of your heart center and allow it to flow naturally. Each time you practice a Sacred Pause think of it as a promise to yourself and a vow to approach life authentically. This creates a path toward emotional truth and to the intelligence flowing through your heart center. Healing unfolds naturally through these simple moments because in so doing we allow the fluidity of feeling to emerge and release, rather than stagnate within.

The Alchemy of Self Inquiry

"Being cut off from our own natural self-compassion is one of the greatest impairments we can suffer. Along with our ability to feel our own pain go our best hopes for healing, dignity, and love. What seems non-adaptive and self-harming in the present was, at some point in our lives, an adaptation to help us endure what we then had to go through.....Hence the need for compassionate self-inquiry."

—Gabor Maté

In practicing the Sacred Pause, we begin to meet our inner experience with greater curiosity and tenderness. Over the years, one of the most transformative ways I've learned to deepen this meeting is through compassionate self-inquiry. My own path has been shaped by many forms of inquiry, from early Satori work to intensive group processes rooted in supported self-inquiry, and most recently through my completion of Gabor Maté and Sat Dharam Kaur's year-long Compassionate Inquiry® professional training program for therapists. Each of these traditions, in its own way, taught me that healing happens when we turn toward our experience with presence and honesty through genuine self-inquiry.

Self-inquiry builds naturally on the Sacred Pause. Whereas the Sacred Pause helps us notice what is happening *right now*, self-inquiry gently guides us toward the past where the root of the emotion lives.

Like all deep work, the process begins in the body. We start by following sensation, just as we did in Chapter Five with the felt sense, and in this chapter with the Sacred Pause. Sensation becomes a trail of breadcrumbs, leading us toward the tender places that once felt too overwhelming.

From here, if we feel grounded and resourced, we move into the heart of inquiry through soft, spacious questions that allow us to trace our experiences back to where the initial pain occurred. We ask:

How far back does this sensation go?
When did I first feel this?
What was happening around me?
What did I come to believe about myself in that moment?
How has this early meaning tried to protect me?

What does this younger part of me need now?

These questions are not meant to analyze or fix. They are invitations, ways of listening beneath the surface to the emotional truths that shaped us. We follow the body's innate intelligence with curiosity.

When practiced slowly and with attunement, self-inquiry becomes healing in motion. The early meanings that once confined us begin to loosen. The old narratives that kept us small start to soften. And the younger self we meet, frightened, lonely, trying so hard to be good, finally has the chance to be held with understanding rather than shame.

Self-inquiry allows us to reclaim the moments where we lost ourselves. It is a path of returning, one gentle truth at a time.

Meeting the Ache Beneath *I Have to Be Good*

During a recent guided session, I sat with a woman as she gently explored the layers of her mother ache. She spoke of a tightness in her chest that felt like a small, unyielding fist clenched whenever she made a mistake or feared she had disappointed someone.

"It's like a knot," she said. "It's been there forever."

We began by returning to the body. I invited her to place a hand over her heart and feel the breath moving beneath it. "Let's stay here," I said. "Just notice what wants your attention."

After a few breaths, I asked, "If this knot, could speak, what might it say?"

She hesitated, then whispered, "I'm scared... scared I did something wrong."

"What might happen if you were wrong?"

Her breath caught. "I won't be loved."

We stayed there with no analysis, no fixing. Only listening. The body already knew her fear, her sadness. Her tears came without effort, naturally. After some time, I asked her:

"Can we ask how old this part of you is?"

She nodded and it was as if she already knew. "Five," she said. "I'm sitting at the kitchen table, coloring, trying so hard to stay inside the lines."

"What did staying inside the lines mean to you when you were five?"

"I just wanted my mom to smile and notice me, praise me."

More tears slipped down her cheek as she sat with this understanding of what she truly needed at five in her childhood kitchen with her mother.

I then asked, "What did you believe about yourself that made staying in the lines so important to you?"

"That I have to be perfect... that if I make a mistake, I won't be loved."

"That's such a heavy belief for a little girl to carry," I said.

"Yes," she whispered.

After a pause to let this truth really sink in, I invited her to speak directly to that small, vulnerable child within, "What would you say to her now?"

"You don't have to be perfect to be loved. It's okay to color outside the lines," she responded immediately.

I watched as her shoulders softened. A long sigh escaped, as her entire being relaxed on its own. The knot that felt like a fist in her chest slowly unfurled.

At the end of the session, she smiled through wet eyes. "I've spent my whole life coloring inside the lines," she said. "Now I want to use every color and no lines at all."

This is the essence of self-inquiry work. We do not analyze the ache; we listen to it. We let the body guide us to the moment *where the story began*. Through presence and compassion, the belief loosens its hold, we feel the hurt we buried within as a moment of truth, and our hearts open to the love that is our intrinsic nature.

Experiential Invitation: Self-Inquiry

Set aside thirty to sixty minutes in a quiet, safe space. Ground yourself: one hand on your navel, the other on your heart. Feel the breath moving between them, weaving your inner connection. This practice is similar to the Sacred Pause you've already learned, but it adds a new element: tracing sensation back in time to when it was first felt.

Just like in the Sacred Pause, think of a troubling situation. Start with your body. Notice where your attention goes, perhaps you sense a tight chest, a tight belly, or a heavy heart. Stay with the sensation.

Name what's here. Gently ask: What emotion is present? Is it fear, sadness, or shame? Let the truth come up naturally.

Trace it back. If you're steady, ask: How far back does this go? Let your body show you. Maybe an image, a memory, or a particular age comes up.

Show compassion. Imagine your younger self who had this experience. What does she need to hear? Whisper softly: *I see you. You are safe now. You are good*. Hold her. Comfort her. Let her be seen and held with your love, as an adult now.

If a memory feels too painful to maintain self-regulation, or you have a hard time connecting to that part of you that had this experience as a child, you can also experiment by picturing a small child of a similar age experiencing the same thing you are remembering, and see if you can offer her the comfort you needed at that age. If even this is too much, let go of this exercise and return to your grounding posture of safety or soft-belly breathing, as we learned in Chapter One. Remember, each small insight into the early experiences that shaped you strengthens the rim of your basket, the container that holds your becoming. If you feel called to explore this work more deeply, you may also find it supportive to do so with a trusted, trauma-informed practitioner.

This slow weaving of self-inquiry becomes easier to understand when seen in lived experience. The story that follows invites you to witness a woman who learned to soften perfection's grip and meet herself with presence.

Mother Ache Healing in the World:

The Girl Who Tried to Get It Right

Annie grew up inside a childhood that felt half-missing. When she asks her family what she was like as a baby, the answer is silence. No stories, no photographs, only a single comment from her grandmother: "You were a beautiful baby, and your mother was a great mom."

What she remembers instead are fragments. A shy woman in the kitchen. A brief moment of warmth when she rode her bike through wet cement and came home sure she was in big trouble. Her mother held her then. It was the first time Annie remembers being comforted.

When she was ten, her parents divorced. What followed were ruptures that left deep imprints on her young nervous system. Her mother, lost in grief and fear, took Annie and a brother across state lines. Weeks later, detectives arrived in the night and brought them back to their father. Annie learned early that life could be upended without warning.

She returned to her mother again in middle school, wanting to support her, parent her. But the home she stepped into was shaped by drinking, sadness, and collapse. By eighth grade, she knew she needed to go back to her father. Soon after, her mother became ill with cancer. By Annie's first year of college, she was gone. What remained was a longing that had nowhere to land.

Her mother had carried her own ache. As a Finnish immigrant raised by a cold, withdrawn mother who punished her by locking her in a dark closet, she learned to survive through blame, bitterness, and collapse. Annie inherited the imprint without the story behind it. She only knew the feeling of absence created by her mother's unhealed trauma.

To cope, Annie adopted the energetic pattern of reaching. Praise was rare, yet she kept striving. When her father teased her about her weight in eighth grade, something tightened inside her. Thinness became proof of worth. Control became a path toward love. The voice in her head told her she was stupid and never enough. It followed her into adulthood like a shadow.

Healing bloomed slowly. Therapy with an attuned woman therapist helped her learn to speak her truth. Writing, art, and journaling gave shape to feelings that had lived wordlessly in her body. A women's group helped her stay connected even when shame told her to withdraw.

When Annie first came to work with me, her focus was not on her mother. She spoke instead about self-esteem struggles, patterns with food, and a persistent sense of insecurity in her relationships with other women. As our inquiry deepened through somatic listening and imaginal work it became clear that these threads all led back to the mother ache.

Hence as we worked together our focus became gentleness. She had spent a lifetime trying to earn love through improvement and perfection. In our work, she began to meet herself with presence instead of pressure. She practiced placing a hand on her heart and greeting the frightened young inner child with empathy rather than criticism. She learned to listen inwardly with patience instead of judgment. Slowly she was able to release suppressed feelings that she had held for years to avoid overwhelm.

A consistent daily yoga practice deepened this shift. Her body that had once been a battleground became a place of belonging. Sweat, breath, and movement softened the hard edges inside her. Prayer and motherhood added their own medicine. Through caring for her three children with tenderness, she learned to offer that same tenderness to the places in her that still felt small and scared.

Today, Annie understands that healing does not come from getting it right. It comes from staying present with herself. The young girl who longed for approval is learning to trust that she is already lovable. Her journey is a reminder that healing begins with the willingness to sit with our own ache and extend compassion inward, one breath at a time.

Journal Reflections: Reweaving Empathy

Empathy Toward Our Mothers

Which emotions did I learn to hide from my mother, and why?
How do those patterns still echo in my relationships today?
What might it feel like to express these emotions now, safely and fully?
What shaped my mother's capacity to feel her own emotions?
Where can I hold empathy for her without abandoning my own truth?
How do I sense the lineage of both ache and love moving through us?

Meeting Your Mother as She Is

What arises in me when I bring my mother to mind as she is today?
How do my boundaries create space for greater self-empathy?
In what ways might empathy for my mother shift how I relate to her now?
What does it mean to honor her as she is while remaining faithful to myself?

Perception and Feeling

How do I most often confuse a perception with a feeling?
What changes in me when I pause to ask, *What is the emotion beneath this perception?*
How does my body help me discern the truth of what I feel?

The Four R's of Emotional Alchemy

When do I notice resistance in my life, and what does it feel like in my body?
How does regression show itself in me: what voice, what age, what need appears?
Where does repression live in me, and how does my body hold what has remained unspoken?
When do I find myself reacting rather than responding, and what feeling lies beneath the reaction?
Which of the new R's—recognize, release, reweave, or respond—feels most natural right now, and which one needs more tending?
How might I bring gentleness to each of these movements, welcoming them as guides rather than faults?
In what ways can I practice the courage to stay with my feelings honestly, allowing them to be seen and felt?

The Sacred Pause and The Alchemy of Self-Inquiry

What sensation in my body most often signals the beginning of a deeper truth?
When I trace a current emotion back to its origin, what early moment or memory arises?
What early meaning formed in that moment, and how has it tried to protect me?
What does the younger part of me need now in order to soften, rest, or feel seen?
How does practicing inquiry change the way I relate to my emotions today?

Annie's Story

Are you aware of any parallels between her patterns and your own?
Do you sense echoes of her longing for reassurance, her striving for worth, or her search for a place that feels safe?
How do you feel toward her as you hold her experience? Warmth, sorrow, recognition, or distance?

Conclusion: Feeling is the Healing

This chapter invited you to rediscover the art of feeling. You traced how perception veils raw emotion, and how empathy begins by turning inward. You explored the ways we avoid our emotions through the Four Rs, and you deepened your understanding of the mother ache, how loyalty and fear muted your truth; and learned to see that these patterns were expressions of your natural longing for true feeling, for empathy.

Through empathy, the Healer within you has been weaving the upper rim of your basket. Each emotion you've reclaimed, including anger, grief, fear, desire, joy, disgust, and excitement, now becomes part of the pattern. What once felt like scattered fragments is now being gathered, softened, and re-woven into coherence. You are relearning how to let emotion flow, to accept what arises and feel it fully. This is the language of the heart, the way the body remembers love. In feeling, there is healing.

"I've learned that whenever I decide something with an open heart, I usually make the right decision."

—Maya Angelo

Part III:
The Alchemy of Presence

In Part II, you have woven your healing basket from base to rim with your intrinsic qualities of acceptance, connection, understanding, and empathy. Each woven strand has taught you how to stay with what is true.

Healing is not a straight line. Some days the weave feels tight and coherent; other days it loosens or unravels in your hands. Yet no strand is ever wasted. Every return deepens presence. The spiral always continues. The basket you weave is your life. Each time you return to the Maiden, the Seeker, the Weaver, or the Healer within, the pattern strengthens. Trust the rhythm. Trust the spiral. Strand by strand, you are remembering how to hold your own life, your own self with love.

Now we begin the work of finishing our healing baskets through the sacred art of transformation. Our baskets must now be sealed. In the chapters to come, we enter the alchemy of transformation where the ache turns to gold. The Alchemist, the Mystic, the Wild Woman, and the Priestess will walk beside you as the sacred fire encourages your journey toward wholeness.

The Alchemist arrives first, binding the rim and drawing in the loose strands. The healing shape is tied off. This is the moment when ache becomes medicine, when pain ripens into wisdom. What once felt like an endless ache begins to ease.

Then comes the Mystic, her touch softening the edges, trimming the roughness, and burnishing the weave with beeswax until it glows. Here, compassion flows. Nothing sharp remains to cut the hand or heart.

Next, the Wild Woman appears, tempering the fibers in the sun. She marks the rim with ash and earth, reminding us that wholeness is inclusive and inherent to us. Her work ensures that the basket holds every strand of our beings.

At last, the Priestess steps forward. She consecrates the vessel, filling it with what gives life and releasing what no longer belongs. Her offering is reciprocity, an act of returning the gift of creation back to life itself. Through her, the circle closes and begins again.

In these final chapters, we meet these archetypes as living forces within us. They show that healing does not end when the weave is finished. It deepens as we bind, soften, temper, and offer. The basket becomes a whole vessel. So do we.

To complete this sacred work is to honor the lineage that wove us into being: the mothers, grandmothers, and foremothers whose hands shaped our becoming. As we finish our healing baskets, we take our place among them, adding our story to the timeless spiral of women who have turned ache into resilience, pain into wisdom, and love into offering.

Chapter Nine:

The Alchemist and the Four Phases of Feminine Transformation

"The archetypal qualities of the Alchemist reveal her to be a mistress of transformation: she's not afraid to burn things back to the bare bones to expose what lies beneath. She's both a visionary and a catalyst for the irreversible changes she conjures into being; in effect, she reimagines, and so recreates, the world."

–Sharon Blackie

The Mother Ache as Base Material

Every transformation starts with something raw and unrefined. For the alchemists, that material was lead. For us, it is ache. The mother ache is the base metal of our lineage, heavy with hurt and longing. It holds both the wound and the wisdom of our maternal line; the sorrow of what was not given; and the fierce love that still seeks a way to flow freely.

We inherit our mothers' stories and their unwept tears, suppressed voices, and unspoken dreams. Our materials for transformation are imperfect and alive. They are the substance through which our wholeness is shaped. The

Alchemist knows that what feels most resistant often holds the greatest potential. The lead must be held to the fire before it can shine.

To bring the mother ache into the vessel of healing is to accept that pain and love are inseparable. They were woven together from the beginning. The same mother who hurt us also gave us life. The ache itself proves our capacity to love deeply; it is love that has not yet found its full expression.

When we turn toward the ache with awareness, we start the work of alchemy. The sacred center becomes the crucible. Breath turns into fire. Presence becomes the vessel. Each time we meet what aches instead of fleeing from it, something dense begins to soften. Each time we breathe into the trembling place, a trace of gold appears in the dark.

The mother ache asks us to remember that nothing is wasted. Even sorrow can be sacred. When we allow it to move through us with honesty and care, it reveals its hidden radiance. The alchemical fire refines. It purifies until what remains is essence: the simple truth of love, stripped of illusion and free to flow again.

The Inner Alchemy of Healing

When I first began writing this book, I did not know where the archetypes emerging would lead me. The Alchemist arrived early, but she remained mysterious. I imagined I might lean on Jung's stages of alchemical transformation, concepts I find meaningful and psychologically rich for my own integration work. For a time, I believed his framework would guide this chapter. But as I kept writing and listening, I realized something essential: the lineage of feminine alchemy does not belong to the masculine language of theory. It belongs to the body. It belongs to the hands. It belongs to the women who came before us.

The Alchemist I encountered as I wove the earlier chapters of this book was not Jung's Alchemist. She was my grandmother. She was the lineage keeper behind every woman who ever tended a wound, swept a hearth, gathered plants for medicine or weaving, or spoke her truth firmly. Her wisdom rose from the eternal ways women have always transformed sorrow into strength and woven brokenness into beauty. In the end, I understood that the alchemy needed here was not symbolic or esoteric. It was feminine, earthly, embodied, and unmistakably human.

As I wrote this book, I often found myself reflecting on the mystery of alchemy. Now, having completed my sixtieth turn around the sun, I feel my own inner Alchemist guiding my hands. Alchemy is no longer an idea for me, it is a lived experience that I practice. The fire that once felt frightening now, at times, feels like grace. I've learned to welcome it because I know that it burns away pretense and reveals what is essential. Writing these words has been its own alchemy: memory becoming meaning, ache becoming offering.

What follows is the Alchemist as I have come to know her through listening intuitively to the mysterious feminine energy that has helped me shape this book. My own inner Alchemist practices the alchemy that reveals itself in the body and in the heart, through intention, truth-telling, and the ache that continues to guide me on my own healing journey.

Inner alchemy is not something we learn; it is something we remember. Like the other inner qualities we have been exploring in this book, it is intrinsic to our very nature. Every woman is born an Alchemist, instinctively moving through cycles of transformation as she grows, loves, grieves, ages, sheds, awakens, and begins again. The only time this process falters is when our protective energy patterns from the past interrupt our natural unfolding. When we live our lives through these old inner patterns, disconnected from our own wiser knowing, our alchemy becomes like a few coals smoldering in a cold hearth, still there but waiting to be tended. When our inner alchemy is smoldering like this, we may gather our materials, but we cannot soften them; we feel the ache that calls for healing, but we cannot transform it. Inner alchemy occurs when we rekindle our inner fire with our healing intentions. When we allow our intention to guide us onto our own healing path and we walk it, the coals that once smoldered within begin to glow again. This is our potential reawakening, the seed we planted blossoming into the radiance of the Alchemist within.

Meeting the Ancient Women of Alchemy

"Alchemy is the Mother of Medicine."

—Prana Gogia

Throughout history, the feminine Alchemist was never a figure removed from earthly life. She did not sit in towers or laboratories. She lived at the center of the village. Her magic was woven into the ordinary, a pot of soup simmering over the hearth fire, herbs drying on rafters, children born by candlelight, grief tended kindly, with comforting touch.

Throughout history, her alchemy emerged subtly in the transformations of life itself: the shifts of the heart, the body, the seasons, and the soul. She was the woman others sought when something in their life was ready to change form; when an initiation was calling; when confusion tangled the mind; or when sorrow felt unmanageable. She appeared whenever the old ways trembled: when wisdom was threatened, when rituals lost their shape, when a lineage risked being swallowed by forgetfulness.[34]

People sought her out for many reasons, but they all shared a longing to be accompanied through transformation because they knew that she was able to listen for the pattern beneath the story, the thread of truth inside the ache. She guarded the ancient ways, the rituals, the wisdom, the magic woven beneath daily life; and tended them whenever they were threatened or forgotten.

She was not separate from the healer, the midwife, the seer, the herbalist, the weaver, or the keeper of ritual. She was any one of these, whichever the moment required. The feminine alchemist belonged to a lineage of women whose work was to accompany, translate, witness, and tend. Her gift was her capacity to see into the heart of things, to sense what wanted to be released, softened, shaped, or honored.

---

34 This archetypal understanding finds resonance in both historical and contemporary sources. In ancient Rome, the Vestal Virgins were entrusted with tending the sacred hearth fire, a role believed to safeguard the continuity and stability of the community during times of transition. In a wonderful, contemporary mythpoetic book, Sharon Blackie describes the alchemist as one face of the "medial woman," a liminal figure who stands between worlds, carrying wisdom that emerges when cultural forms are breaking down (*Hagitude*). These references are offered as echoes of a recurring human pattern rather than as a historical or theoretical claim. Sharon Blackie, *Hagitude: Reimagining the Second Half of Life* (London: September Publishing, 2016).

In this sense, the ancient feminine Alchemist was a threshold-keeper. She stood at the edges of birth and death, endings and beginnings, grief and renewal, belonging and selfhood. She held space for what our culture rushes past: the dissolving, the reshaping, the moments when the fire of inner truth melts old identities and allows new form to emerge.

In every village, there was a woman others turned to when life became too heavy to carry alone. In seeking the Alchemist, they were seeking a presence capable of holding the in-between, the liminal space where something is ending and something new has not yet formed. She knew how to stay with what others avoided. She trusted the process even when the person could not.

This is the work your inner Alchemist is now being asked to take up. Just as the ancient women held space for what was dissolving and what was about to emerge, you are being invited to accompany yourself through this same threshold. A threshold of cohesion. Our healing basket is almost whole. Its rim waits to be bound, which is the final act that keeps the entire weave from unraveling and brings all the work beneath it into cohesion.

Here, the Alchemist arrives, steady-handed, tending the inner fire of transformation. She knows that completion requires refining what has already been woven by binding the final fibers at the rim so the work does not unravel. Every strand she touches has already been tended with care; her task now is simply to secure the form that has been woven, protecting the integrity of the work so it can support the healing still to come.

Binding the rim is your work now as you invite your inner alchemist to join your healing journey. For us this is the moment when the ancient idea of alchemy shifts from story to embodiment, from myth to practice, from something women once did to something we are doing now.

The Alchemist binds the rim of the basket, the final gesture that brings the whole weave into cohesion. Gold light gathers around her fingers as the four phases—gathering, softening, shaping, and offering—rise within her as living possibilities. She knows that completion requires refinement. In this last binding, she honors both her inherited fibers and the ones she reshaped, each essential to the gold now woven through her hands.

The Four Phases of Feminine Alchemy

"Alchemy is not a ritual. It's a rebirth.
Not a trick. A truth.
You are not here to ascend away.
You are here to descend fully—
And transmute this life into light.
Be the Alchemist.
Burn it all.
Rise as gold."

—Yeshua Ben Yosef

All through this book, you have been practicing alchemy without naming it. Each time you turned toward your ache, each time you softened the body's defenses, each time you told the truth or reclaimed a lost part of yourself, you were already doing the ancient work of transformation. What we name here is a remembering of the craft that has been unfolding beneath every chapter you have worked through.

And, just as the basket weaver follows the natural arc of her craft, the feminine Alchemist guides us through the same four essential phases: gathering, softening, shaping, and offering. These are not linear steps. They are living processes, spiraling and deepening with every return. They form the foundation of your own inner alchemy. They are the fire within that fuels your capacity to meet your ache with presence, soften what has been guarded, shape your life with truth, and offer the wisdom that emerges back into your world.

The four phases that follow arise from this feminine understanding of alchemy: a way of naming the alchemy that women have carried for generations without ever calling it alchemy at all. If it supports your understanding, you may imagine these phases as mirroring the moon, the ancient companion of women's rhythms. Gathering echoes the New Moon: the beginning in darkness, when what is needed rises softly to the surface. Softening reflects the Waxing Crescent: a first illumination that reveals what wants to open. Shaping resonates with the Full Moon, the moment of clarity and emergence when truth stands bright. Offering aligns with the Waning Moon, the cycle of release and integration, when what has been transformed is returned to life as wisdom. Like the moon, you will return to each phase again and again. This is the art of inner alchemy. Let's explore.

Gathering—The Phase of Beginning

Traditional alchemists began by gathering the raw materials they would later try to transform, such as metals, minerals, salts. Our ancient village alchemist gathered her own materials such as wild plants for teas and remedies. And now, our inner Alchemist gathers still more delicate material, the lived texture of our own lives. She gathers our stories, our memories, the roots of our mother ache, so that nothing needed for our inner healing work is left behind.

In this phase, you are meeting your life in all its glorious, messy, wonder. And, the Children within you that you have recalled, the Innocent, Magical, and Wounded, have each been fueling the fire of our inner Alchemist. The Innocent brings her pure awareness. The Magical brings her innate curiosity. The Wounded brings her brave honesty about where it hurts. Throughout our journey together, we have asked them to help honestly gather what is real, sensing what wants to be collected, what stories still live in the body, and what patterns have been inherited from our mothers and grandmothers.

This gathering is the first phase of inner alchemy. Gathering is an act of awareness, wonder, and curiosity. It is the simple but powerful acknowledgment: *This is where I begin. This is what I have to make magic with.*

Not only have these children been practicing the art of inner alchemy within you they have also been cultivating an important alchemical tool within you as well. This quality is deep listening. It arises naturally through the awareness, curiosity, and honesty of the three children you have been remembering within. Deep listening is a soft and steady receptivity that allows truth to emerge in its own time.

The fire of transformation does not announce itself. It requires deep listening, revealing its secrets only when we slow down enough to hear them inside. Deep listening is a return to a more natural way of wisdom. With intention, it appears in meditation, in the breath, and in the ordinary moments of daily life. As you continue this work, you may begin to notice that listening becomes a way of being, a gentle attunement to your inner world that supports everything that follows. When we practice the qualities of awareness, curiosity, and honesty of these three young archetypes within us deep listening unfolds of its own accord.

Softening—The Phase of Opening

Fibers cannot be woven until they have been softened. The ancient alchemists tended the hearth, and in your own way, you tend the heart. Softening is the phase in which feeling is allowed to thaw and move again, so that your healing becomes real and embodied. This is something you have already begun in the preceding chapters, again without naming it as alchemy.

Throughout this journey, the Orphan within you has been slowly preparing you for this moment. She carries a teaching passed down from the Great Mother to the grandmothers who came before us: that every soul is entrusted with a portion of human pain, a strand of the collective story to heal. This entrustment is meant to be a rite of passage for you in this precious human life that you have been given. It is part of a greater cycle of evolution, part of your very soul's unfolding across lifetimes.

Alongside this entrustment comes an endowment: the inner capacity to meet what has been placed in your hands. You have been building this capacity step by step, breath by breath, as you learned to stay with yourself through earlier archetypes. Softening deepens when you recognize the truth of this teaching within yourself and turn toward the work that is yours to do. Here, the Orphan has guided you toward trust, the inner knowing that you have the capacity to walk this path.

As the Orphan opens the doorway for our softening, the Healer within steps forward, and we have been learning genuine empathy through her archetypal presence within: sitting beside what once overwhelmed you, allowing your heart to open so that you can feel your emotions and allow them to flow.[35] She reminds you how to feel what once you could not, name the emotions that lived unnamed for so long, and offer them to the inner fire where they can loosen, soften, and change form.

The Healer belongs to an ancient lineage of women who understood that emotion is a sacred element. They knew that tears are prayer, that trembling is a form of release, that ache finally felt in the heart is the sign of life stirring again. The Healer in you carries this memory. Her empathy is the warmth that allows softening to unfold from the inside with the assurance that nothing arising within you is beyond your capacity to meet.

Her work is simple and profound: to stay, to witness, to warm, and to let the ache speak until it is ready to change. Through her, the heart remembers how to soften without collapsing, how to open without losing itself, and how to let feeling become fuel for transformation.

Softening opens the inner space where transformation becomes possible. When the body trusts and the heart no longer hides, the fire you carry can reach what has been waiting for warmth. Softening is the threshold between surviving and becoming. It is the inner turning that prepares you for the next phase, where the shape of your life begins to shift from within.

---

35 You may be wondering about the difference between the Healer and the Alchemist, and it is subtle. The Healer tends what hurts, while the Alchemist shapes what is ready to evolve; their work interlaces so completely that they often feel like one presence guiding you toward wholeness.

Shaping—The Phase of Becoming

Once the fibers have softened, they can be shaped. This is where clarity enters and you begin to sense the difference between who you truly are and who you were conditioned to be. In this movement, you are not reinventing yourself; you are remembering yourself. The Seeker within you is also an alchemist that brings her growing inner connection to this work. Throughout our journey together, she has been learning to turn inward rather than outward and to trust the truth in her body. Her alchemy is the courage to stop seeking herself in the world around her and to discover the self that has been waiting within.

Alongside her, the Weaver of Life steps forward, practicing her alchemy by seeing the patterns of the mind as energy rather than identity. She understands the four protective energy patterns as energy movements she adopted in her outer world in order to survive. She notices the old narratives, the conditioned fears, the inherited roles and she helps you work with them alchemically, transforming them into clarity and choice.

This gentle reorientation is the third movement of inner alchemy. Shaping is an act of truth and self-regard. It is the steady inner knowing that says: *This is my authentic self. This is what I choose to carry forward. This is what I release*. In both weaving and alchemy, this is the moment of emergence, when the basket rises from the ground and the inner shape of your life begins to stand. The shaping fire burns away illusion, revealing what has always been true.

Offering—The Phase of Returning

Offering is the final phase of feminine alchemy, where your healing becomes reciprocity, a giving back to life from the fullness you have cultivated within. True reciprocity cannot be forced; it emerges from the steady inner ground shaped by meditation. All the work you have done, including the gathering, the softening, the shaping, has been a form of meditation. Healing arises through meditation because meditation allows the inner world to reorganize itself. It brings you back to the sacred center again and again until that center becomes the place from which you live.

Meditation is not limited to sitting quietly with your eyes closed. It is present in the way you breathe before you speak, in the pause that softens reactivity, and in the awareness that accompanies you through ordinary moments. It is the attention that returns you to your body and your breath. Meditation is the alchemist's key, the fire that warms the ache and the field in which transformation becomes possible. When you practice it regularly, even for brief moments, it begins to ripple through your life. It shapes how you listen, how you speak, and how you see yourself and others. This is why the phases we have explored are meaningful. They prepare you to carry meditation off the cushion and into your relationships, your choices, and your presence in the world. Through this steady returning to the sacred center, the archetypes that follow in the next chapters become embodied. Without meditation, they remain distant ideas. With meditation, they become lived expressions of your inner radiance.

We sit down to meditate not only to rest in stillness, but to learn how to meet life more fully when we rise again. Practice attunes us to the quiet intelligence moving through ordinary moments. It softens the mind's urgency and sharpens our capacity for wonder. In a world that constantly pulls attention outward, choosing stillness is a courageous devotion. And each time you return, something in you remembers how to listen.

Every alchemical process reaches a final fire, the flame that transforms what has reached completion into offering. In this phase, you allow the process to finish its cycle. Offering arises naturally when presence deepens. It is the way your healing begins to touch the world around you like a ripple in still water after a pebble has been tossed in. Offering is the threshold into the chapters ahead.

From here, the inner alchemist places the gold of your transformation into the hands of the archetypes who will guide the next stage of your journey. Each one carries a different expression of offering. The Mystic offers compassion as a way of seeing. She recognizes the humanity in all beings and allows your healing to expand outward as unconditional love. The Wild Woman offers wholeness by welcoming every part of you, including the tender, the fierce, and the forgotten. In doing so, she creates space for the wholeness of everyone you encounter. Her offering is the permission to be fully human and to allow others the same. The Priestess offers embodied presence. She carries the transformative fire that moves through generations, the kind of presence that restores balance and allows healing to travel far beyond your own life. Her offering is devotion expressed through embodied presence.

Together, these archetypes reveal the final phase of inner alchemy, which is the turning of your healing into medicine. Offering arises from a life lived close to its sacred center. It appears when the ache has been transformed into understanding and when your inner spaciousness becomes large enough to hold the experiences of others with clarity and care. It is the moment when you sense that what you have lived has shaped you and that you are ready to return its gold to the world.

Experiential Practice: Mirror Gazing

Mirror gazing is one of the oldest forms of feminine alchemy. Long before written teachings, women sat before still water and watched the face that looked back at them shift, soften, and reveal what lived beneath the surface. This practice invites you into the same terrain where identity loosens, truth emerges, and the fixed idea of who you are begins to dissolve.

Choose a quiet evening.

Sit in a darkened room with a single candle slightly off to the side, so only your face is illuminated, not the flame. Sit comfortably, spine steady, breath soft. Bring a mirror to eye level.

Gaze into your own eyes.

Do not blink if you can.

Let your gaze be steady, receptive, open.

Stay for forty minutes.

As you gaze, something subtle will begin to happen. Tears may arise from the intensity of the gaze. Let them come. Continue looking into your eyes without blinking or turning away.

Over time, your face may begin to shift.

You may see new expressions, new versions of yourself, flashes of faces you have worn and shed. You may see the child you once were, the elder you are becoming, the woman you have not yet lived into. You may see masks, the roles, the defenses, the inherited images, rise and fall across your features like smoke.

If you stay with the practice long enough, even your own face may begin to disappear. Do not be alarmed. This is the alchemy.

For the deepest experience, mirror gazing must be practiced over time. Eleven days, twenty-one days, or forty days will reveal the full arc of the meditation. The longer you remain in the ritual, the more fluid your sense of identity becomes. The mirror shows you what the mind forgets: that nothing in you is static. Not your face. Not your story.

After forty minutes, blow out the candle. Sit for a moment with the quiet that follows. Let the fluidity you witnessed remind you that transformation is not a departure from who you are. It is your nature.

I once practiced mirror gazing for forty days.[36] It was profound, strange, magical. The faces that appeared offered me an unexpected wisdom: that my sense of self is not a single, solid thing but a shifting constellation. What I call *me* is a river of moments, shapes, and possibilities. Seeing this in the mirror taught me something essential about the phases of my own becoming. The self I protect is only one small moment in a much larger, more fluid unfolding. Allow the mirror to be your teacher too.

There is another doorway through which many people encounter this dissolution of the fixed self. Like mirror gazing, it loosens the boundaries of identity and reveals the deeper movements of the inner world. For thousands of years, women have entered this doorway through sacred plants: tending, preparing, and working with them in ceremonial ways that supported healing, vision, and the rewriting of inner truth. Entheogens are one thread in the long feminine lineage of altered states, a lineage in which plants served as mirrors, and guides. They are not necessary for the alchemical work we are doing, yet they often illuminate the same truths we meet through meditation and presence. What follows is an exploration of how these ancient practices intersect with the transformation already unfolding within you.

The Fire That Teaches: The Alchemy of Entheogens and the Mother Ache

I want to honor one more path through which many people encounter these phases of inner alchemy. Some arrive at them through meditation and

36 I discovered this meditation in the following book and it appealed to my own inner Alchemist: *The Orange Book: The Meditation Techniques of Bhagwan Shree Rajneesh* (Pune: Rajneesh Foundation International, 1978).

presence, and others glimpse them through the altered states opened by psychedelics and entheogens. This work is about healing, and it would be incomplete without honoring the sacred medicines that have helped so many remember their wholeness. Sacred plant teachers and consciousness-expanding medicines have, for millennia, served as gateways to revelation, release, and communion with the divine. Medicines such as ayahuasca, huachuma and psilocybin still carry the songs of the mountains, forests, and deserts from which they originated. Today, new expressions of consciousness altering healing modalities are emerging, such as ketamine and MDMA-assisted psychotherapy, which are modern consciousness altering pharmaceuticals that promote healing. Organizations like MAPS are helping to advance these modalities, and many practitioners are learning to hold them with integrity.

Healing rarely arrives through reason or logic. Sometimes it appears as a dream, a prayer, a storm, or in the quiet of the forest. Sometimes it arrives through the opening of perception that these medicines provide. No matter how it arrives, the transformation occurs through softening the boundaries that once kept us separate from self-love and the living pulse of existence.

For many women, psychedelics and sacred consciousness-altering plant medicines, also called entheogens, have served as alchemical teachers, wise allies that bring to the surface what has been hidden within. These medicines can help to dissolve old defenses and release that which is not ours to carry. Yet true lasting transmutation doesn't happen during the medicine experience itself; it occurs afterward, in the integration. It resides in how we bind the rim of our basket with presence, humility, and care. A plant medicine ceremony may open the door, but integration requires us to cross the threshold and walk the path revealed. This is the essence of alchemy: to take what was dissolved in the fire of revelation and shape it into something strong enough to hold our healing.

The sacred plant medicines of South America, especially ayahuasca, have been profound teachers and allies in my journey. I encountered them when I was truly ready, when the call came from within me. Such readiness cannot be rushed; it comes from inner wisdom, the deep knowing that the heart is prepared to receive what will be revealed. Over the years, I have helped many women integrate their consciousness-altering experiences, and time and again, I have seen that real transformation depends on the readiness of the participant rather than the power of the substance imbibed. These experiences are not final destinations; they are doorways that open for us, hopefully only when the wiser self within is ready.

When women ask whether these medicines can help with the mother ache, I neither encourage nor discourage their use. Instead, I invite them to listen inwardly and trust their own inner wisdom. For those who feel the genuine call, these medicines can offer profound healing, especially in the realm of the mother-daughter bond and the ancestral feminine lineage. Ayahuasca (often referred to as Grandmother) in particular, carries a deep intelligence for mending these wounds, guiding us toward remembrance and reconciliation within the great web of the maternal line.

Like the Alchemist's fire, entheogens dissolve old structures of identity and allow new light to enter. Yet the Alchemist reminds us: the gold is not found in the flame itself. What is melted must cool and integrate into the whole. The true magic of these medicines lies not in what they show, but in how we live what they reveal. Without integration, their wisdom fades like smoke. With it, they strengthen the rim of the basket, sealing, shaping, and completing the vessel we have been weaving.

No medicine can attune you to yourself; only presence can. Entheogens may open doors, but they cannot walk you through them. Transformation is not in what you see; it's in how you stay with what you have seen.

For this reason, discernment is sacred. The container is just as important as the medicine. If you feel called, proceed slowly. Choose facilitators who are humble and ethical. Seek spaces that prioritize safety, preparation, and follow-through. Always listen to your own inner call, not the echo of someone else's story. Healing does not require entheogens. Breath, body, silence, nature, the meditations, and other self-exploration tools we have explored thus far in this book, are also medicines.

The Alchemist understands that when the rim of the basket feels fragile, fire can sometimes soften the weave enough to tighten it. She knows that the fire itself is never the point, the weaving is. If you choose this path, remember: the real alchemy is in your ability to stay present with what unfolds after the ceremony and to weave the vision into everyday life until pain becomes healing and vulnerability transforms into wholeness.

Entheogens are powerful. They can open long-closed doors and be an immense gift when experienced with safety and love. They can also be overwhelming without these. Always, in my experience, the true ceremony is how we live once the vision fades.

Held by the Mother Beneath All Mothers

The first time I drank ayahuasca, I wasn't seeking visions, healing, or ancestral contact. I simply followed an inner yes that surprised me as much as anyone. Months earlier, when a friend first mentioned the medicine, I had no interest at all. But on a flight home, I opened Isabel Allende's memoir to the page I'd left years before and found myself reading about her desire to reconnect with her maternal lineage, her *abuelas*, and her journey to South America to drink ayahuasca. Something in me recognized the call. It was unmistakable.

A few months later I found myself on a traditional *dieta* (sacred plant retreat) in the Amazon rainforest, drinking ayahuasca for the first time in a traditional ceremony. During that first ceremony in the jungle, as the medicine began to move, time loosened its hold. One moment I was sitting in darkness, listening to the curandero's song; the next, I was at the bedside of my maternal Dutch grandmother, Effie, as she lay dying.

I experienced myself rubbing her cold feet, telling her everything I had never said: how much I loved her, how grateful I was that she was my grandmother, how she had given me a sense of belonging during years when I felt untethered and unseen, so hurt, so afraid. In the vision, I held her hand. I stayed until she was ready to go and experienced her passing as a gift, a holy transition, rather than a loss to grieve.

In waking life, when I was nineteen, I hadn't been able to do any of this. A stranger hovered over her bed, and I didn't have the courage to ask for space alone with her. I whispered "I'm here," from a distance and fled the room in tears. She died later that night. That unfinished goodbye lived in my body for years, without me knowing it.

Ayahuasca brought me back to her as a retrieval of something my younger self couldn't face. It allowed me to step into the moment that shaped me and soften its imprint.

Later in the same ceremony, I found myself lying on the warm earth. As my tears flowed into the soil, I felt *Pachamama* (Mother Earth) holding me. I felt the pulse of something vast, ancient, steady. In her embrace, the boundary between my grief, my tremendous gratitude and the ground I was resting upon dissolved.

It was then that I sensed, perhaps for the first time, the larger field of the Mother: the Great Mother who holds all lives and all endings; the Divine

Mother whose compassion does not waver; the archetypal Mother who is both the ground beneath us; and the presence behind all healing.

In later journeys, this presence appeared often, sometimes as Pachamama, sometimes as the Divine Mother, sometimes as the vast and luminous Great Mother. Each face carried a different quality, but the message was the same: you are held, you are known, you are loved. You are part of a lineage of women far larger than your ache.

This encounter did not erase my grief. It revealed its place in a wider web of belonging.

It showed me that the mother ache does not begin or end with our personal mother. It lives in the ancestral line, in the collective feminine, in the archetypal Mother who holds every wound and every strand of repair.

The medicine didn't give me something new. It returned me to something ancient, something that had always been mine that I recognized as an intrinsic part of me.

And the real healing came afterward, in how I let this experience reshape the ache I had carried, how I let my grandmother's love become a strand of strength that I had long forgotten.

Entheogens open the door. The true, embodied healing happens in the life we live afterward, walking the walk.

The ripple of transformation is not abstract; it moves through real stories and real bodies. The next story invites you to witness how one woman stepped through darkness and emerged carrying light for others.

Mother Ache Healing in the World:

The Girl Who Walked Out of the Fire

Lyra's childhood is held in fragments, as if smoke passed through her memory and softened the edges. When asked what she remembers, she says, "My childhood feels erased. I remember very little."

Her mother was only twenty-four when Lyra was born, still carrying the tremors of unhealed trauma. Her parents lived inside the fading remnants of the hippie movement in San Francisco, a world of drugs, music, and unpredictability. Lyra was unplanned, yet she likes to imagine her soul choosing that moment with certainty, whispering, "I am coming in anyway."

Her body moved fast, walking at nine months and climbing out of her crib before she could speak. Even as a baby, she seemed to sense danger in the home. When she was four, a younger brother arrived, bringing a strand of sweetness. Together they weathered what was ahead.

At this same age of four, she remembers lying awake while her parents fought, feeling as if her spirit hovered above the room. At seven, her parents separated. Her father turned toward a strict Christian faith, while her mother rebelled against anything that resembled control. With three hundred dollars to her name, her mother fled with the children. The next decade unfolded as a long corridor of instability, with many homes, volatile partners, guns in drawers, screaming in hallways, and a mother whose mind unraveled under unhealed trauma. Lyra learned to comfort her brother in locked bedrooms, whispering steadiness into the dark.

When Lyra was still quite young, her mother told her that Lyra's grandfather had raped her throughout childhood and that Lyra needed to stay alert. Lyra did not understand the words but felt the fear. Holidays with him carried a silent dread.

By her teens, Lyra resisted her father's church and lost his affection, as her rejection of his strict God caused him to cancel all visitation with her. At seventeen, she left home for good, painfully being forced to leave her brother behind. The years that followed echoed with loneliness, depression, and the sense that she had slipped through all the cracks.

Yet inside the wreckage lived a spark. Sacred plants became early allies. By twenty, she was participating in lineage-held ceremonies where the medicines met the pain she had been carrying alone. An elder eventually brought her to the Amazon. There, the jungle taught her what her childhood could not: safety, connection, and the possibility of a life rooted in truth rather than fear.

During our work together, Lyra began to understand her pain through the lens of alchemy. She came to see how her early relational environment—particularly the absence of consistent maternal safety—had shaped her defenses, and how those defenses had once saved her. Even her numbness, she discovered, held intelligence. Through compassionate inquiry and somatic practice, she learned to stay present with sensations that had once overwhelmed her. Through sacred medicine work, she learned how to let old terror move without collapsing into it. Over time, the girl who hid in locked rooms began to open to the woman she was becoming.

Her music became a bridge very early in her life and has helped sustain her healing journey. Singing continues to allow what had been frozen to thaw. Rhythm and breath gave shape to emotions she had never been able to name. Slowly, her story transformed from something that happened to her into something she could carry with dignity.

Lyra now serves others from the ground she once struggled to find. She mentors at-risk youth, teaches music to teens, supports the dying, and guides people through healing journeys with honesty and devotion. What she once longed for in her own mother, she now embodies for others. Her life is a living prayer, shaped by reciprocity and the fierce tenderness of one who has met the fire and walked forward with wisdom intact.

Alchemy reshaped her. Pain did not vanish; it changed form. The fierce girl who survived became a healer who understands that transformation arises when we meet our wounds with presence, breath, and an unwavering willingness to remain true to the soul beneath the story.

Journal Reflections: Reweaving Inner Alchemy

Meeting the Ancient Women of Alchemy

What qualities of the ancient feminine alchemist do you recognize in yourself, even in subtle ways?
When in your life have you held space for transformation, for yourself or others, without naming it?
What inner knowing awakens in you when you imagine yourself as part of a long line of women who used alchemy for daily weaving?

Gathering—The Phase of Beginning

What truths, memories, or patterns are rising to be seen right now, without needing to be fixed?
Which of the inner children, Innocent, Magical, Wounded, feels most present as you begin this phase?
What are you noticing in your body as you pause and say, *This is where I begin?*

What have you been carrying that is now asking to be acknowledged?

Softening—The Phase of Opening

What feelings have you been bracing against that are now inviting you to soften toward them?
When you imagine the Orphan receiving the teaching of being entrusted and endowed, what arises in your heart or body?
What does softening feel like for you, physically, emotionally, or energetically?
What might become possible if you allowed warmth, breath, and presence to meet the places that still ache?

Shaping—The Phase of Becoming

What truths about yourself are becoming clearer as you release inherited stories or identities?
Where do you feel the Seeker's inner connection strengthening in your life?
What patterns mental, emotional, energetic, are you now able to see without becoming them?
What is the shape of the life you feel called to create from this deeper clarity?

Offering—The Phase of Returning

In what ways is your healing beginning to ripple outward naturally, without effort?
What does reciprocity mean to you at this stage of your journey?
What gold are you beginning to recognize in yourself, and how might you offer it gently back to your life or the world?

Mirror Gazing

What arose in you as you gazed into your own eyes without looking away?
What faces, expressions, or versions of yourself appeared, and how did they speak to you?
What sensations did you notice in your body as your sense of identity began to loosen or shift?
What did this practice reveal about the fluidity of your inner life and the stories you hold about who you are?
How does witnessing your own changing face alter your understanding of the phases of your becoming?

Lyra's Story

Do you sense any familiar patterns in her longing, her resilience, or her search for safety and belonging?

How do you feel toward her as you hold her journey? Tenderness, sorrow, admiration, recognition?

Conclusion: From Alchemy to Devotion

"Someday, after mastering the winds, the waves, the tides and gravity, we shall harness for God the energies of love. And then, for the second time in the history of the world, man will have discovered fire."

—Pierre Teilhard de Chardin

To bind the rim is to complete the circle and give back what has been received. This is the Alchemist's offering: gratitude made visible. Each act of kindness, each truth spoken softly, becomes another thread of gold returned to the Great Mother's universal weave. The healing basket you have woven with your heart and way of being now becomes medicine for the world.

Binding the rim creates a sense of wholeness. Transformation doesn't require new materials; it asks us to nurture what already lives within us. Every emotion, memory, and fragment carries the gleam of gold. Awareness is the flame; presence is the vessel. Together, they turn shadow into light, anger into courage, grief into love, and fear into wisdom. Nothing within you goes to waste. The Alchemist understands that true transformation involves the willingness to hold opposites by letting sorrow and joy, shadow and light coexist in one heart.

This is how we heal, by encompassing all that we are. Our baskets are strong because nothing is left out. In this inclusiveness lies a sense of completion. The ache softens into radiance; the ordinary becomes sacred. What remains is stillness in the soft glow after transformation, when gold no longer needs to prove its worth. Here, the Alchemist steps back, and the Mystic begins to stir, her gaze turning inward toward the light now burning at the heart's center.

The work of doing becomes the art of simply being. The spark of transformation becomes the fire of compassion.

Chapter Ten:

The Mystic and the Path of Compassion

"Compassion is the most precious of all gifts. In times of sorrow and bewilderment, it is what restores us and offers refuge.... It is compassion that rescues us from despair and helplessness, that provides a refuge of peace and understanding inwardly and outwardly. Compassion does not claim to be a quick-fix for the age-old causes of suffering, nor is it a magic wand that will sweep away sorrow. But it is our commitment to compassion and our willingness to nurture it in every moment that gives meaning to life."

—Christina Feldman

You have been walking a sacred spiraling path toward compassion. Each chapter has been a turn inward, softening what was once guarded and preparing the ground for this unfolding. With every turn, you have drawn closer to your sacred center, which is the innate space within from which compassion arises naturally.

We started with awareness, learning to see what is. Then came curiosity, the gentle willingness to look closer; honesty, the courage to name what we find; and trust, the steadying root that helps us stay present. Through acceptance, we made space for what had been resisted; through connection, we remembered that when we turn inward, we discover we already know that which is. Empathy taught us to feel without avoiding, awakening the heart's sensitivity. Alchemy invited us into an inner openness where what we feel can change form, allowing sensation, emotion, and meaning to move and reorganize.

Now, as the spiral draws you inward, these qualities weave together like strands of light. Together they reveal what was never lost: the understanding that all life aches and all life longs, and that your tenderness is part of the world's great heart. This is compassion, to hold each ache, each truth, with love.

Compassion is a way of being that emerges when empathy and presence come together. Through self-compassion, we start to face our pain with kindness and wisdom. It is the warmth that appears when feeling is met with awareness, when the wisdom of the navel, the empathy of the heart, and the sacred center move as one.

In this chapter, your inner guide is the archetypal energy of the Mystic. She is the one who perceives beyond appearances and feels her deep connection with all that exists. Every woman carries this energy within her. The Mystic reminds us that compassion arises through remembrance: the awareness that nothing within us is separate, and that all parts, stories, and sorrows belong to the same living whole.

In old stories, the Mystic often reaches upward, seeking union with the divine beyond the ordinary world. Our Mystic also seeks the divine, but she does so by turning inward. She reveals that the sacred is not only in the heavens but also within our own hearts. She does not withdraw from life, she participates in it fully, meeting each moment with presence. She teaches that compassion is the way we experience the divine in the most human of places: our bodies, our relationships, and our daily lives.

As we have been weaving our baskets, we have needed to add new strands when the first ones grew short. Their ends are rough and sometimes poke out. Now, with the hands of our inner mystic, we carefully trim these so the outer surface is smooth. Then, we burnish the basket with beeswax. The wax seeps into the fibers, polishing and strengthening them. It protects the weave from breaking and keeps the contents within safe. This is the work of compassion. It is the art of strengthening and preserving what is real while smoothing our rough edges.

Our inner Mystic is not a saint. She also has rough edges. A saint often lives above the world, untouchable, pure, and removed from our everyday humanness. The Mystic differs. She doesn't rise above life; she flourishes within it. She welcomes her own light and shadow, her clarity and doubt. To the Mystic, embracing her miraculous, imperfect humanity is where her compassion takes root.

The Mystic rubs beeswax onto the inner and outer basket weave, anointing it with love. The wax seeps into the fibers, softening, sealing, and blessing her healing with compassion.

Women Who Embody the Mystic's Compassion

Green Tara and Mary Magdalene represent the essence of the feminine Mystic I invite you to awaken within yourself. In Buddhism, Green Tara is the bodhisattva of compassion. Although we may think of her as an ancient and distant Goddess, she is actually forever leaning toward the cries of the world, quick to respond. Her compassion is alive, rooted in presence and action.

In truthful Christian mysticism, Mary Magdalene embodies this same archetype. She is not the Beloved yet somehow unreachable Virgin Mary. Rather, she is the woman who experienced love and loss, devotion and grief as a true seeker following Christ. When called to speak, she maintained her voice and flame of truth despite being doubted, minimized, and cast aside.

The Bodhisattva Who Stayed

I have a deep and personal connection with Green Tara. For over twenty years, I have kept her close to my heart in the form of a small pendant I found at the Norbulingka Institute in Dharamsala, India. Her mantra, *Om Tare Tuttare Ture Soha* was the first song I ever sang aloud during a ceremony. I was never a musician, and for a long time, the idea of singing seemed impossible. Yet through this mantra, my voice found me. Tara's prayer became a bridge and an invocation for protection, healing, and the courage to face fear with love within me. Over the years, it has been a steady companion, a thread of devotion guiding me through uncertainty and into the refuge of the heart.

Tara was once a woman devoted to spiritual awakening.[37] In a previous life, she was a princess who practiced meditation with great discipline and love. Her heart was so steady that she nearly reached the threshold of enlightenment. At that moment, others told her she should pray to be reborn as a man to complete her journey.

She refused. Tara pledged to stay in female form for all her lifetimes until every being was free from suffering. With that pledge, she became Tara, the liberator, guiding others across the ocean of sorrow.

Green Tara symbolizes life and movement. She embodies compassion through action. Her image reflects this truth: one leg folded in meditation, grounded in stillness; the other extended, ready to rise. When suffering calls, she is already moving toward it.

Lotuses bloom above her shoulders, pure and unblemished despite growing from mud. The flower reminds us that compassion is born from suffering. Pain becomes the soil from which love rises.

Her hands tell a story: one open in generosity, the other raised in protection. She gives freely and shields without fear. Tara became the Goddess of Compassion not by transcending humanity, but by remaining within it. Her compassion is immediate, embodied, and awake.

She teaches that compassion isn't about escaping pain. Compassion is staying with it until it transforms into love through the heart center.

37 Rachael Wooten, *Tara: The Liberating Power of the Female Buddha* (Boulder, CO: Sounds True, 2020)

Compassion begins as a whisper in the heart, but when you answer it, the sacred divine feminine moves through your hands, your words, your life.

The Apostle of the Heart

Mary Magdalene holds a sacred place in the story of Christ. She was the only woman among his disciples and his closest companion. She stood at the foot of the cross and was the first to witness his resurrection. Because of this, she was later called the "apostle to the apostles," entrusted to speak the message when others had fled.

Yet for centuries, her image was desecrated. She was named a prostitute, which became a false patriarchal myth passed down through art and teaching for generations. The church finally corrected this error in the late twentieth century, though shadows of the distortion remain. Today, her true image is reemerging as a teacher, leader, and mystic in her own right.[38] The Gospel of Mary was left out of the Bible and intentionally destroyed, yet fragments survived, hidden for centuries in clay jars. I also like to imagine in ancient woven baskets. Although incomplete, these surviving pages reveal her deep understanding of inner vision, freedom from fear, and the soul's journey back to rest. When the disciples doubted her, she spoke with calm authority and love. Her gospel portrays her as Christ's most awakened disciple and possibly his beloved.

Mary's story is one of erasure and recovery. She was silenced, misnamed, and diminished, yet her voice endures, carrying the courage to speak truth with compassion. She stands as a mirror for the Mystic within us all.

This is the essence of the Mystic: the grace that dwells within all life and within us. This grace dissolves what is false, the shame, the slur, the old names that never belonged, and reveals what is true: steadfast love and a sure voice even when doubted. Mary invites us to face our ache, listen inward, and speak from love.

These two feminine Mystics, Tara and Mary Magdalene, have walked with me for many years. They embody both the earthy nature of women and the divine current flowing through. Many other women carry this balance of Earth and spirit. You might already know one. She could be a goddess, a

38 Meggan Watterson, *Mary Magdalene Revealed: The First Apostle, Her Feminist Gospel, and the Christianity We Haven't Tried Yet* (New York: Hay House, 2019)

saint, a teacher, or a grandmother who has lived her life with fierce tenderness and honesty. Or she might be someone who simply shows up each day with presence and care.

The Mystic holds all these strands. She does not ask you to be pure or unblemished. She asks only that you soften toward yourself so that you can know your own nature, your own truth. To trim the rough ends of your story. To polish your life with the beeswax of tenderness. This is compassion: tending the basket of your being so it can hold not only what you love but also what once felt unbearable. Ultimately, the Mystic is within you. She awakens through remembrance, breath, and love. Tara and Mary Magdalene serve as mirrors, and the reflection they offer always guides you back to your own heart, to you.

"For women mystics, contemplative life is not so much a matter of transcending the illusions of mundane existence or attaining states of perfect equanimity as it is about becoming as fully present as possible to the realities of the human experience. In showing up for what is, no matter how pedestrian or tedious, how aggravating or shameful, the what is begins to reveal itself as imbued with holiness. How do we make space in our lives for this kind of sacred seeing?"

—Mirabai Starr

The Mystic's Seal is Compassion

The stories of Green Tara and Mary Magdalene show us that compassion is not reserved for saints or sages. It is the fragrance released when pain is met with presence, when love becomes stronger than fear. Compassion does not belong to another realm; it blossoms right here, within the heart that has endured and remained open.

We all yearn to be compassionate toward ourselves and others. In Chapter Eight, we examined empathy and our inner Healer, turning inward to face the emotions that once felt too heavy to bear. Empathy is the capacity to feel the actual emotion, to fully sense it within your own body and respect its truth. We also focused on attunement. Attunement is about meeting what emerges at the same vibrational frequency, resonating with it so it can be acknowledged and held without distortion.

Now we come to compassion, which is something more. Empathy feels. Attunement resonates. Compassion holds. Empathy and attunement draw us into the wound so it can be tended. Compassion steps back just enough to offer breath and spaciousness. Where empathy trembles with sorrow, compassion places a steadying hand over the trembling to let it know it is held.

In this way, compassion seals our basket. It prevents the contents from leaking and keeps what is alive within us from spoiling. Compassion widens the heart and whispers: *I can feel this and stay whole. I can endure this and remain rooted in love.*

For healing, this is essential. Empathy helps us reveal what has been hidden. Attunement encourages us to be honest with what we discover. Compassion teaches us how to hold it all with love. Through compassion, the parts within us can stay present with pain without needing to shut down or escape. This steadying process strengthens our healing basket so it can carry what is heavy without breaking.

Compassion isn't a distant ideal or virtue to strive for; it is the native language of the heart. To experience it directly, we turn to an ancient meditation practice called Tonglen, meaning *sending and receiving*. Through simple breathing, we tap into the secret alchemy of the heart. We breathe in suffering and breathe out love.

Why would we breathe in pain? The Mystic within us already knows. When we resist suffering, it tightens its hold. When we welcome it into the heart, it transforms. The heart serves as the bridge, and breath is its messenger.

Breathing the World into the Heart

Tonglen Meditation is among the oldest compassion practices in the Buddhist tradition. At its essence, we breathe in suffering and breathe out love.

To the mind, this might seem strange. Why would we breathe in pain? But the Mystic within us knows the secret. When we resist suffering, we give it more power. When we welcome it into the heart, something miraculous occurs. The heart, vast and wise, begins to transform what it receives. The breath becomes a bridge between fear and love.

The heart does not break from feeling too much; it breaks from being closed. When we breathe into what we have avoided, the heart opens wider. Through this opening, compassion begins to move through us like light through water.

Tonglen teaches us that compassion is a living current. It's the movement of love entering what hurts. As the heart receives suffering, it does not hold onto it, rather, it transforms it. The breath draws the ache inward, and love flows outward. Each inhale softens what is hard; each exhale blesses what was bound.

Think of this practice as polishing the healing basket you've been weaving. The weave is strong, but the edges may still be rough. With each breath, you smooth those edges, sealing and strengthening the vessel of your heart. Over time, it becomes supple enough to hold life's pain without breaking.

When you practice Tonglen, you become part of a long lineage of mystics and wisdom keepers who have discovered that the heart can endure what seems unbearable when it moves with each breath. Pain becomes the raw material of love. The rough edges of your being are polished with strength.

Experiential Practice: Tonglen Meditation

Duration: 30 to 60 minutes. I use the Osho Heart Meditation soundtrack, available on all streaming platforms or enjoy the resonant tones of Tibetan bowls or other meditative music. There are many forms and variations of this practice, so feel free to experiment. This is the one I use regularly. Find a comfortable place to meditate.

Step 1: Arrive (5 minutes)

Sit comfortably and close your eyes. Allow your breath to flow into your heart center. Feel your body settle as if the basket of your being is already holding you. Let yourself arrive.

Step 2: Start with yourself (20 minutes)

Bring to mind your own suffering, a current worry, a memory, or your own mother ache you are working to heal. As you breathe in, gently draw this ache into your heart. Hold it there without resistance. As you exhale, feel it soften into ease, kindness, and love. Continue: inhale the ache, exhale compassion.

Step 3: Expand to others (20 minutes) Bring to mind someone you love. See their face, feel the pain they hold. Inhale their suffering with tenderness, exhale compassion. Gradually expand your circle to include acquaintances, strangers, and ultimately, all beings. Inhale the world's pain, exhale love. Imagine your breath as beeswax sealing the great basket of life, smoothing its rough edges and softening what has become hard.

Step 4: Return to yourself (5 minutes)

Gently bring your awareness back to your own heart. Rest there, breathing softly. Feel the subtle hum of connection and the pulse of compassion that now moves through you.

Daily weaving keeps the basket of the heart supple and strong. You can practice for only a few minutes whenever you feel triggered, closed, or disconnected. When I feel triggered, I often breathe in my own anger or judgment until it softens into a big compassionate exhale and then include the other person's pain as well. Sometimes it takes quite a few breaths for me to get there, but I always find that the heart always knows how to transform when given the chance.

The Inner Flame of Compassion

True compassion is the earthly emanation of love. Love itself is the essence beneath all other essential qualities we have explored. It lives at the center of our being, constant and unbroken. Yet, for this love to flow through us, it must first be experienced within us. We can only love others as much as we love ourselves.

This journey we've traveled together is essentially an invitation to practice self-love. Now, the spiral turns again. How does self-love grow? Through self-care. Each act of care deepens our capacity to love, and as love expands, care becomes more natural, more rooted in daily life. Simple, but not easy.

Compassion paves the way. Love is what we discover as we walk through it. Self-love is a state of being. It's the understanding that you are worthy, complete, and free to be exactly as you are. Yet it is also an action. Every step you've taken here has been an act of self-love: turning toward your pain, bringing awareness to early meanings, softening protective patterns, and allowing feeling to be felt. Each practice has brought love from essence into form, helping to ease your mother ache and anchor compassion in your body.

What is Self-Love

"If your compassion does not include yourself, it is incomplete."
—Pema Chödrön

Explore the following expressions of self-love. Notice which ones resonate with you and which ones feel challenging. Invite your inner Mystic to guide you as you read each one slowly, allowing the words to resonate within your being.

Agency

Self-love is the felt understanding that your life is worth your own care. It is a steady warmth at the center that does not depend on praise or achievement. It is an affirmation that I am allowed to be myself, and I am responsible for how I live.

Presence

Self-love is presence, the willingness to sit with your ache without turning away. It is the breath that reaches the navel, the calm that emerges with intention.

Protection and Nourishment

Self-love manifests through actions that protect and nurture you. It means feeding your body, resting deeply, and moving with awareness. It includes setting boundaries that maintain your wholeness and choosing relationships and routines that help you flourish. It speaks in honest inner dialogue and in the honoring of your own intentions.

Humility

Self-love is humility. It is not indulgence or superiority. It accepts reality as it is, admits mistakes, and repairs what can be repaired. It allows you to stand within your humanity with grace.

Courage

Self-love is courage. It recognizes fear as a threshold, not an enemy. It helps you face what you've avoided, speak when silence seems safer, and ask for help when needed.

Discipline

Self-love is discipline. It keeps simple promises: breathe, rest, nourish, move, reflect. It repeatedly guides you back to the practices that sustain your aliveness.

Acceptance

Self-love is acceptance. It welcomes who you are while supporting who you are becoming. It holds your history without letting it define you. It meets the mother ache with compassion and patiently weaves new patterns, strand by strand.

Relationship

Self-love is relational. It doesn't make you smaller or withdrawn; it opens you up. It makes you kinder. It allows you to give without feeling depleted and to receive without guilt. It transforms empathy into compassion and compassion into reciprocity.

Embodiment

Self-love lives in the body. You can feel it in the breath that deepens, in the rooted navel, the relaxed jaw, and the upright spine. Your posture itself when erect, heart lifted says *I belong*.

Cyclicality

Self-love moves in a spiral. Being fuels doing; doing deepens being. Presence gives rise to care, and care strengthens presence, cycling endlessly through the seasons of your life.

Creativity

Self-love is a craft. You tend to lose ends, polish rough edges with beeswax tenderness, and weave your story into coherence.

Remembrance

Self-love is the remembering of your original essences: awareness, curiosity, honesty, trust, acceptance, connection, inner alchemy, and compassion; and the willingness to claim these qualities as your true self.

Remember: self-love is not something to achieve. Self-love is a rhythm to return to again and again, like breath weaving through the body of your life.

Tending the Sacred Vessel

Compassion begins with self-love. Self-love develops through self-care. For many women carrying the mother ache, self-care can be the most difficult act of all. Old adaptive patterns whisper to us*: Give until you fade. Stay busy. Don't rest. Don't claim space. Don't listen to your needs.*

When we connect with the Mystic within, a new voice begins to emerge, whispering instead: *Give to yourself from abundance. Care for the sacred vessel that is your body here and now*. Self-care is not indulgence; it is devotion in action. It is compassion made visible, love translated into action. Love cannot truly be shared with others until it is felt within first and we manifest this inner love through self-care.

Start small. Think daily. Simple gestures, genuine intention. That is all that is required.

Self-care may appear as rest, nourishment, breath, boundaries, movement, time in nature, or touch. It lives in practices you may already know and in those we've explored together in these pages: soft belly breathing, returning to sensation, walking in nature, Kundalini meditation, noticing early meanings with curiosity, recognizing protective energy patterns, rooting in navel strength, trusting the felt sense, pausing, inquiring gently, attuning inwardly, and practicing Tonglen. Each is a thread in the weave of self-care.

If you take away only one thing from this book, let it be this: practice self-care consistently. Choose one practice and commit to it daily. Healing happens through consistency, perseverance. Set a time each day. Show up.

The commitment itself becomes an act of love, self-care. Each time you pause, breathe, and tend to yourself with presence is an act of self-care. Let this understanding remind you that caring for yourself is how you keep the weave of your being supple and strong.

The Body as Sacred Ground of Compassion

One reason self-care feels so challenging is our relationship with the body. For women carrying the mother ache, this connection is often tangled and sensitive, as we explored in Chapter Six. Here, in our bodies, for those of us healing our mother ache, compassion, self-love, and self-care meet most directly.

The Mystic within you encourages you to view your body as a sacred temple. Your body is the form through which your spirit, that part of you that is eternal, experiences life here, now. It is the altar of embodiment, the living ground of your awakening.

Begin with kindness. Remember that your body has undertaken the huge job of holding your experiences until you're ready and able to heal them. Your body carries both the ache of loss and the power to alchemize that loss into love. It has endured the weight of harsh words and still contains the warmth of tenderness. Meeting your body with compassion means loving it without condition or demand.

Your body is the basket that contains your life. It is woven with muscle, bone, breath, and blood. Messages about beauty, worth, and weight often take root early in the body. Many of us inherited them from our mothers, some spoken, others silently lived. Approval became entangled with appearance, and in seeking love, we abandoned and or punished the body that is our true home. Aging can awaken and exacerbate this ache. In a culture that worships youth, lines and softness are viewed as flaws. But every mark tells a story of living, each crease a record of love and loss.

Your body is not the problem. It is the sacred container of your story and strength. Self-love here is a courageous act. To say, *I will not abandon myself because I age. I will not reject myself because I change.* This is the vow of the Mystic: to bless the body as it is.

The Mystic within helps you keep this promise. She brings openness in your reflection, care in your daily rituals, and wisdom in the inner voice that whispers, *Bless this body. Honor its strength. Love its softness. Trust it's knowing*. By keeping this vow, you end an ancient cycle of pain and the lineage of judgment and shame by replacing it with reverence.

Experiential Invitation: The Beeswax Blessing

In our basket weaving metaphor, our mystic is tasked with rubbing beeswax onto the basket, sealing the weave and deepening its glow. The wax does not hide the fibers; it softens them, giving strength. The Mystic brings this same tenderness to her body. She understands that care itself can be prayer. This simple ritual invites you to bless your body as the living vessel of your becoming.

Find a time for self-care, where you will not feel hurried and can honor your aloneness. Have some scented essential oil available for this ritual. These can be purchased at health food stores or through local apothecary shops. Choose an oil that speaks to the moment: rose for the heart, sandalwood for grounding, or frankincense for prayer. Warm a few drops between your palms and inhale the scent before touching your skin. Let the fragrance remind you that the sacred is not elsewhere; it lives here, in the body you bless.

Warm a small amount of natural oil between your palms.

Name three places you appreciate about your body. Touch each place with gratitude and rub the sacred oil into these places.

Now, identify one area that feels ignored or judged. Place your hands there.

Breathe in any ache. Exhale softness and warmth.

Whisper: *I will not speak harm to you*. Make slow circles with your hands, as if polishing the rim of your basket, applying the oil gently with care and love. Continue to other areas that have experienced your discontent.

Finish by placing one hand on your navel and one on your heart.

Sit quietly for a minute.

Inner Beauty: The Radiance of Simplicity

The Mystic understands that true beauty isn't something to be acquired or displayed. Inner beauty is the luminosity that appears when we are rooted in truth. It doesn't depend on youth or perfection. It comes from a woman who knows herself and has chosen what truly matters.

The woman connected to inner beauty perceives truth clearly. She remains steady, wary of anything that pulls her away from her center where her truth resides. Her strength is firm. Through her healing journey, she has shaped herself into someone authentic.

A woman connected to her inner beauty has shed what is false, both inside and out. She has retained only what is vital, let go of what weighs her down, and done so without regret. In her, the unnecessary has fallen away, and what remains is her intrinsic essence, which has always been luminous, true.

This refinement, this return to the center, is the practice at the core of every awakening path. The Mystic lives by this rhythm of shedding and returning. She knows that a lifetime's work is in remembering that to dwell in the center of one's being is to dwell in beauty itself.

Inner beauty is born from finding alignment through self-attunement. When you're centered, your energy stops scattering in self-doubt or constant striving. Instead, it gathers in your heart and radiates through your presence. This is the glow of authenticity. It is a subtle flame that cannot be imitated through our masks of adaptation.

To cultivate inner beauty, look inward. Ask yourself: What have I been holding onto that no longer belongs to me? What truth feels beautiful because it is real? Then, let go of what is no longer relevant and honor what remains. The Mystic understands that to be centered is to shine. Remember: true beauty is what moves through you when you live aligned with your essence.

Mother Ache Healing in the World:

The Daughter Who Inherited the Mystic's Path

Natasha learned early how to live without being held. Her mother sent her away to live with her paternal grandparents when she was three.

When she was five years old she returned to her father's home, and she immediately sensed that the woman who had become her stepmother did not like her nor welcome her. No one said this aloud, yet her body knew. The house felt unfamiliar, watchful, tight. Natasha learned quickly to read the room, to stay out of the way, to take up as little space as possible. Safety required self-containment.

What she did not yet know was how carefully this moment had been shaped by love.

Before Natasha was sent away at three years old, her mother had already been living inside the awareness of mortality. Her own mother had died of breast cancer at thirty. Her primary memory of being mothered was illness, fragility, and loss. When she herself was diagnosed, she made a decision born of fierce protection. She did not want her daughter's earliest memories to be of a dying mother. She wanted Natasha to be held inside steadiness rather than fear. So she sent her to live with her paternal grandparents, believing this would spare her daughter the imprint she herself had carried.

During those years, Natasha's mother wrote weekly letters to the grandparents. They were careful, reflective, alive with longing. She described her days, her inner life, her devotion to meditation, her desire for peace. There were also a few letters written directly to Natasha. One of them asked a simple question: "Do you remember going with me to the red mailbox?"

Natasha does remember.

It is the only memory she carries of being with her mother. The feel of walking beside her. The red metal door. The moment of posting something into the world together. This memory lives in her body as tenderness, love.

Three months before she died, Natasha's mother also recorded hours of tapes. In them she spoke openly about her childhood, her struggles with food and control, her spiritual longing, meeting Natasha's father, and the devotion that had become her ground. These recordings, along with the letters, were given to Natasha by her grandfather when she became a young woman.

Through them, she came to know her mother who died so young, and to feel the mother-daughter continuity that had never been broken.

Natasha's mother had always been a seeker. As a teenager she traveled abroad with spiritual missions. Later, during the cultural opening of the 1960's, she encountered a Zen teacher and recognized a truth she had been circling for years. Meditation became her home. As her body weakened, her devotion intensified. Shortly before her death, she edited a book on meditation, offering what remained of her energy to the path that had steadied her.

That orientation did not vanish with her passing.

Meditation entered Natasha's life as inheritance rather than instruction. It offered steadiness where attachment had been interrupted. It taught her how to sit with what could not be repaired. It also shaped her protective patterns. Without a mother available for attunement, Natasha learned containment. She required little. She asked for nothing. Independence became second nature. Those closest to her later sensed a distance, a quality of presence that felt self-contained and unreachable. This pattern once kept her safe.

In adulthood, she started her journey with meditation at a very young age because it connected her to her mother. Off and on, she attended therapy and much later in her life she healed through profound psychedelic journeys, which allowed long-held grief to surface. Waves of laughter and sobbing moved through her body when her system finally permitted release. Long-standing friendships with women offered another form of medicine, rooted in witnessing and shared history. These relationships provided continuity where early life had fractured.

In our work together, Natasha began to explore the quality of detachment that had organized her inner world, a pattern shaped early in relationship and the loss of her mother energetically at the age of three and to death at the age of five. Through somatic practices and inquiry work, she discovered how deeply grief had been held beneath her steadfast aloofness and the composure in her cellular body. Slowly, with patience, she allowed feeling to return. Her energetic pattern of guarding softened. Presence widened.

She came to understand her mother's absence through a larger lens. Her mother had been living inside urgency, illness, and a desire for peace before time ran out. The devotion that drew her away also formed the lineage Natasha now carries forward. What passed between them was not abandonment. It was transmission. A true gift.

Meditation remains central to Natasha's life. It is the place where compassion continues to deepen, where embodiment unfolds at its own pace, where the heart learns how to stay. Through devotion, inquiry, and the courage to feel what once exceeded capacity, she transforms inheritance into wisdom. This is the Mystic's work. To carry grief without closing. To remain present where love was interrupted. To let compassion become a living lineage.

Journal Reflections: Reweaving Compassion

Invoking Green Tara

Before you begin, take a few slow breaths and imagine a soft green light surrounding you. This is the color of renewal, of compassion made active. Tara's presence is not distant; she lives within every impulse to ease suffering, to reach out, to help. Let this reflection become a conversation with that living compassion inside you.

What does it mean to me that Tara pledged to remain in female form until all beings are free?

Where in my own life do I long for compassion that is active, quick, and fearless?

When I imagine Tara stepping down to help, what part of me feels seen or protected?

Remembering Mary Magdalene

Before you begin, take a slow breath and bring to mind the image of Mary, as the woman of wisdom and devotion she truly was. Let her presence remind you of every voice that has been silenced, every truth hidden beneath misunderstanding. As you write, listen for the power that stirs within your own being, the part of you that knows your own truth.

What does it stir in me to know that Mary was once silenced, misnamed, and erased?

Where in my own life have I been doubted or dismissed when I spoke my truth?

How do I respond when my authority or inner knowing is challenged?

What part of me longs to reclaim a voice that has been hidden?

How does Mary's story of erasure and return inspire and support me now?

My Mystic Teacher

Before you begin, take a slow breath and imagine the line of mystics, healers, and wise women who came before you. Those who walked between worlds, tending the unseen. Some you may know by name; others live in your blood and bones. This reflection invites you to remember the teachers, seen and unseen, who help you listen to the divine within the human.

Who in my lineage, culture, or spiritual path embodies both the earthly and the divine for me?

What woman can I call on when I feel the deepest ache?

What would it mean to trust that I am a Mystic, a seeker of truth and bearer of compassion?

When you finish, close your eyes and feel the soft pulse within your heart. Imagine a thread of light connecting you to those who have walked this path before. Their wisdom lives in you. The Mystic is not separate from you, she can be found in your own awareness, remembering yourself as sacred.

Tonglen Meditation

Before you begin, take a few slow breaths and notice the rhythm of your inhale and exhale. Tonglen meditation, sending and receiving, invites us to breathe with the suffering of the world, to soften the boundaries between self and other. As you write, reflect on how it felt to let breathing into the heart center become a bridge to your natural intrinsic compassion.

What did I notice when I began with my own suffering?

What feelings arose as I held the pain of someone I love?

How did my body respond as I widened the circle to all beings?

What was most difficult for me to breathe in?

How did returning to myself at the end feel different from when I began?

Self Love Is The Gold Within

Which of these expressions of self-love feels most alive in me right now? How does it reveal itself in the way I move, speak, or care for myself?

Which qualities feel like seeds still waiting to sprout? What small gestures or practices could help them grow?

When I imagine living from the wholeness of these qualities, what might begin to shift in my body, in my relationships, in the rhythm of my days?

The Practice of Care

Which self-care practices feel natural to me?
Which ones do I resist, and why?
How can I incorporate one practice into my daily routine and stay committed?
Make a list of practices you can return to when you feel frayed or on edge.

Honoring the Body as Temple

Which parts of my body do I already cherish?
What act of care is my body asking for today?
How can I soften my attitude toward my changing body so that it feels more welcoming, more kind?
What would it mean to shift my perception of the body from something to manage or improve into a sacred temple to tend with reverence?

Inner Beauty: The Light Within

What qualities in myself do I recognize as expressions of inner beauty?
What am I ready to release so that my inner light can shine more freely?
How does it feel in my body when I am centered and at ease?

Natasha's Story

What aspects of Natasha's story stirred recognition or emotion in me?
How have loss, impermanence, or early grief shaped my inner life or spiritual seeking?
Where do I sense that something meaningful has been passed to me through lineage, even through absence?
How has contemplation, meditation, or inner inquiry helped me stay connected to what truly matters?
As you work this these reflections, remember that compassion is a practice. Each time you meet yourself with honesty rather than judgment, each time you soften toward another without abandoning your own truth, the Mystic is alive within you. Compassion becomes a way of seeing that widens the heart without losing discernment. Carry this way of seeing with you as a living practice, one that continues to unfold long after these pages end.

Conclusion: The Fragrance of Compassion

"I wish I could show you, when you are lonely or in darkness,
the astonishing light of your own being."

–Hafiz

When compassion ripens, it becomes more than a response to pain. It turns into gratitude. Initially, compassion is simply the willingness to remain with what hurts, meeting it with love rather than judgment. But as this presence deepens, we begin to sense the sacredness of what we are holding. The wound that once felt unbearable reveals itself as a teacher. The ache becomes scripture. The struggle becomes the path that leads us home.

In this light, gratitude doesn't need to be forced; it naturally arises from understanding. Compassion shows us that every step of the journey, especially the painful ones, has been guiding us toward awakening. We start to thank what we once resisted. Gratitude blossoms not because life becomes easier, but because we have learned that everything belongs.

In the spiral of healing, gratitude is the fragrance of compassion. Gratitude is the subtle aroma that fills the heart once it learns to embrace life with love. The Mystic within us understands this. When we meet our own suffering with tenderness, the veil lifts, and we glimpse grace in all things.

Compassion always starts with the self. Without it, the mother ache remains raw. With it, the mother ache becomes part of the weave. Self-love isn't something we learn; it's something we remember through the steady rhythm of self-care. Love is our true nature. To embody this truth, we must live it through small daily actions, through each breath, each boundary, each blessing of the body. This is how compassion becomes embodied as a way of life. Not distant. Present. In your hands. In your breath. In your weave.

Sometimes I look back on my own spiral of healing and see that gratitude rarely arrived when I expected it. It came later, in stillness, like light returning after a long night. What once felt like failure revealed itself as initiation. The moments I resisted most fiercely became the thresholds that opened my heart the widest. I have learned that gratitude cannot be forced; it ripens when we stop fighting what is.

Even now, when I touch the small Green Tara pendant that rests against my heart, I whisper thank you—not because everything is resolved or I am fully healed. I whisper thank you because I have learned to trust the weave of my life as I weave it more and more consciously. Gratitude hums beneath the ache, reminding me that love and sorrow have always belonged to the same fibers of my own being.

Chapter Eleven:

The Wild Woman and the Fire of Wholeness

"Within every woman there is a wild and natural creature, a powerful force, filled with good instincts, passionate creativity, and ageless knowing."

—Clarissa Pinkola Estés

Wholeness isn't perfection. It is not the erasure of pain or flaw. Wholeness is the embrace of all that we are.

In the weaving of our healing basket, this is the moment when the rim gently flares open. The vessel opens wider and reveals its true shape. Then it is placed in the sun. The warmth hardens the beeswax our Mystic selves applied to the weave, giving it strength and permanence. Nothing is hidden. Nothing is erased. What was fragile becomes resilient through light and heat.

The Wild Woman is our guide here. She calls us back to instinct. She reminds us that no part of us belongs in exile. She is fierce and tender at once, claiming her power without apologies, living free of shame. Her archetypal energy belongs to every woman; it has always been our birthright. *Wholeness*.

Our culture feared her. Stories called her dangerous: witch, hag, madwoman. Yet she endured. She lived underground within our bodies, our longings, in the places we could not reveal to our mothers or even ourselves.

Now she rises again. She rises to witness the work you have done. She rises to bless the fertile ground of your healing. She rises to remind you that you are not meant to be small.

Wholeness means opening to every thread: the grief and the joy, the rage and the tenderness, the child, and the crone. Like the basket rim in the sun, the Wild Woman strengthens you through warmth, not denial. She shows that wholeness is fire and light, strength and softness, all woven into the shape of your becoming.

Walking with the Wild Woman is walking home. It says: *I am all of this. I am not broken. I am whole.*

The Wild Woman carries the basket into the sun. She sets it down upon the earth, allowing wind, warmth, and time to complete what her hands began. The elements gather in harmony—sunlight curing, earth grounding, air and fire blessing the weave. Her teaching is wholeness. In offering the basket to the earth, she recognizes herself in all things: the maker and the made, the weaver and the woven form. Through her, life remembers its unity.

Women Who Run with the Wolves

I first read *Women Who Run with the Wolves*[39] by Clarissa Pinkola Estés in my early thirties. It planted a seed in me that helped me step onto my path and begin to embrace my truth. This is a book of powerful women's stories, myths, and legends handed down over millennia and carefully resurrected to remind us of what must be remembered. Looking back, I see that reading it gave me permission to imagine stepping outside the box I had built around myself for safety, a box that had also become a trap.

When I reread it in my late forties, I was struck by how differently it spoke to me. Having walked a bit of the Wild Woman's path, I no longer read it as a distant inspiration but as a reflection. In my thirties, I thought: *If only I had the courage... if only my life would allow me to.* In my forties, I found myself whispering: *Yes, I know this woman. She is me.*

I was grateful to include this archetype in this book and encourage you to explore it further by reading Estés' book. It is a wise woman's gift to all women.

To illustrate, Clarissa Pinkola Estés shares the story of the Wild Woman as the Bone Collector, La Loba. An old, gnarled woman who lives in a hidden place wanders the desert collecting bones, especially those in danger of being lost to the world. Piece by piece, she gathers them, arranging them in order. When the skeleton is complete, she sings over it. In her song, the bones transform into a wolf. The wolf rises, shakes the dust from her fur, and runs across the desert. As she moves, she becomes a cackling woman *who runs free*. The Wild Woman returns.

This story teaches that nothing is ever truly lost. The bones symbolize the indestructible life force within each of us, and it is our sacred task to recover what has been scattered. What feels buried or broken is not gone; it is always there, waiting to be found. Even what seems too fragile or long forgotten can be called back with courage. The Wild Woman inside you remembers the song that brings these lost strands home. She reminds us that wholeness is not the absence of loss. It is the courage to gather what has been scattered. It is the faith to sing over our own bones until they rise again.

---

39 Clarissa Pinkola Estés, *Women Who Run With the Wolves: Myths and Stories of the Wild Woman Archetype* (New York: Ballantine Books, 1992).

During your healing journey through the mother ache, this is the moment to fully gather yourself. The strands you once left behind and the pieces you thought were too much or too little all belong here. The Wild Woman teaches you to reclaim them, open completely, and allow the sun of your own presence to strengthen the vessel of your life.

How the Mother Ache Teaches Us to Tame Ourselves

As we have explored throughout this book, The Mother Ache often teaches us to tame ourselves, to be acceptable, and to stay small. A daughter learns early that her wildness is too much. She is told she is *too loud, too angry, too free*.

Sometimes this happens through words. A mother warns her not to be selfish or dramatic. Sometimes it happens nonverbally. A mother withdraws when her daughter shows too much fire. Either way, the lesson is learned: hide what is untamed.

As we have learned together, what is suppressed does not vanish. It goes somewhere else. The Wild Woman does not vanish from our psyche. She goes underground. She becomes rage stored in the body. She becomes longing wrapped in shame. She becomes the voice that whispers secretly, *I want more*. Healing the mother ache means calling her back. It means listening for the instincts buried under fear. It means letting the body move, letting the voice rise, and allowing the truth to be spoken.

Reclaiming the Wild Woman is not rebellion against the mother; it is the restoration of the self. She reminds us: wholeness is not about hiding what makes others uncomfortable. Wholeness is about embodying every part of who you are.

Trusting the Voice That Rises From Within

The Wild Woman lives by intuition. She does not seek permission or follow old maps. She listens to what arises from within. She trusts the whisper that comes before thought.

When we say *trust your gut* or *my gut response is…* we are referring to this inner knowing that is rooted in the navel center we explored in Chapter Five. The Maiden's task was to reconnect with this center, restoring the bridge between body and instinct.

> *"Trust your instincts. Intuition doesn't come to an unprepared mind."*
>
> —Toni Morrison

Yet instinct alone is not enough. To truly hear what the navel has to say, our sacred center must also come online. The navel is the seat of intuition; the meditative mind is the field of awareness that enables us to listen. When these two centers work together, our intuition becomes clear, grounded, and trustworthy. Without our sacred center, we may confuse reactivity for intuition. With it, we can discern the truth that arises from deep within the body.

Every step you've taken since the start of this healing journey has been about turning inward to hear your own authentic voice, the voice that emanates from the navel and is rooted in love, not knowledge. You have learned to slow down, feel, and soften around beliefs. This inward listening has prepared you for something deeper: a voice not shaped by the mind or conditioned by fear. It is the voice of inner knowing.

In the basket-weaving metaphor, the Wild Woman places the vessel in the sun and flares its rim. This moment is about letting go and trusting. The weaver cannot control how the sun will harden the weave. She can only prepare the basket, lay it out, and let the warmth do its work. Intuition is much the same. It arises through openness, not effort. It speaks when space is created for it to emerge.

The Wild Woman reminds you that you were born with this knowing. You may have silenced it to survive. You might have learned to distrust, ignore, or dismiss it as silly. You may have lost touch with it when you disconnected from your body, your navel intelligence, your sacred center. But it has never left you.

The Wild Woman teaches that listening to the inner voice isn't about being right. It's the art of living from the inner light rather than conforming to expectations. This voice doesn't come from the mind; it emerges from the depths of being.

Like every process in this book, intuition unfolds as a sacred spiral. The more you listen, the more it speaks. The more you honor what it says, the stronger it becomes. Each turn of this spiral brings you closer to wholeness.

Reclaiming intuition involves trusting what you feel deep in your bones. This is the Wild Woman's gift: to know without needing proof; to follow the thread of inner truth; and to walk in harmony with your own rhythm.

The Wild Woman and the Return to Nourishment

The Wild Woman awakens as you start to meet your own needs. She is the one who refuses to beg for love. She does not barter. She does not plead. She remembers that your needs are not luxuries; they are your birthrights.

Animals understand this. They eat when hungry. They curl up when tired. They tremble out of fear, then return to stillness. The Wild Woman restores this same knowing in you. She shows that presence, safety, nurturance, guidance, acceptance, autonomy, and validation of feelings are not favors someone else must grant. They come from the Mother Earth beneath your feet, and they reside within you.

The mother ache taught you to wait, hope, and perform. The Wild Woman teaches you to act, feel, and trust your instincts. She reminds you that you are both daughter and inner mother now. You can tend to your own needs directly. You can stop abandoning yourself.

Meeting your needs isn't selfish, it's sacred. It's how wholeness becomes real. When you are nourished, rested, guided by your own wisdom, and free to feel your true emotions, your inner life becomes the light you've been seeking. This is the Wild Woman's gift. She takes the seven needs out of theory and into flesh.

She says: *Begin now. Feed yourself. Protect yourself. Rest when you are weary. Speak your feelings aloud. Trust your choices. Stand in your worth.*

Each time you do, you weave another strand of wholeness. You heal the mother ache and strengthen the vessel of your life.

Our Seven Needs Revisited

As we explored in Chapter Five, every daughter comes into the world with seven essential needs: presence, safety, nurturance, guidance, acceptance, encouragement of autonomy, and validation of feelings. These are the strands from which trust and love are woven.

When a mother cannot provide them, whether partially or completely, the daughter adapts. She learns to guard herself, to please others, to rebel, or to go numb. The weave holds, but with gaps. Now, in wholeness, we return to these needs with new eyes. You are no longer just the daughter who needed more than was available; you are the Wild Woman who makes whole. To step into wholeness is to take responsibility for meeting these needs within yourself, because your healing now requires it.

You can establish presence by showing up daily with attention and breath.

You can create safety by setting boundaries that keep you steady.

You can nurture yourself with food, touch, rest, and warmth.

You can guide yourself by listening to your inner wisdom.

You can practice acceptance by softening judgment when old wounds resurface.

You can encourage autonomy by trusting your choices.

You can validate your feelings by allowing them without shame.

Each act transforms the ache into wholeness. This is not a checklist of tasks to complete. It is a rhythm to practice. Some days you'll forget; some days you'll resist. That, too, belongs. Wholeness isn't perfection. It is the steady devotion of staying with yourself until these needs are met by you.

Rekindling the Sacred Fire of Creativity

The Wild Woman is the guardian of creative fire. She howls and sings, paints on cave walls, and brings new ways of being into existence. When the mother ache pressed you into smallness, that fire dimmed. You learned to suppress imagination, set aside play, and repress your inner artist.

Wholeness restores this fire. As you meet your needs and reclaim your instincts, the flow of creativity begins to move again. It may manifest as words, colors, movement, song, or the joy of tending to something you love. The form doesn't matter. What matters is that energy flows once more.

The Wild Woman reminds you that creativity isn't a luxury; it's breath for the soul. It is how you remember your aliveness. It is the exhale after repression, the rising howl that reshapes your world. Every time you create, you show yourself that the ache doesn't define you. You are more than what was missing.

Creation is not separate from healing; it *is* healing. When you create, you allow your life force to flow through your body and transform what was once frozen. Breath becomes a brushstroke. Movement becomes prayer. Story becomes medicine.

This is the alchemy of the Wild Woman, turning loss into art, silence into song, and ache into rhythm. She reminds you that creativity isn't about making something good. It's about letting energy come alive again. It's about trusting your impulses, your body, your joy. This is the Wild Woman's blessing, the fire that both softens and strengthens, returning you to your natural rhythm. Each act of creation, no matter how small, is a gesture of freedom and a thread in the weave of your wholeness.

Totality: Living the Creative Force of Life

Wholeness is the embrace of all that you are. Totality is how you live from that place. Creativity is the spark; totality is its expression. When the Wild Woman's creative fire is reclaimed, it naturally seeks to flow, through art, music, or writing; and also, through the simple act of being fully alive. Totality is creativity embodied in life itself.

When you move in totality, you give yourself fully to what is before you. If you laugh, you laugh with your whole body. If you grieve, you grieve with your entire heart. If you dance, you dance without holding anything back. Nothing is half-lived. Nothing is restrained.

Wholeness and totality spiral together. When you allow yourself to be whole, you stop hiding parts of yourself. You feel complete. From that completeness, you step into life with totality. And when you live in totality, your wholeness deepens. You begin to see that nothing in you needs to be cut off or contained.

This is when life-force returns. The energy once trapped in shame or repression begins to flow again. Vitality rises. Radiance glows from within. The basket shines because it is alive with every thread.

Totality doesn't mean control. It doesn't mean always feeling joyful or strong. It means being fully present with what is here. Total in anger. Total in grief. Total in joy. Total in love. When you are total, every part of you has permission to exist.

The Wild Woman understands this. She does not ration her energy. She does not perform for approval. She immerses herself fully in life as it unfolds. Her strength lies in abundance. She reminds you that living authentically and completely is the key to freedom.

This is the spiral: wholeness allows for totality. Totality deepens wholeness. Together, they restore the natural flow of your being. They also heal the mother ache, which taught you to fragment, to shrink, and to half-live. Together, they weave you back into your true self: vital, radiant, and whole.

Experiential Invitation: Nataraj Meditation, Dancing into Totality

The Wild Woman doesn't hold back. She moves from instinct, not effort. She embodies a flowing river of energy that moves through every part of her body. To meet her is to surrender control and let movement become prayer, to trust the body to lead and the mind to follow. This meditation practice encourages you to embrace totality through dance.

Set aside a full hour. Find a space where you can move freely, unobserved. Dim the lights. Close your eyes. Allow the music to become your teacher and your muse. You can use the traditional Osho Nataraj Meditation soundtrack or create your own hour-long playlist that evokes a sense of freedom and depth, inviting movement.

First Stage—The Dance (40 minutes)

Begin by standing still. Listen as the music starts to resonate within you. Take a few slow breaths. Feel the ground beneath your feet. When you're ready, allow movement to happen naturally. Don't steer it. Don't choreograph. Let your body move as it wishes. Allow each cell to join in. Dance as if you've disappeared, as if only life itself is moving. There is no watcher now, only the dance. Be total.

Second Stage—The Silence (20 minutes)

When the music stops, allow your body to find stillness. Lie down on the ground with eyes closed. Feel the echo of movement vibrating through you, the vital energy that danced beyond the mind. Let the silence absorb you. Rest in the center of your being, where motion and stillness meet.

Third Stage—The Celebration (5 minutes)

When the final music starts, stand up slowly. Let joy move through your body. This last dance is a celebration of life, of embodiment, of your willingness to fully show up. Smile. Laugh. Be wild.

When the practice ends, sit quietly for a few minutes. Feel your heartbeat, the hum of being alive. Notice how totality brings peace and how surrender awakens strength. The Wild Woman lives here in reverence, in wholeness. Every time you dance like this, you loosen the chains of self-consciousness and remember the freedom woven into your bones. This is your body's wisdom. This is your totality.

Mother Ache Healing in the World

The Daughter Who Inherited the Path: Finding Her Voice

We met Natasha in the previous chapter and continue her story here. As Natasha's guarding continued to soften, something else began to stir beneath the layers of steadiness and composure. It was not grief this time, but longing. A desire to feel more alive. To move energy outward rather than hold it in. To let sound, breath, and emotion take form beyond the stillness of meditation.

For much of her life, Natasha had lived efficiently and capably. She accomplished what needed to be done. She stayed busy. Yet beneath that competence lived an unexpressed current. The Wild Woman within her had been waiting patiently, to animate her devotion.

The first opening came when she answered the call to take private singing lessons, chosen almost tentatively, which offered a place where she could explore sound without being seen. At first, her voice felt unfamiliar in her own body. Breath caught. Notes wavered. Emotion rose unexpectedly. Singing asked something different of her nervous system. It invited presence without containment. Expression without apology.

Over time, the practice expanded into weekly group singing. Being witnessed in her voice awakened both vulnerability and pleasure. Sound moved through her chest and belly, loosening old holding patterns. Where words had once failed, tone carried truth. Where guarding had protected her, song offered liberation. This was not performance. It was embodiment.

As Natasha sang, she felt herself reclaim a birthright that had been paused rather than lost. The Wild Woman does not rush expression. She waits until the body is ready to speak. Through rhythm and breath, Natasha discovered that joy and grief could coexist. That devotion and desire were not opposites. That life-force long held in reserve was safe to release.

When Natasha eventually recorded her first song, it emerged from this place of integration. Unsurprisingly, the song was about her mother and her energetic presence in her life. The song is about her maternal lineage carried forward through voice. It holds tenderness, longing, devotion, and life all at once:

Can you see me?
Can you feel me?
Living through me
'Cause I feel you in my bones

—Natasha

This is the Wild Woman's medicine. She returns what has been contained back into the world as creative force. She reminds us that healing is about stillness and movement in equal measure. It's about meditation yes, and expression. When guarding relaxes enough for desire to surface, the Wild Woman steps forward to claim her place. Natasha's voice is no longer waiting. It is living. It is free.

Journal Reflections: Reweaving Wholeness

Recognizing the Wild Woman Within

Before you write, close your eyes and breathe into the wild ground beneath you. Imagine roots unfurling from your spine into the Earth, drinking from the same ancient pulse that moves through rivers, tides, and moonlight. The Wild Woman lives there at the meeting point between nature and us. She is the rhythm beneath your breath, the one who remembers how to move, feel, and trust without restraint. These reflections invite you to listen for her voice and welcome her home to the weave of your life.

How do I recognize the Wild Woman within?

How might I connect with her?

How does embodying this energy ask me to move differently in my life?

How might my life change if I allowed her energy to be part of the weave of my life again?

Intuition

These reflections invite you to remember the ways your inner knowing has always been present and to listen for how it wishes to guide you now.

When have I heard my inner voice and chosen not to follow it?

When have I listened, and what was the result?

How might I create more space in my life to let my intuitive knowing guide me?

The Creative Fire

Before you write, take a slow breath and imagine a small flame glowing at your center. This is the Wild Woman's fire. It is the creative pulse of life that burns with aliveness. For the Wild Woman within each of us, creativity is her way of remembering wholeness, of transforming what was once constrained into movement and flow. These reflections invite you to listen for where that flame longs to travel, and how it wishes to shape your life from within.

Where is my creativity most eager to flow right now?
What part of me represses or judges those impulses?
What would happen if I allowed myself to create just for me, without worrying about it being good?
How might my creative expression become part of my daily rhythm of wholeness?

Dancing in Totality

Totality is the Wild Woman's prayer of wholeness, the dance where body, emotion, and spirit move as one. Let these reflections help you listen for what your dance revealed.
What did totality feel like in my body?
Where did I notice resistance, hesitation, or control?
Did any emotions or memories arise as I danced?
How does my body feel now, after movement and silence?
What truth about my Wild Woman revealed itself through this dance?

Natasha's Story Part Two

What longing for freedom, expression, or voice do I recognize in Natasha's journey?
Where in my life have I kept parts of myself contained or quiet for safety?
What creative impulse feels ready to emerge now, even if it feels tender or unfamiliar?
How might reclaiming my voice be an act of wholeness rather than performance?

Wholeness asks you to welcome all of yourself. As you complete this chapter, notice what feels more integrated, more trusted, more alive in you. The Wild Woman holds life's contradictions without trying to resolve them. She teaches you to stand inside your full humanity without apology. From this place, you move forward as a woman learning how to live what you already are: whole, complete, perfect because of every wild, wooly imperfection that makes you uniquely you.

Conclusion: Wholeness and the Mother Ache

"We must strive to allow our souls to grow in their natural ways and to their natural depths. The wildish nature does not require a woman to be a certain color, a certain education, a certain lifestyle or economic class . . . in fact, it cannot thrive in an atmosphere of enforced political correctness, or being bent into old burnt-out paradigms. It thrives on fresh sight and self-integrity. It thrives on its own nature."

—Clarissa Pinkola Estés

The Mother Ache is the wound of disconnection. It taught you to fragment yourself to stay loved. It taught you to hide your anger, soften your desire, and quiet your voice. It left you feeling partial, never enough, always searching.

Wholeness is the answer to that ache. It is the state you were born into. The child came whole. The ache came later.

To heal the Mother Ache is to reclaim the silenced parts, to welcome the cut-off strands, and weave them back into the basket. The Wild Woman knows this path. She is the one calling you home. She remembers the natural state beneath the wound. She whispers, *You were never broken. All of you belong*.

Like La Loba, the Bone Collector, she gathers what was scattered. She finds the pieces you thought were lost, arranges them tenderly, and sings them back to life. Her song is your own breath, your movement, your voice rising again. As the bones assemble, the wolf runs free, and you, too, remember your original rhythm.

For me, a felt sense of wholeness arrived subtly. For years, I wondered when I would become creative, when I would finally feel that wild, inspired flow I imagined might be possible within me. But creativity didn't come as a single event; it developed as a way of life. It showed itself in my daily rhythm: in the garden, where my hands move with the earth; in the kitchen, where I stir warmth into food; in the space between breaths with my clients; in the song that rises unbidden during a walk. Without noticing, I was already living in the flow I longed for. Wholeness had become creativity itself, life expressing through me in a hundred simple ways.

When you embrace the Wild Woman, you find that healing isn't about becoming someone different. It's about reconnecting with who you have always been: whole, vital, and alive. The ache softens here. The past is not erased. The ache is integrated into the story. It no longer tears the weave apart; it makes it stronger. This is why wholeness is a journey. It is a homecoming where the ache itself becomes the very strength of the basket holding your life.

As wholeness takes root, something begins to steady within you. What you have integrated now asks to be lived. In the next chapter, we meet the Priestess, the one who teaches how wholeness becomes embodied presence.

Chapter Twelve:

The Priestess and Embodied Presence

"Your body is the temple of the divine. Dwell there in reverence."
—Sri Aurobindo

The Priestess, our final inner archetypal teacher is the circle within the circle of our healing journey. Here, the weaving of your healing basket appears complete. The base is sturdy, the sides are shaped, and the rim has been bound with care. Each thread of your being has been softened, polished with light, and laid in the sun to cure. For a moment, the basket rests in your hands. The ache that once drove your search now hums at the center, transformed into a pulse of understanding.

Yet the Priestess whispers, this is not an ending. Wholeness is not static. The weave continues. Each breath renews it. Each moment of awareness tightens or loosens the rim. Healing is a spiral, ever-turning, ever-returning, always revealing new depths of presence through the familiar strands of your life.

The Priestess thus teaches us that *embodied presence* is a rhythm to remember. It is a way of living as a prayer: movement, breath, connection, and stillness flowing together as one seamless current. You will forget and return, open and close, lose and find the strands of your healing journey. The Priestess stands within you during these moments of return. She reminds you how to bow to the ordinary, to the pulse of the sacred center where ache becomes devotion.

The Priestess is the guardian of thresholds. She dwells between the visible and the unseen worlds, and her body is her temple. She embodies the parts of you that have ripened through every stage of the spiral: the Innocent Child's awareness, the Magical Child's curiosity, the Wounded Child's honesty, and the Orphan Child's trust; the Maiden's acceptance, the Seeker's connection to self, the Weaver's understanding, the Healer's empathy, the Alchemist's fire, the Mystic's compassion, and the Wild Woman's sense of wholeness. Now she gathers all these facets of her being and holds them in her gaze, inviting them to sing together.

In ancient lineages, the Priestess tended the fires that marked the turning of the seasons. Her task was to keep the flame alive through every darkness and every dawn. The same applies within you: the Priestess within you maintains the light of these qualities burning as your life continues to spiral for you and your healing journey. She is not the culmination of your healing but the presence that keeps it sacred as you uncover more healing layers to alchemize into love.

In her hands, the basket becomes an offering of reciprocity, returned to the lineage that wove you and to those who will follow. She blesses what has been crafted, knowing it will someday unravel, and she blesses that too.

Through her, you realize that healing has never been about fixing the past or preparing for the future. It has always been about learning to live at the threshold, where breath meets breath, where life meets itself. Here, now.

The Priestess teaches that the fruit of healing is presence. Communion. To live with ache and grace, always opening to more becoming.

The Priestess and the Mother Ache

The mother ache fractures our trust in life. It teaches us to seek love through pleasing, to mistake approval for safety, and to abandon ourselves for belonging. The Priestess offers another way. She remembers that love cannot be earned; it is revealed through being. Her worth does not depend on what she offers but on the radiance of her presence. She knows that to inhabit herself fully is to pray with every breath.

When the Priestess awakens within you, old patterns start to soften. The desire to be chosen loosens its hold, revealing the truth that you have always been held. The need to prove your worth gives way to a steady rhythm of self-trust. Where you once gave from depletion, you now give from abundance. Where you once sought recognition, you discover the gaze of your own soul meeting you from within.

The Priestess lives in communion with her body. She listens to its messages, honors its seasons, and trusts its cycles. She moves with life's rhythm rather than against it. She rests when rest is needed, rises when the current calls her forward. In this rhythm, she heals the ancestral pattern of the legacy of women who poured themselves out until nothing was left.

Her way is in establishing right relationships. She understands that presence depends on boundaries. She no longer shrinks to ease others' discomfort or molds herself to what is familiar. She engages with others as equals—heart to heart—without losing herself. Through her presence, the mother ache is continually rewoven: transforming fear into trust, abandonment into belonging, silence into song.

The Priestess teaches that true authority is about the inner harmony of body, heart, and spirit. When these are in alignment, your life becomes a sacred temple. She also reminds you that coherence is not a fixed state; it is a living balance that you renew each time you return to yourself. Living this way means embodying prayer and offering your life from devotion rather than depletion.

Each time you forget, you will remember. Every time you close, you will open again. The weave continues. This is the practice of the Priestess: to live in rhythm with what is real, to let love flow through what once ached, to serve the sacred by being fully human.

At the end of the spiral, the Priestess lifts the basket and offers it back to nature. Her gesture is both culmination and return. What began as gathering and weaving becomes giving. She stands in stillness, vessel in hand, knowing the circle is whole. The basket is no longer hers. It belongs to the living field. In this offering, she fulfills her vow to live as the weave itself, where creation and Creator are one.

The Orphan and the Priestess

For much of my life, I carried an ache of loneliness. It wasn't visible to others. It lived deep inside, like a small, echoing chamber where no one could quite reach me. Even in love's company, I felt a veil between us, a subtle sense of being apart. I mistook that feeling for being unworthy of love, believing that something in me was missing, lost.

But through the slow practice of presence and the courage to stay with myself, I discovered that beneath the ache was not emptiness, but spaciousness. In that vast, tender silence, I began to feel accompanied by existence itself. Aloneness revealed itself as belonging. The ache had always been the doorway to grace.

Now, when I sit alone, I feel embraced by kinship in the wind's breath, the heartbeat of the earth, and the presence of the Great Mother who has never left. Silence becomes a companion, and my aloneness, a sanctuary. I no longer seek to be completed; I remember that I already am.

This is the Priestess's gift. She teaches that solitude is initiation. When we stop fleeing from aloneness, it becomes a sanctuary. In that stillness, we become strong, clear, and luminous vessels of grace.

The Orphan taught you how to face loneliness without fear, to stand in your own company and begin the gradual process of trusting yourself. She showed that healing starts when you no longer wait to be rescued. You learned that your life is in your own hands.

Now the Priestess steps forward, blessing what the Orphan began. Where the Orphan learned to trust aloneness, the Priestess learns to *serve* it. She sits in stillness not because she has never known loss, but because she has made peace with it. She understands the difference between loneliness and aloneness, which is the vast quiet that opens when you inhabit your being fully. What once felt like emptiness becomes presence. What once felt like exile becomes home.

In the weaver's art, the final act is consecration. Here, we might hold the basket close to our hearts and whisper blessings over its rim. The Priestess within each of us embodies this blessing. She gathers all that we've woven—our ache, our courage, our love—and seals it with presence. To bless what we've made does not mean it is finished. We are simply honoring the mystery that continues. As we do so, perhaps we make a vow: *I can hold myself, my life. I can offer it back in reciprocity.*

Some years ago, I sat in a circle with seekers who had just emerged from deep meditation, each carrying their own ache. One woman began to weep. The part of me trained to comfort wanted to reach out, to soothe. But a quieter voice within whispered: *Just be with her*.

So I placed a hand over my heart, took a breath, and remained still. No fixing. No rescuing. Only presence. Slowly, her breathing steadied; the air softened. When she looked up, her eyes were clear. "For the first time," she said, "I didn't feel alone in my pain."

That moment revealed the Priestess's deepest teaching: healing does not come through effort but through embodied presence. The Priestess serves not by doing, but by being, embodying the spacious, grounded love that allows life to recognize itself.

Experiential Invitation: Consecrating the Basket that is Life

The Priestess honors what has been woven, not because it is finished, but because it is alive. She understands that healing occurs in spirals, always returning to the sacred in new ways. This ritual invites you to consecrate the basket that is your life as a living altar by naming its purpose of healing and offering it back to life with gratitude. It is not an ending, but a pause within the weave, a way to remember the holiness already present.

Preparation

Return to the altar you created earlier in this journey. Refresh it with what feels alive now: a candle, fresh flowers, a stone from a recent walk, a feather, a strand of woven fiber. Let these be reminders of your ongoing relationship with the elements of earth, water, fire, air, and ether that continue to support your becoming.

Arrival

Sit or stand before your altar. Close your eyes. Breathe slowly. Feel the ground beneath you, the breath within you. Sense that you are being embraced by the earth, the altar, and the unseen presence of the Divine that sustains you. Whisper softly: *I am here, now*.

Remembering

Let your awareness gently move through this spiral of healing, the journey we've shared. The ache that called you. The archetypes that guided your path. The healing strands you've woven. See them gathered in the basket of your life: strong, imperfect, shining with love. Bless what remains unfinished. It too belongs.

Anointing

Light the candle. Place your hands on your heart and belly. As you breathe, acknowledge your body as the living altar of your journey. You may speak these words, or your own:

This body is my altar. This breath is my prayer. This life is my offering, ever weaving in the sacred spiral that is life.

Let these words echo inside you until they feel like truth.

Offering

Lift your hands above your heart in a gesture of giving. Offer gratitude to your mother, your lineage, the Great Mother within and around you, and the earth that holds your becoming. Imagine a soft golden light radiating from your center, blessing not only what has been woven but also what is still waiting to take shape.

Rest

Blow out the candle or watch its flame flicker and fade. Feel the warmth of the ritual settle into your body. You have not completed your work; you are living it. The Priestess breathes through you now, reminding you that consecration is not a one-time act; it is the daily act of showing up with reverence for what is.

Consecration is never final; it's a beginning wrapped in gratitude. Each time you bless your life, something new awakens in the silence, a subtle current longing to be expressed. The Priestess senses this movement inside and recognizes it as the next rhythm of devotion, her voice. What was woven in stillness now desires to be heard in the world as prayer.

The Priestess and the Power of Voice

There was a morning years ago, just before dawn, when I sat beside a river wrapped in my shawl. Mist rose from the surface like breath. I had come with a question I couldn't name, something about direction, something about finding my true voice, the one beneath all the layers of ache and adaptation. For years, my voice had been the first to go silent when I felt unsafe. As a child, I learned that staying small could protect and shield me quite effectively. Reclaiming my voice has been a long, uneven road and a slow remembering that to speak, sing, or write is to allow myself to be seen.

That morning, I found myself simply listening to the water and to the pulse of my own heart beating quietly in rhythm with nature. Then, in the stillness, I heard words, not through my ears, but from within: *Your voice is not yours alone. Speak for the ones who cannot.*

It wasn't a grand proclamation. It was a whisper, steady, ancient, and sure that carried the weight of remembrance. In that moment, I understood that voice, when aligned with truth, is a responsibility. The Priestess does not speak to be seen; she speaks to serve. Her words are not for applause, but as offerings of healing and authenticity for others.

From that day forward, I began to treat my voice as a sacred instrument that must be tuned in silence before it can sing. Each time I sing, teach, or write, I remember that silence, that river, and the long road that brought me home to my own voice.

As healing deepens, the voice begins to rise. Our words come from presence, not performance. Through our Priestess, we learn that voice is meant to be a current of clarity flowing from the heart, guided by inner wisdom.

Healing the mother ache involves reclaiming this voice. When your voice was dismissed, or shamed, you learned to hold it back. The Priestess restores it. She invites you to speak confidently, from the center of your being, your sacred center.

This voice may not always be loud. Sometimes it is a whisper that says, *no more*. Sometimes it is a prayer that says, *yes, I'm ready*. Sometimes it is gratitude breathed into the world, *thank you*. Sometimes it is a shared song. Whatever form it takes, it carries dignity because it arises from the depth of your truth.

The Priestess teaches that voice is devotion. When you speak from presence, your truth becomes an offering that liberates not only yourself but also those who hear it. Your words turn into medicine, born of silence and woven with love.

Voice, like weaving, is a continuous practice. Each word, each silence, adds another thread to the spiral of presence. You will forget, then remember; speak, then return to listening. The Priestess reminds you that truth resides in the ongoing dance between silence and sound, between what is spoken and what is felt.

When voice emerges from silence, it becomes prayer. When it returns to silence, it becomes devotion. The Priestess understands this rhythm well, to speak from the heart, then to sing it back into stillness. Her voice is an offering from her healing. It is also an exhale of all that is woven within her as she continues to heal. This is the voice beneath the voice, the one that has always known how to speak in alignment with truth.

Experiential Invitation: Singing Yourself Home

The Priestess understands that voice is vibration, a bridge between the seen and unseen worlds. When sound arises from presence, it becomes prayer. This practice encourages you to reclaim your voice as sacred sound. It's not about performance or perfection. It's a way of remembering that the vibration of your being is holy.

For me, this practice started many years ago with the mantra *Om Tare Tuttare Ture Soha*. It was the first sound I ever dared to share aloud. Over time, other mantras and healing songs came to me. Each one arrived as medicine for a particular moment, some for grief, some for courage, some for healing. The more I lifted my voice, the more these songs arrived as truth within me, as if singing itself opened a channel for healing to flow. Your own voice will call its companions in the same way.

We start by choosing a mantra. Mantra is the language of vibration and the meeting of breath, intention, and sound. Each syllable shapes the subtle body, tuning it like an instrument. As you chant, let meaning arise not only from the words, but from how they feel as they vibrate through you.

There are countless mantras and sacred songs across traditions, each carrying its own vibration and medicine. You may already have one that lives in your heart, or you might let one of these call to you. If you wish, explore recordings that speak to your spirit. Many can be found on your favorite streaming platform. I've shared a selection of my own healing mantras and chants on my Spotify account, including a few of the ones that continue to accompany my practice. A few of my favorites include:

Om Tare Tuttare Ture Soha

The mantra of Green Tara, the Goddess of Compassion. Invoking her energy invites healing, protection, and swift liberation from fear and suffering.

So Hum

"I am That." A reminder that your essence and the essence of life are one, the breath whispering your connection with all that is.

Ma

The simplest and oldest prayer, the sound of the Great Mother herself. A vibration of comfort, belonging, and surrender.

Ra Ma Da Sa Sa Say So Hung

The healing mantra of the Golden Chain, chanted to call upon the sun, moon, earth, and infinite Spirit. It restores balance in the body and radiates light to those in need of healing.

Om Shanti Shanti Shanti

A prayer for peace within the self, in relationship, and in the world. Each repetition softens the edges of separation.

Om Mani Padme Hum

"The jewel is in the lotus." A Tibetan mantra for awakening compassion and recognizing the sacred within every experience.

The Mul Mantra

A chant of remembering: that beneath our wounds, identities, and inherited stories, there is a core of truth that cannot be broken. This mantra brings us home to that sacred center.

Allow the mantra to choose you. There is no right or wrong. What matters is the feeling that this sound resonates within your heart.

Once you have selected a mantra to sing aloud, find a space where you feel comfortable and at ease. Sit comfortably with your spine straight and your heart open. You might light a candle on your altar and hold your hands at your heart in prayer mudra. Take a few slow breaths and notice your body as an instrument of resonance, with your chest, belly, and throat all gently open to produce sound.

Listening

Begin in silence. Listen inwardly for the tone that wants to emerge as you play the mantra. This listening is the first note of prayer.

Chanting

Begin softly, repeating your chosen mantra as a whisper and gradually let your voice rise. Allow it to move through your breath and body, not your mind. Feel the vibration travel along your spine, through your heart center, and down to your navel center, as we did in the humming meditation. If emotion arises, let it flow. This is sound becoming healing. Continue for several minutes, or as long as the vibration feels alive.

Silence.

After chanting, rest in stillness. Let the sound echo through you. Feel the resonance of the mantra lingering inside your body as a hum of belonging that needs no words.

Integration

You might want to practice this daily, singing to yourself as an act of devotion. Your voice becomes both a vessel and a prayer. I often sing on my walks as a way to pray and express my felt sense of gratitude. When you finish, rest your palms over your heart or throat and take one slow breath. Notice the stillness that follows the song. Feel the silence that holds it all. This is the true mantra: the living pulse of awareness singing itself home through you.

Each sound you make is a thread of remembrance, weaving you back to the Great Song of Aum that exists beneath everything. Some days, your voice might tremble or fall silent. Still, the vibration continues, echoing in the body of the world.

This is how healing ripens. We do not arrive somewhere. We inhabit where we are and offer gratitude for this very moment. You will spiral through these teachings again and again: awareness, curiosity, honesty, trust, acceptance, empathy, alchemy, compassion, wholeness, presence. Each turn refines the gold already within you. Each breath is another prayer. The Priestess bows in devotion. She understands that embodied wholeness is not a place we reach; it is a rhythm we learn to live.

Experiential Invitation: Where Ache Becomes Devotion

When I am deep in prayer, I often find myself in this posture: knees pulled close, arms wrapped around, head bowed, spine curved inward, rocking gently to the rhythm of my breath or music in ceremony. I do not plan it; it simply happens, as if some ancient memory awakens within my body. I imagine that long before words, this was how we prayed: not by reaching upward, but by folding inward and bowing to the mystery that holds us all.

You might find yourself here as well. It's also the posture of the Wounded Child, protective, small, seeking safety. And yet, as the spiral shows, what starts in pain can turn into reverence. The same body that once curled for defense now bows in devotion. The posture stays the same, but its meaning changes.

Find a space to meditate. Gently draw your knees toward your chest. Lower your head until your forehead tilts toward your heart. Feel the curvature of your spine and the comfort of your own embrace. Breathe softly into your belly.

Seated once more in stillness, we return to the posture where our journey began. As we bow, the gesture is one of remembrance, a humble offering of our self to the mystery that has always held us. The basket, now complete, resides within our heart. In this devotion, we become both prayer and the one prayed for, the weaver and the woven, the Priestess who knows that every breath is sacred.

This is the oldest prayer. You don't need to lift your face to be seen, nor speak to be heard. The earth beneath you knows.

Here, the spiral completes itself. You return to where you began, but now you arrive with a sense of wholeness, of belonging to the whole. The wound has become a doorway. The ache has become prayer.

Stay here as long as you need, breathing with the Great Mother, letting Her breath move through you. When you are ready, lift your head slowly. Unfold gently, like a fern uncurling in morning light. Let your spine rise, your heart open, and your gaze soften. Bow once again. Notice this is not from deficiency, but from devotion. Remember this posture, as it holds both the ache of your wounded child and the devotion of the priestess within. This is how we heal by embracing the full spectrum of our lives.

Embodied Presence: From Ache to Offering

The mother ache once fractured your trust, teaching you to confuse love with approval and safety with smallness. Embodied presence restores that trust. It brings you home to your sacred center, where choices arise from attunement rather than fear. It teaches you to belong to yourself while remaining in relationship with all of life.

When presence ripens, it naturally overflows into reciprocity. There is no effort involved, only the gentle rhythm of giving and receiving that life itself embodies. You give without losing yourself, serve without betraying yourself, and offer without erasure. Embodied presence is alignment in motion, guided by love. It moves with integrity and grace. It listens through the body, breathes with the spirit, and walks in rhythm with truth. It neither denies nor defends; it integrates.

All wisdom traditions echo this idea. Buddhism teaches compassion through presence. Nondual paths remind us that the Self is already whole through presence. Indigenous teachings ground embodiment in reciprocity through gratitude, stewardship, and service to future generations, through presence. All come together in one truth: embodied presence is genuine prayer that results in reciprocity, which is genuine devotion.

Moving from ache to embodiment means shifting from seeking approval to living with devotion; from fragmentation to coherence; from projection to participation; from numbness to feeling and wise response. The ache taught you to earn love. Presence reveals that *you are love*.

Indigenous wisdom reminds us that reciprocity is a way of living. Gratitude fills every breath and choice. We belong to one another, to the land, to the unseen weave of being. Living this truth means allowing love at the center of our being to circulate freely through our own selves, our loved ones, and the world.

Simple gestures keep this rhythm alive: a conscious breath before action, a pause before speech, a prayer before eating, a candle lit in remembrance, a gentle no to guard your fire, a wholehearted yes to what opens you. Service becomes a way of being, a kind word, a shared meal, a silent blessing. True reciprocity values interdependence. It gives from abundance, not from depletion, and receives with humility. Reciprocity is the knowing that embodied presence is never solitary. It is reciprocity and moves through you, to you, and from you in an endless spiraling weave of grace.

The Innocence of Wisdom

The Priestess's final teaching is that beneath it all through embodied presence we return to innocence. The spiritual journey of healing brings you home to right relationship with your body, your lineage, your community, and the sacred. Embodied presence matures into reciprocity, where gratitude and offering flow as one. What once required effort transforms into devotion.

And so, we return to the beginning. The Innocent Child we met at the start of this journey has never left you. She is the pulse beneath every transformation, the awareness that witnessed it all. What began as innocence has become wisdom; what began as presence has become prayer. The destination, it turns out, was never elsewhere. It has always been here, within.

The Priestess stands in that knowing, firm in her promise. Her power is bestowed by the unseen hands of those who came before and by the trust of those who will come after. Your healing is not solitary. It flows in both directions: back to your mother and lineage and forward to those yet unborn. This is how ache becomes medicine, and how the basket of your life becomes a living prayer.

> *"We are not human beings having a spiritual experience. We are spiritual beings having a human experience."*
>
> —Teilhard de Chardin

Journal Reflections: Reweaving Embodied Presence

Before you work with these prompts, take a few breaths and feel the weight of your body supported by the earth. Imagine a temple within you, your own sacred center, where the heart burns steady as an altar flame. The Priestess lives here, in the stillness that listens and the presence that radiates without effort. These reflections invite you to meet that presence within yourself.

Living from Presence

If I trusted my own worth completely, how would I move or speak differently?

What does embodied presence feel like in my body?
How can I offer the basket of my life as devotion, not depletion?

Consecrating the Basket

Consecration is the reminder that devotion and everyday life are woven from the same thread. Let these reflections help you sense how that holiness now resides within you.

What feelings arose as I blessed my life as sacred?
How might I carry this devotion into ordinary moments?
What does it mean to live as a consecrated being in motion?

Reclaiming the Voice

Before you write, take a few slow breaths and rest one hand over your throat and one over your heart. Feel the current that moves between them, between expression and compassion. Your voice is not only sound; it is vibration, presence, and prayer. These reflections invite you to meet your voice as something sacred that is both fragile and strong, both wholly yours and part of the greater song of life.

Where in my life do I still silence my voice?
What truth longs to be spoken, even if only to myself?
How can I honor my voice today as a sacred instrument of love and clarity?

Mantra: Singing Yourself Home

Before you write, sit for a moment in the afterglow of sound. Feel the subtle vibration that lingers in your body, perhaps the hum beneath silence, the echo of your own devotion. Mantra is both ancient and intimate, a way of remembering your belonging through breath and tone. These reflections invite you to honor how the sacred sound moved through you and what it awakened.

Which mantra or sound resonated most deeply with me?
How did it feel to let my voice vibrate through my body?
Did any emotions or memories rise through the sound?
How might I bring this vibration of devotion into my daily life?

Reciprocity

Reciprocity is the natural flow of life when you embody presence. These reflections invite you to sense how that balance lives in your body today.

What does reciprocity mean to me in this season of my life?
How does gratitude open the space for reciprocity to flow?
What does it mean to offer reciprocity to myself with care and respect?
Where in my life am I being invited to give back to what has nourished me?
How might I embody reciprocity as a daily practice of offering kindness or care?

The Final Homecoming

Homecoming is the final turning of the spiral. It is the return not to where we began, but to a deeper way of being within it. It is the realization that everything we sought, including love, belonging, meaning, was never outside of us. It lived beneath the ache, waiting for us to slow down enough to feel it and remember.

For so long, I believed home was a place I had to find, something I might reach after enough healing, enough traveling, enough becoming. But the further I went, the more I discovered that home was not somewhere I could arrive. It was the breath inside me and the earth beneath me, wherever I find myself, here, now.

Homecoming happens when we stop trying to be someone else's version of whole. When we soften around our scars and allow the ordinary to become sacred again. It's in the morning light, in the scent of rain on the soil, in the laughter that breaks through grief.

To come home is to inhabit your own rhythm. It is to trust your body's wisdom, to honor your emotions as teachers, to live as though the Divine were moving through your hands in every small act of care. You do not need to travel far to find the sacred. The same wisdom that calls from temples and jungles also whispers in your kitchen, in the breath between tasks, in the moments when you choose tenderness over striving.

Healing asks that you enter your life fully, with awareness, honesty, curiosity, and compassion. Each act of presence while washing dishes, lighting a candle, listening to the body's felt sense is a thread in the weave of remembrance. The Divine Mother meets you there in participation.

The Great Mother does not ask us to be perfect; She asks us to be present. Homecoming is Her embrace made visible through our lives. Each time we return to the breath, we return to Her. You are already within the circle, already under Her wing. The journey home is not outward, but inward, to the heart that has been waiting, patient and luminous, all along.

And so, we continue, thread by thread, remembering that every act of love is another step home. My story is only one of countless weavings. Yours, too, is part of this greater tapestry—a living thread in the spiral of remembrance. As you close these pages, may you feel the rhythm of your own story continuing, soft but sure, carrying you home to the wisdom that has always been yours.

Chapter 13:

The Daily Weaving of a Living Prayer

"Do not worry if your basket is not perfectly made. Weave with the materials you have, in the moment you are in. Let the weaving itself become your prayer."

—Jigme Khyentse Rinpoche

Every weaving must come to an end, yet our healing basket is also never truly finished. Life keeps adding new strands, the wind reshapes its curve, and sunlight deepens its color. So, it is with your healing. The healing basket you have created here is a living vessel, one that will keep evolving alongside you.

You have gathered the fibers of your story, some delicate, some thorny. You have sorted them, softened them, and shaped them with breath and patience. You have faced the ache that lay beneath the surface and discovered the gold hidden within. You have remembered that healing is not a destination but a relationship, a practice of returning again and again to what is true.

Now the basket rests in your hands, warm from the sun and entrusted with purpose. It is strong enough to hold your life, yet supple enough to keep growing. The weave of awareness, curiosity, honesty, trust, acceptance, connection, understanding, empathy, inner alchemy, compassion, wholeness, and embodied presence is now yours. Each thread remains alive within you.

Your sacred center blesses this moment. You stand between worlds, rooted and receptive, your presence a bridge between what has been healed and what still needs attention. You know your healing basket is neither complete nor perfect. It doesn't have to be. Perfection closes the weave; presence keeps it open to life and the ever-unfolding nature of existence.

The Practice of Daily Weaving

Healing continues in the ordinary. Every day presents small invitations to reweave what matters. You don't have to look far; the sacred is woven into the simplest acts.

When you wake up, pause before getting out of bed. Feel your breath and quietly say, *I am here*. When you eat, bless your food and remember all the hands and ingredients that nourished it. This is connection. When you walk, let your feet touch the earth gently. This is trust. When you meet someone's eyes, soften yours. This is compassion. When you feel pain, take a moment. Place a hand on your body and breathe deeply. This is empathy. When you falter, come back to awareness. This is honesty. When you create, whether it's a meal, a journal entry, or a craft, do it with love. This is alchemy. When you rest, let your rest be complete. This is acceptance. When you feel alone, look up at the sky, the trees, the stars. Remember the Great Mother, who holds all. This is presence.

These are not tasks, they are touchstones, ways to keep weaving. Over time, they turn into rhythm, devotion, prayer. Your life becomes the ceremony itself.

Every basket, once finished, is meant to serve. Healing, too, ripens into offering. When you live from embodied presence, you give naturally, your voice, your care, your attention, your gratitude from abundance.

This book is my gift to you; your life will be your gift to others. The path of love advances through simple acts: listening intently, speaking truth with kindness, caring for the earth, forgiving the past, and blessing the present.

Reciprocity doesn't require grandeur. It begins with thank you. Thank you to the body that carries you. Thank you to the ancestors who dreamed you. Thank you to the teachers, seen and unseen, who guide your steps.

Thank you to the ache that became the doorway. May you walk in the spiral of the Great Mother: bright and forever held.

A Note from the Weaver

There is a moment, after the basket is finished, when I set it down and simply look at it. The weave is uneven in places; some strands are thicker, others thinner. Yet when the light hits it, I see how every imperfection fits. It reminds me that healing, too, is handmade.

I did not write this book as an expert, but as a woman remembering her way home. Each strand comes from lived experience, silence, tears, breath, and the women who have sat before me with open hearts. Together, we have remembered that the ache itself is sacred, and that it guides us back to love.

Healing has taught me that nothing is wasted. The pain, the longing, the moments of loss, all of them become strands of wisdom when met with tenderness. What started as an ache becomes a prayer. What once felt broken turns into a blessing.

If you've walked even part of this spiral with me, know that you are woven into its living fabric. You have spun your own fibers, softened them with breath, shaped them with courage. You have remembered that presence, not perfection, is what keeps the basket open to life.

So, when you forget, place your hands on your heart and listen. The Great Mother is still breathing through you. The strands of your healing can never be lost.

As you continue your journey, return to the practices we have explored whenever you feel called. Healing is not linear; it moves in spirals, deepening with each season of your life. Some practices may speak to you now, while others will reveal their medicine later. Trust your timing and the intelligence of your own unfolding.

You'll find a list of our shared practices in Appendix A: Daily Weaving Practices, a summary to support your ongoing journey of remembrance, embodiment, and devotion. In Appendix B, you'll find gentle worksheets for working with triggers and the protective energy patterns that arise along the way. Appendix C offers a glossary of the terms and working models I use throughout this book. In Appendix D, you'll find a short history and further reflections on the ancient craft of basket weaving. Let these offerings be your strands of return, guiding you back to center whenever you forget the way.

May your basket hold what you love. May your hands never forget their remembering. May your life become a song of belonging. Each breath, a blessing. Each act, a prayer.

Appendix A:

Daily Weaving Practices

The practices offered here are the same ones you have been introduced to throughout this book, gathered in one place for ease and encouragement. They are simple ways to weave presence into daily life, and while they may appear modest, they carry profound healing potential when practiced with care and consistency. You are not meant to do all of them at once. Choose one that calls to you and return to it gently, day after day.

You may find it supportive to practice each one for a period of time: eleven, twenty-one, or forty days. These time frames invite a fuller relationship with the practice. Eleven days can help establish consistency and build trust. Twenty-one days can allow a rhythm to settle. Forty days can support deeper integration in the body and heart.

If you miss a day, nothing is lost. Weaving a daily practice into your life is an act of devotion that, above all else, asks for self-compassion. Let them support you in staying connected to your body, your inner knowing, and the rhythms of daily life.

Breathwork, Grounding, and Regulation

Soft Belly Breathing

Allow the breath to move naturally into the belly, softening the nervous system and restoring a sense of safety from the inside out.

Long, Slow, Deep Breathing

A steady breath supports regulation, agency and self-connection, especially during moments of stress or transition.

Anchoring In A Posture Of Safety

Return to the posture of safety you explored in Chapter Six, a position in which your body feels supported and held, and allowing the nervous system to settle.

Mini Self-Regulation Practices

Brief somatic practices used gently throughout the day to support balance and ease, including simple tapping or pausing to connect with your surroundings or with nature, as explored in Chapter Six.

Breath of Fire (Navel Activation)

A short, rhythmic breathing practice that gently pumps the navel to awaken vitality, courage, and inner strength. Sit in sukhasana in prayer pose or with the hands in gyan mudra, and practice for one to three minutes with an even, steady rhythm, inhaling and exhaling through the nostrils, emphasizing steadiness rather than force.

Intention, Awareness, and Inner Listening

Working With Intention

Setting intention is an ongoing process of self-reflection rather than a fixed goal. You may choose to reflect on intentions during each new moon, using smaller intentions to support larger ones over time.

Attending To The Felt Sense

Listening for subtle bodily knowing beneath thought and story, allowing sensation to guide understanding. The felt sense may show up as warmth or coolness, tightness or ease, tingling, pressure, heaviness, or movement. Rather than interpreting these sensations, the practice invites gentle curiosity and presence, trusting the body's quiet intelligence to reveal meaning in its own time.

Mini Self-Inquiry Sessions

Ask inward questions with curiosity rather than urgency, allowing insight to arise organically. If you have time to try to trace your experience back to it earlier manifestation that is also helpful: *How far back does this tightness go?*

Non-Dominant Hand Journaling

A great way to get to know your wounded child in a playful but powerful way. Non-dominant hand journaling allows access to early experience and inner knowing by bypassing habitual cognitive pathways.

Embodiment and the Navel Center

Navel Awareness

Practice navel awareness while sitting, standing, or walking, sensing movement, vitality, and inner authority arising from the body's center. Navel awareness may be supported through long, slow, deep breathing or brief activating practices such as breath of fire, and it cultivates qualities of courage, grit, and disciplined presence by rooting awareness in the body rather than the mind.

Navel Strengthening

Practices such as yoga, Pilates, strength training, or other forms of functional movement that build core stability and inner strength.

Sitting In Sukhasana With Prayer Mudra

A simple hand position in which the palms are pressed together at the heart, supporting balance between the left and right hemispheres of the brain, yin and yang, feminine and masculine currents. Prayer mudra can be practiced on its own or paired with natural breathing, long slow deep breathing, breath of fire, or mantra singing. It is especially supportive when feeling overwhelmed, scattered, or disconnected, offering an immediate way to gather attention, stabilize the nervous system, and return to center.

Meditation and Contemplative Practices

Vipassana Meditation

A contemplative practice of clear seeing that involves observing bodily sensations, thoughts, and emotions without judgment or interference. Often practiced in short daily periods such as eleven minutes, Vipassana cultivates steadiness, discernment, and the capacity to remain present with experience as it unfolds.

The Sacred Pause

Brief, intentional pauses woven into daily life to restore presence and choice. The Sacred Pause can be practiced consistently at specific times or before transitions, such as before speaking, eating, responding, or moving from one activity to another, allowing awareness to return to the body and interrupt habitual reactions.

Mirror Gazing Meditation

A meditative practice that uses sustained, gentle eye contact with one's own reflection to cultivate self-recognition, compassion, and presence. Mirror gazing can soften ego identification and support a felt sense of fluidity within.

Tonglen Meditation

A compassion practice that involves consciously breathing in suffering and breathing out relief, care, or spaciousness. Tonglen strengthens the heart's capacity to remain open in the presence of pain without turning away, allowing the intelligence of the heart to transform it into love.

Mantra Singing

An ancient contemplative practice that uses sound, breath, and repetition to support healing and regulation through the voice. Mantra can serve as an anchor for the mind, helping to steady attention, soothe the nervous system, and gently interrupt habitual or distressing thought patterns. When practiced with sincerity, mantra allows vibration to move through the body, restoring coherence and a felt sense of inner support.

Movement and Energy Flow—Active Meditations

Kundalini Meditation

An active meditation practiced widely around the world, often in the early evening, to support the transition from the outward demands of the day into a more inward, receptive state. It unfolds in four stages—shaking, dancing, sitting in stillness, and deep relaxation—allowing energy to move through the body, release accumulated tension, and settle naturally into integration and presence.

Nadabrahma Humming Meditation

An active meditation practice that uses vibration and resonance to harmonize the body's three centers of intelligence. It unfolds in three stages: thirty minutes of humming creating a deep vibration up and down the spine, fifteen minutes of simple hand mudras of giving and receiving, and fifteen minutes of deep relaxation. Humming is an ancient meditative technique found in Tibetan traditions and used by wisdom keepers across cultures to quiet the mind, balance energy, and support integration.

Nataraj Dance Meditation

A dynamic dance meditation centered on totality: the invitation to move with full presence and abandon. The practice unfolds in three phases: approximately forty minutes of free, spontaneous dancing; twenty minutes of deep rest and stillness; and a final five minutes of gentle movement to support integration and celebration. Through complete expression followed by rest, Nataraj allows energy to discharge, settle, and reorganize, supporting embodied aliveness and clarity.

Dynamic Meditation

An active meditation practice designed to mobilize stuck energy and allow repressed emotion to be expressed within a structured, contained field. The practice unfolds in five stages: chaotic breathing to activate energy and break habitual patterns; catharsis to release held emotion such as anger or grief; navel activation through jumping and the *Hoo* mantra; a period of stillness or freezing to witness the effects; and a final stage of celebration and integration. Practiced with care, Dynamic Meditation supports emotional discharge, vitality, and embodied clarity.

Sensory Presence and Nature Connection

Connecting with the five senses

Returning from story into immediate experience through conscious engagement with sight, sound, touch, taste, and smell. This practice anchors awareness in the present moment and gently interrupts mental looping by orienting the nervous system to what is here now.

Connecting with nature

Spending time walking, sitting, or resting outdoors to reorient the nervous system and restore rhythm. In addition to a daily twenty-minute walk, nature can be approached as a teacher and healing path through observing, listening, and allowing the living world to inform and steady you. Let nature meet you where you are and let it teach you in its own quiet way. Nature has been my most profound teacher, let Her teach you, too.

Care and Creativity as Daily Weaving

Daily journaling

Daily journaling offers a simple way to listen inward and give language to what is unfolding beneath the surface. Write without editing or urgency, allowing words to emerge as a form of witnessing rather than problem-solving.

Daily walking

A daily walk of twenty minutes or so can serve as a moving meditation, supporting regulation, reflection, and connection with the rhythms of the body and the natural world. Let the pace be unhurried, using the walk as a time to sense, breathe, and gently settle.

Play

Play supports aliveness and regulation by inviting movement, curiosity, and sensory engagement without productivity or performance. Let sensation lead rather than outcome, stopping before exhaustion and noticing how your body feels afterward. Choose simple forms of movement, creativity, relational play, or everyday playfulness that feel accessible in the moment.

Daily acts of self-care

Rest, nourishment, movement, touch, and supportive boundaries form the foundations of regulation and repair. Because self-care is often one of the hardest practices for women to prioritize, approach it with kindness allowing exercise, pampering, or simple comforts to count as meaningful acts of care rather than indulgence.

Daily acts of creativity

As healing deepens, creativity often returns as a quiet but powerful force of vitality. Everyday creative acts such as drawing, cooking, knitting, gardening, dancing, writing, and singing offer simple ways to let life-force energy move and be expressed.

These practices are not meant to be mastered. They are ways of remembering—returning to the body, to presence, and to the quiet intelligence that unfolds through daily attention and care.

Appendix B:

Weaving the Work into Daily Life

Working with Triggers: A guide for recognizing when the past overtakes the present.

A trigger occurs when a present-moment cue touches an old wound, and the nervous system responds as if the past is happening again. The intensity belongs more to memory than to the moment. Nothing is wrong with you. This is your system protecting you with tools learned long ago. If you find yourself thinking, *I'm overreacting again*, this worksheet is an invitation to slow down and gently meet what is underneath.[40]

Three Signs You've Been Triggered

I have developed a simple rule of three to help identify when we are triggered:

---

40 The trigger chain described here of *spark, surge, story, and strategy,* along with the identifying signs of *speed, size, and sameness*, reflect my own original framework, developed through years of somatic, relational, and trauma-informed work with my own triggers and others.

Speed: the reaction happens before thought (beating heart, shaking hands, urge to flee).

Size: the reaction feels much bigger than the situation.

Sameness: the feeling is familiar across people or contexts.

The Trigger Chain

Triggers tend to move quickly through a familiar sequence: Spark > Surge > Story > Strategy. Let's explore. Take a moment to reflect on a recent trigger and trace its sequence:

Spark: What happened? What was the cue?

Surge: What sensations arose in your body?

Story: What meaning, belief, or interpretation appeared?

Strategy: What protective energy pattern from Chapter Eight came up:

Reaching: pleasing, over-explaining, clinging, performing.

Guarding: withdrawing, shutting down, numbing.

Judging: arguing, blaming, escalating.

Collapsing: freezing, helplessness, wanting to disappear.

After identifying the protective energy pattern activated you can gently explore what early meaning, as we explored in Chapter Three, was touched? For example: *I am alone, I am not enough, I am too much, I am unsafe*, etc.

Returning to the Sacred Center

Place a hand on your heart or belly and breathe slowly. You might say inwardly:

I feel your fear, or *I am here now*. Then ask gently: *What were you afraid was about to happen?* or *What do you need right now?* Remember, triggers are invitations to notice where the past still lives in the body through our Wounded Child and longs to heal. Awareness is what loosens the pattern and restores choice.

Recognizing and Working with the Four Protective Movements

This worksheet is designed to help you recognize the four protective energy movements of reaching, guarding, judging, and collapsing, as they arise in daily life. Each movement once served to protect you. Through awareness and compassion, you can begin to meet them differently and restore choice. Move gently. There is no goal here beyond noticing with awareness, curiosity, compassion.

Reaching

Reaching is the movement toward something or someone for safety, worth, belonging, or soothing. You might notice reaching as: grasping for reassurance or approval; overexplaining, fixing, or managing others; or moving outward before turning inward.

Did I notice reaching today?

What was I needing in that moment?

What happens when I pause and offer that need to myself first?

Guarding

Guarding is the movement that creates distance to prevent hurt. You might notice guarding as: bracing in the body; withholding truth or emotion; or pulling back when closeness appears.

Did I notice guarding today?

What feeling was I protecting myself from?

What softens when I acknowledge, *I feel vulnerable here*?

Judging

Judging is the movement that uses criticism or control to avoid feeling something underneath. You might notice judging as: harsh self-talk, criticizing others, needing to be right, perfect, or in control.

Did I notice judging today?

If I look beneath the judgment, what tenderness or emotion is present?

What shifts when I meet that tenderness instead?

Collapsing

Collapsing is the movement of shrinking, giving up power, or disappearing when things feel overwhelming. You might notice collapsing as: feeling small, foggy, or powerless; shutting down or going quiet; wanting to disappear or avoid; believing there is no choice, agency, or way forward.
Did I notice collapsing today?
What felt too big or too much in that moment?
What happens when I place a hand on my heart and say, *I am here with you*?

Returning to the Sacred Center

Take a slow breath. Sense your navel center. Feel the steadiness beneath what rises and falls within you. What becomes possible when I return to my center before responding? What daily weaving practices support your connection here?

Guide to The Four Rs of Emotional Alchemy

When triggers arise or protective energy patterns take over, emotion is often shielded rather than felt. These responses are not mistakes; they are intelligent strategies shaped early to keep you safe. Once the intensity has passed, emotional alchemy becomes possible.

The Four Rs—Recognize, Release, Reweave, and Respond—offer a way to return to what was protected beneath the reactivity of the Four Rs of protection: Resist, Regress, Repress, and React. They are not steps to complete, but invitations you can move through slowly, in your own timing.

You might explore one or two of the reflections below, allowing them to open awareness rather than resolve anything.

Recognize

What am I able to see now that I could not see in the moment?
What pattern, belief, or protective movement became visible?

Release

What is ready to soften or move through the body now, through breath, sound, tears, rest, or movement?

What happens when I allow the body to let go a little?

Reweave

What new understanding or resource wants to be woven in?

How might this experience be held with more truth, compassion, or choice?

Respond

From this steadier place, what feels like an honest next response, internally or externally?

What action, boundary, or care aligns with my center now?

These reflections are not meant to be answered all at once. Return to them as you feel ready, trusting that integration unfolds in layers and overtime.

Appendix C:

Glossary of Terms

This glossary offers gentle orientation to the language used throughout *The Mother Ache*. Much of the language and most of the terms named here have emerged from my own way of listening, working, and making meaning through lived experience and relational practice. They are my own names and working models, developed and used in my work with clients to help articulate felt experience and support embodied understanding. They are not meant to be definitive or diagnostic. Use them as guides, translating the language as needed to meet your own lived truth.

Mother Ache

The mother ache refers to the relational wound formed through early experiences of mis-attunement, absence, or unmet need in the mother–child bond. It is not a diagnosis or a judgment of mothers, but a shared human initiation shaped by dependency, longing, and early belonging. When met with presence, the mother ache becomes a source of wisdom rather than deprivation.

Sacred Center

The sacred center refers to an embodied place of alignment and wholeness within us: a living intelligence that emerges when instinct, heart, and awareness are in relationship. It is rooted in the navel center, where intuition, vitality, and inner authority are felt as visceral knowing. From there, the heart opens into emotional truth and compassion, and awareness widens into a subtle, neutral clarity, the still point beneath thought. Healing unfolds as a return to this center through the body, breath, and lived presence, allowing us to respond from wholeness rather than habit or protection.

Early Meanings

Early meanings are body-based understandings formed in our earliest relationships before language or conscious choice. They arise as the nervous system makes sense of safety, belonging, and connection. These meanings are adaptive understandings that can soften and reorganize when met with awareness and care.

Feminine Alchemy

Feminine Alchemy describes an embodied process of transformation rooted in relationship, presence, and lineage. Rather than striving for transcendence or perfection, it emphasizes openness, integration, and the capacity to let experience change form. Alchemy here is the inner condition that allows sensation, emotion, and meaning to move and reorganize.

Navel Center

The navel center is the body's seat of agency, courage, and grounded presence. It governs instinct, boundary, and the ability to act from inner authority. Rooting here supports intuition, self-trust, the capacity to stay with experience, and courage.

Heart Center

The heart center is the seat of feeling, empathy, and relational intelligence. It allows us to sense, receive, and respond emotionally without becoming overwhelmed. When protected or shut down, feeling becomes constricted; when supported, the heart returns to its natural fluidity.

Mind Center

The mind is the center of meaning-making, perception, and pattern recognition. It organizes experience through interpretation and memory, often in service of safety. In this work, the mind is an ally that can soften and realign when grounded in the body and heart.

Protective Energy Patterns

Protective energy patterns describe how the system organizes survival when safety is compromised. The four patterns explored in this book of reaching, guarding, collapsing, and judging, are adaptive responses shaped early in life. They are intelligent adaptive strategies that can be rewoven into wholeness as awareness grows.

Reaching

Reaching is a protective movement toward something outside the self for relief, reassurance, or completion. It seeks connection, soothing, or validation when inner resources feel unavailable.

Guarding

Guarding is a protective movement of holding back or controlling experience to prevent further hurt. It may appear as rigidity, self-reliance, or emotional containment.

Collapsing

Collapsing is a protective movement of withdrawal, numbing, or shutting down when experience feels overwhelming. It conserves energy by reducing sensation and engagement.

Judging

Judging is a protective movement that turns against the self or others through criticism, comparison, or blame. It attempts to regain control through evaluation rather than feeling.

The Four R's of Emotional Protection

The Four R's describe how the heart responds when feeling begins to surface within a given protective energy pattern. They are reflexes that once helped manage what felt unbearable. With awareness, these responses can transform into new movements of emotional alchemy.

Resistance

Resistance appears as tension or armoring against what is being felt. The system braces to stay safe by tightening the body and heart.

Regression

Regression involves slipping into younger states of coping, such as freezing, pleasing, or hiding. The nervous system returns to familiar childhood strategies.

Repression

Repression pushes feeling out of awareness, storing emotional energy as tension, fatigue, or illness. What cannot be felt is carried silently in the body.

Reaction

Reaction projects feeling outward through impulsive action, blame, control, or withdrawal. Emotion moves quickly into behavior rather than being felt directly.

The Four R's of Emotional Alchemy

The Four R's of Emotional Alchemy describe the natural movement through which feeling transforms when met with presence and care. They are capacities that emerge as protection softens and the heart regains its fluid intelligence.

Recognize

Recognize is the act of naming what is present without judgment. "This is sadness." "This is anger." "This is fear." By naming our feeling simply and honestly, we bring it into awareness without becoming overwhelmed or identified with it.

Release

Release allows feeling to move through the body in its own time and way, through breath, sound, tears, or sensation. Rather than forcing expression, release trusts the innate intelligence of emotion to complete its movement when it is safe to do so.

Reweave

Reweave is the integration of what has been felt. Through empathy and understanding, we sense how an experience shaped us in the past and how it may no longer need to define us in the present. What was once held in isolation is woven back into wholeness.

Respond

Respond is action that arises from presence rather than pattern. It reflects choice, alignment, and self-trust, allowing us to meet life from a place of clarity instead of reactivity.

Appendix D:

Ancestral Basketry—The Materials of Maternal Love

"The marvel of a basket is in its transformation, its journey from wholeness as a living plant to fragmented strands and back to wholeness again as a basket. A basket knows the dual powers of deconstruction and creation that shape the world. Strands once separated are rewoven into a new whole. The journey of a basket is also the journey of a people."

—Robin Wall Kimmerer

This weaving began not in metaphor but in memory. I have always loved baskets, their scent of grass and dust, the soft rasp of their fibers, the curve shaped for human hands. My grandmother kept hers on high shelves, filled with buttons, thread, and folded cloth. As a girl, I would empty her baskets and sort through the small treasures inside, studying their contents: stray ribbons, buttons, spools of thread, seashells.

Many years later, during my morning sadhana, I read a short passage by Jigme Khyentse Rinpoche called *Advice for a Basket Weaver*. His words landed like an old remembering. He spoke of weaving with patience, of softening fibers before bending them, of shaping something that could hold both water and light. In that moment, I realized the basket had always been my teacher.

To honor this metaphor faithfully, I began studying the ancient art itself—both as craft and as lineage. Basketry is one of humanity's oldest languages, spoken through the hands of women for tens of thousands of years. Long before clay was fired or metal shaped, women bent beside rivers and marshes, gathering reeds, roots, bark, and grasses. They spent days preparing and sorting their materials before ever beginning to weave, believing that what was gathered by one's own hands carried a particular vitality. The basket was not decoration. It was survival. It was the womb made visible.

Across continents and cultures, the gestures were strikingly similar. In the deserts of the Southwest, women split yucca and agave. In the wetlands of Africa, they coiled raffia and palm. In Asia, bamboo sang beneath the knife; in Europe, willow bent and whispered. Girls learned by watching their mothers and grandmothers, playing at weaving, imitating what they saw until their elders recognized readiness and began to teach them. Skill was understood not only as technique, but as something transmitted through presence, story, and sometimes through ritual. Some traditions spoke of a guardian spirit of basketry, an intelligence that could be passed from woman to woman through the hands themselves.

Baskets were woven for every aspect of life. They carried food and water, seed and grain. They served as cooking vessels, cradles, sifters, and storage. They held medicines, offerings, and ceremonial objects. Some were made to accompany the dead, burned as funeral offerings so the weave might travel with the soul. To weave a basket was to participate in ceremony, one that joined the practical and the sacred without distinction.

Perhaps this is why the basket endures as metaphor, and why it resonated so deeply as I wrote this book. Each of us carries within the body the memory of these gestures: gathering, softening, shaping, and holding. Every act of tending the heart is an act of weaving. Each boundary is a rim. Each moment of forgiveness is a softened reed.

Remembering the basket is remembering the mother line: women bending to the rhythm of rivers, gathering what was near, transforming it into what could both hold and endure. They did not separate survival from sanctity. They wove both into a single vessel, strong enough to hold life.

Your basket—the life you are shaping—is part of that lineage.

Each time you breathe into your belly, bless your body, and tend your inner landscape, you continue their work. You are the weaver and the vessel, the hands and the prayer.

May you remember the women who wove before you, their patience, their songs, their wisdom whispered into the weave. May the basket of your life be strong enough to hold your ache and open enough to let the light through.

If you wish to explore the art of basket weaving further, these were among the texts that informed my understanding while writing this book: Ruby Taylor's *Wild Basketry: Making Baskets and Natural Cordage from Foraged Plants* offers a visually rich and accessible entry into basketry, blending practical instruction with historical context and beautiful imagery. Frank W. Porter's *The Art of Native American Basketry: A Living Legacy* remains a foundational and deeply researched text for those interested in Indigenous basket traditions, while *Daughters of the Earth* provides a meaningful cultural and symbolic lens through its thoughtful chapter on basket weaving.[41]

41 See *Daughters of the Earth*, ed. Miriam Robbins Dexter and Josephine McCarthy (Boston: Beacon Press, 1997), particularly the chapter on basket weaving, which explores weaving as both a practical craft and a symbolic expression of feminine knowledge, continuity, and care. Additional texts that informed this section include Ruby Taylor, *Wild Basketry: Making Baskets and Natural Cordage from Foraged Plants* (London: Herbert Press, 2025), and Frank W. Porter, ed., *The Art of Native American Basketry: A Living Legacy* (Westport, CT: Greenwood Press, 1990).

Acknowledgments

This book was shaped by the hands and hearts of many women.

I want to begin by honoring the women I have never met, whose words have walked beside me like lanterns. Books have always been my faithful friends, and in seasons when I felt alone, I found companionship in the pages of women who spoke with courage, clarity, and devotion. I carry deep gratitude for the voices that have nourished and steadied me, among them: Tara Brach, Pema Chödrön, Clarissa Pinkola Estés, Robin Wall Kimmerer, and so many others, far too many to name. Your work helped me trust my inner life. It helped me remember.

I also bow to the many women who have guided my healing path through retreats, teachings, and fields of practice where presence itself becomes medicine. Alima Cameron gave me one of my first lived experiences of an attuned woman speaking from the wisdom of her heart. She led my first Path of Love Retreat, and I have been blessed to keep learning with her over the decades as both teacher and friend. Studying Gurdjieff sacred dance movements with Amiyo Devienne, I experienced presence transmitted with rare integrity and depth. I am grateful as well for the retreats that shaped me in lasting ways, including Satori with Ganga Cording and Primal Therapy with Puja Lepp in India. These women, and so many others, helped me trust the power of feminine leadership rooted in unconditional love, devotion, and lived truth.

I also offer my deepest gratitude to Sat Dharam Kaur, cofounder of Compassionate Inquiry®, a training that has profoundly shaped the work I offer others. Though I have not worked with her individually, her steady presence, humility, and clarity of transmission throughout the year-long training were a true inspiration to me.

I also want to honor the many women I have worked with over the years. Your courage, honesty, longing for healing, and willingness to turn toward what hurts have taught me more than I can say. So much of what lives in these pages was inspired by what I have witnessed in you: the devotion it takes to feel, soften, name the truth, and begin again. Thank you for trusting me with your stories, your tenderness, and your becoming.

To the women in my personal life—my friends across seasons and years, near and far—thank you for walking with me. Thank you for your honesty, humor, and willingness to stay.

With all my heart, I thank my editor, Emily Graf, who first invited me to write this book and then helped me become more fully myself on the page. Your care, precision, and steady guidance made this book clearer, braver, and truer. Thank you for seeing both the forest and the trees when I could see only one leaf at a time.

My gratitude also goes to Sentient Publications and to Steven Harrison for trusting me with this work and believing in what I had to offer. Your support made this book possible, and I am deeply grateful. Thank you to my book designer Laura Waltje. This is the second book we have created together, and your patience, talent, and creativity helped bring my vision to life. Thank you, Stephanie Hempel, for your meticulous copyediting and care.

To my teachers and the Indigenous wisdom keepers who have shared their medicines and healing ways with such generosity, I am forever indebted.

And finally, to Samir and Ben—thank you for keeping the fire burning at home while I disappeared into my creative den. Thank you for the love, the meals, the tea, the laughter, the walks, and the gentle reminders that life itself is the ceremony. I love you.